1993

SPIRIT AND EXISTENCE

LIBRARY OF RELIGIOUS PHILOSOPHY
Thomas V. Morris, General Editor

Number 4

Spirit and Existence

A Philosophical Inquiry

Michael Gelven

UNIVERSITY OF NOTRE DAME PRESS
NOTRE DAME

Library of Congress Cataloging-in-Publication Data

Gelven, Michael.
　Spirit and existence : a philosophical inquiry /
Michael Gelven.
　　　p.　cm.—(Library of religious philosophy : no. 4)
　　ISBN 0–268—01736–0
　　1. Spirit.　2. Spiritual life.　I. Title.　II. Series : Library of
religious philosophy : v. 4.
　　BD423.G44　1990
　　128—dc 20　　　　　　　　　　　　　　　　　　89–40754

To
HERMAN STARK
and
FRAN MAYESKI

Contents

Acknowledgments

With such a book as this it seems almost impossible to do justice to the task of thanking those who have inspired, helped, worked, and endured so much to bring this essay to its finished form. There are too many to name them all, but a few deserve mention. My thanks to Herman Stark for working on the manuscript and contributing spiritual support; to Donald Livingston, whose careful criticism of my earlier manuscript proved so beneficial to this one; to Fran Mayeski, Sharon Sytsma, Annette Mumma, and Frank Gonzalez for reading all or parts of the manuscript and contributing their responses. My thanks also to Professor Thomas V. Morris for his invaluable assistance as editor.

The chapter on suffering contains some material which is included in an article I wrote earlier for the *Journal of Value Inquiry*, 1988, entitled "Is Sacrifice a Virtue?"

PART I

Setting Up the Problem

1

Who Are We?

They eat. They sleep. They drink. They find pleasure rutting in the ditches. They sweat and they stink. They giggle like silly geese, and when they herd themselves together in time of stress, their eyes bulge with the thought and fear of death. When hurt, they howl in anguish and outrage, and strike out against anyone who is near, indifferent to justice or to right. They even kill each other, and whimper for reprieve when these acts of darkness are uncovered. They deceive with such wantonness it seems they delight in deception for its own sake. They are driven by pleasure, indifferent to all restraints against the gratification of their unholy wants. Some of them are clever indeed, using and manipulating others to increase their private gain. Nor are they all ugly; some possess bodies of remarkable allurement which they exhibit shamelessly and often, snagging the lusts of those who respond to their greed. The lovely seduce, the powerful rape, the rest connive. They are greedy, selfish, desolate, and base; they are cunning, treacherous, sly, and adroit. Their stench is occasionally concealed by the thick sweetness of artifice, but it is always there, in reeking defilement. When they intoxicate themselves beyond all sense, which is often, their harsh and bestial laughter becomes a cacophony of madness. But always, always, their desires must be fulfilled, and when they are fulfilled, they moan and snort, sigh and grunt, like pigs. They threaten to suffocate themselves in their own fecal waste. They are animals.

They are us.

We are indeed animals. Aristotle assures us of it. The twin pillars of our carnal fate, lust and mortality, support us all and can be avoided by no one. It is a truth which none save the fool-

3

ish deny. As animals we are flesh. We are also flesh and blood, but blood speaks of death and sacrifice; flesh speaks of pleasure and venereal gratification, and in moments of unsmiling lethargy, flesh also speaks of weakness.

The spirit indeed is willing, but the flesh is weak.

The good man who said that, along with the wisest philosophers, as well as the pimp, the whore, and the jailer, know this is true. The flesh is weak. And so, we being flesh are weak.

But granted that we are flesh, and that we are weak, and that we are animals in behavior as well as in kind, is that all? One of us, perhaps one of the most favored, spoke about this; and he speaks for us:

> What is a man,
> If the chief good and market of his time
> Be but to sleep and feed? a beast, no more.

Even in the pits of the most scarlet debauchery, there remains that question. Is this all we are? Animals? Flesh? We do not, and cannot, deny we are flesh. We dare not, at the cost of being judged fools, deny we are animals. But the question remains; is that *all*? Does our bestial nature explain us entirely? Do beasts ask such questions?

The flesh is weak, that good and holy man once said. But he also spoke of spirit. And Hamlet, too, wrenched in the agony of his own self-betrayal, cries out, protesting.

> Sure he that made us with such large discourse
> Looking before and after, gave us not
> That capability and god-like reason
> To fust in us unused.

A good word, that: fust. It means to grow moldy from disuse; in earlier English a fust was a wine-barrel, old, grey, musty, cobwebs surrounding the molded curve of the ancient oak. Is our spirit then musty and moldy, lying in the dark, cool, forgotten cellars of the mind? Perhaps with a radiant, secret wine lurking redly within?

Flesh and spirit. They belong together, but as opposites, like twin siblings of different sexes: where there is one, the other is at least remembered. But Hamlet's cry was a question, not an answer. Are we only beasts? If not, then we must also be . . . what?

Spirit? But what is spirit? Whatever it is, it surely accounts for Hamlet crying out like that, questioning the meaning of his nature in an anguish provoked by the very animality that he opposes. And if our animality disgusts us, as it must now and then, then what is it within us that is disgusted? Disgust may be the beginning of redemption. For unless Hamlet were disgusted with the riotous animality around him and in him, he would not be Hamlet.

But 'spirit', you say, is a fusty word. It does not belong on our modern tongues; it is an old word, a word of quainter, gentler, more foolish times, a word of superstition and dark religion. We scorn the farmer's wife as she tosses salt over her shoulder for luck when she drops a utensil. And at the farmer himself, as he doffs his cap and bows his head when the Angelus is rung from the village church. They are alike, the superstitious and the religious: they are unscientific, unsophisticated, and unenlightened.

But are they really alike? We may not share his humble faith or know of the same kindly god he worships, but is his bowing truly the same as his wife's tossing the salt? Perhaps we think about his act of spirit a little differently than her act of superstition. Perhaps Hamlet, in crying out against his own bestial nature, overcomes it somehow. *Somehow.* If he could not, somehow, overcome it, why does he cry out? Perhaps that is what spirit truly means: a crying out against the awfulness of the beast. The etymology of the term *spiritus* means "breath"—perhaps a sigh or a cry? Perhaps spirit begins right there, with disgust. Unless we are disgusted, we have no spirit.

No less a scoffer and maligner of religion than Friedrich Nietzsche, self-yclept as the Antichrist, astounds us with the same thought. Our greatest moment, he claims in *Thus Spoke Zarathustra,* is when our own happiness fills us with disgust. Why? Why should our happiness fill us with disgust? And even if it does, why should it be our greatest moment? Perhaps Zarathustra is as crazed as Hamlet. But if Shakespeare and Nietzsche agree on something, it must be worth at least a moment's consideration. They too were animals, but when they speak, we listen, for truth, no less than beauty, is a rare commodity among us beasts.

If all we do is sleep and feed, if all we want is the fun of rutting in the ditch, if all that matters is our satisfaction or our happiness, then, these fellow-beasts ask: What does it mean? Disgust. But, why does our own nature disgust us? What were our expectations? What else could we possibly want save that which satisfies our wanting?

This disgust is the origin of spirit.

It begins, then, as a negation. It is the reaching out beyond ourselves; it is a denial. It is a No, wrenched from us when we look upon ourselves. We may not grasp it fully, perhaps we must remain forever unfulfilled, but it cannot be denied, this primordial, fundamental, basic No. So primordial is this original No that it does not permit of being questioned. For, if the pedant demands to know why we are so sure, why we may not, perhaps, be seduced by an illusion, we hush the protest by the very anguish of the question. Disgust is not an argument, it is not a scientific procedure, it is more fundamental than these devices of reason; disgust is a way of being. Disgust is not a mere emotion, a whim from within; like Reason it is a power, like Will it is a reality. It cannot be dissuaded or distracted by a clinical protest or a delicate refinement of doubt. If I am only animal, I am disgusted; deeply disgusted, fundamentally disgusted. And this disgust is the very birth of thought.

As animals, however, this disgust with the flesh becomes self-disgust, and hence achieves a far deeper and far more demanding seriousness. For we cannot remain content with this revulsion against ourselves. Unlike the experiences of external disgust, from which we can turn away and simply leave behind, self-disgust gnaws continually at our existence, threatening to undermine the entire edifice of our satisfaction and contentment. Self-disgust cleaves us from ourselves, forcing us to think; it unsettles the settled tranquility of our existence. There is no other word for it; it is our existence that is provoked. Could it be, then, that the disgust with flesh which parts the placid sea of unreflective being is fundamentally an existential phenomenon? Is the question provoked by this self-disgust anything less than the fundamental question about the meaning of our existence?

Let us probe this suggestion further. "The spirit indeed is willing but the flesh is weak." When we hear this, we are not committed to any theology; we do not find ourselves affirming any particular metaphysics. An atheist, who believes in neither God nor soul, can understand and appreciate the sentence: he knows exactly what it means. Flesh, then, is not 'body', nor is spirit 'mind'. We must resist these metaphysical reductions. Body and Mind are metaphysical entities, they either exist or do not exist. But flesh and spirit are ways of being, they are not entities which exist as independent things. When he returned from his agony in the garden of Gethsemane, he found them sleeping, and in sadness he sighed that their spirit was willing but their flesh was weak. By flesh he meant that which is tempted by the narcotic of weariness; by spirit he meant the wakefulness that was due him and which they owed him as friends even when their eyes were heavy. They should have remained alert. Flesh and spirit are ways in which we understand our existence, and so they are existential.

Flesh is not the same as body since I can rejoice spiritually in an erotic passion for the beauty of another in carnal love. Spirit is not mind, for mind is a formal faculty, a source of dispassionate rules which guide our inferences; it provides us with principles with which to calculate and reason. But passion is necessary for spirit. Thus we must avoid the reductionism so common among the contemporary thinkers who insist that everything be identified as an entity. I do not first believe in an entity called 'soul' and then seek to achieve spirit; rather I am first spirit, and then perhaps I may seek to understand my spirit in terms of soul. One does not first believe in God and then become spiritual; it is because one is spiritual that one believes in God. The existential thus is prior to the metaphysical.

But this existential torment of self-disgust needs to be explained, or at the very least examined, for unexamined this self-disgust will render us impotent philosophically. Provisionally we may leap ahead of the inquiry and suggest that flesh disgusts us because to be merely flesh is to be without meaning. This existential self-disgust is thus a necessary protest against the dread of nihilism. For if we are merely responses to stimuli, if our conduct and our existence is completely intelligible by reference to cause and effect, replaceable levers and cogs in mindless mechanism, then we do not mean anything. We simply do not count. Our disgust with ourselves, this fundamental, existential self-disgust, is a purgative against the nausea of meaninglessness. We are disgusted because we matter. We reject the picture of ourselves as mere recipients of pleasure because we are meaningless in such a picture. We do not reject this description of ourselves because we *want* to be meaningful, but because we *are* meaningful. And so this fundamental self-disgust is the beginning in which there is, suddenly, light.

The present inquiry is an attempt to grasp the fundamental meaning of spirit; thus it does not concern itself primarily with whether there is a thing called 'a spirit' or even 'a soul'. Consideration as to whether something exists must surely wait upon an analysis of what the thing is, or what a concept means, for how can I wonder if something exists unless I first know what it means? However, the inquiry is not merely an analysis, it also seeks to determine a judgment. After we understand what it means to be spirit, we can then ask: Is it more rational to be spiritual than not? This form of the question, as an existential inquiry, comes before any metaphysical claim about the existence of anything, whether spirit, soul, or even God. But this beginning seems dubious: we are suggesting that the origin of our understanding of spirit comes when we are disgusted with the flesh. Is this truly the proper place to begin? And even if we do begin with the disgust we have for our own flesh, where does it lead us? Surely we need guidance in this quest. For disgust, especially self-disgust, is an uncomfortable phenomenon. By its very nature disgust is something from which we want to turn away. How does this turning away reveal anything that is philosophically sound?

One who is disgusted in this fundamental way is a charming, eager, even fiery Greek youth named Glaucon. His disgust provoked one of the greatest thinkers of all time to explore the consequences of his young friend's revulsion. It is perhaps fitting, then, that we initiate the inquiry by considering in some depth the true significance of the handsome young Glaucon's disgust; first, because his disgust is ours, or at least it becomes ours when we study it carefully; and, second, because the Socratic approach to these great questions is a part of our heritage, and we overlook it only at the danger of misunderstanding ourselves.

Glaucon, we are told, was a younger brother of Plato. But at the time of our original encounter with him, he and his other brother, Adeimantus, are discussing the virtue of justice with their mentor, Socrates, in the venerable dialogue called the *Republic*. Glaucon is no slouch. He is eager to learn whatever wisdom he can glean from the inspired Socrates, but he is not so awed by him that he will not interrupt or even challenge the sage of Athens. From the dialogue we learn about Glaucon's character: he is quick-witted, lively, thoroughly Greek, and vehement in his challenge to what he does not accept. Unlike the more scabrous Thrasymachus, when thwarted he does not grow sullen and ominous, but eagerly questions his own errors so as to learn from them. We can imagine him, sitting with the others at the house of Cephalus, scarcely able to restrain his youthful impulses as the more senior members of the gathering carefully explore the early definitions of justice. It is not until Book II that he enters the dialogue with any energy. There is no doubt that Socrates is fond of him, and as the discussion begins to settle into the great central argument, the two younger brothers become the central focus of attention, leaving the older questioners like Polymarchus quiet and almost forgotten.

To appreciate Glaucon's philosophical disgust and its existential significance, we must recall, at least briefly, the sketch of the argument. In seeking to understand the true nature of justice, they have constructed, by means of language only, an imaginary state. They do this because they have agreed that the state is simply a larger, more easily read version, of the human soul. In the beginning, the reason for the emergence of the state seems obvious and simple: the lives of the individuals are improved when each produces that which he is most skilled in doing, so that if the shoemaker makes shoes for both himself and the tailor, and the tailor makes clothes for them both, they will both have better shoes and better clothes. In this simplistic manner, the state is expanded so that all of man's basic wants and needs are accounted for. Life in this simple community is bucolic, honest, and plain. They have no refinements because they need no refinements, and this is a state based upon needs. They go naked, at least in summer, and eat boiled greens. The young Glaucon, who has participated in this discussion with growing reluctance, finally can stand it no more. He bursts out in ridicule and disgust at the state which Socrates has been developing. What, he cries, is this *all*? You have given us little more than a state of pigs, Socrates! And the astonished lover of boys asks meekly, Well, Glaucon, what would you have us do? And Glaucon responds by demanding that the people be given spices to enhance their food, and meat and silks and couches to lie on.

And of course, this is the turning point of the argument, so subtly introduced that many commentators simply overlook it. First Glaucon is disgusted. But why his disgust? Everyone in the state is provided for. The simple, almost sylvan life seems very attractive; it certainly is innocent enough. But in this basic state, this state founded on needs, there is, even by Socrates' own admission, no excellence. There is indeed no virtue of justice at all. It is, in short, unbecoming the status of a man. Yet, the demand by the hotheaded and youthful Glaucon is dangerous. By introducing spices and luxury, Glaucon has also introduced greed and guile, the need for rules governing commerce and ownership, and finally, he has introduced war. To be sure, the introduction of luxury upsets the tranquility of the pig-state, but unless it is upset, there is no justice, because there is no excellence. Glaucon's disgust starts the entire inquiry off in a new direction.

Socrates admits the introduction of luxury, but with it he also introduces a new class, a new *kind* of man altogether: the warrior. Without the warrior, who enters the state alongside the poet, there can be no excellence. At first it seems that the warriors are separated from the citizens for purely practical means. They are denied any private property, even private sex, lest they accumulate private interests and private concerns. They are, after all, the young, the bold, the courageous, the strong; unless they are specially trained, what is to keep them from usurping the rights and properties of the citizens? But they are trained to revere, not their own private interests, but the good. However, the term 'good' here no longer is identified with private benefit. What it means will be shelved for further discussion later on. At the moment it is essential only to realize that Glaucon's disgust with the sheer gratification of wants, what he calls the pig-state, has produced a new kind of being, a warrior, whose unnatural training results in his sacrificing his own private interests for the good of the whole.

From this new class, the warriors, eventually a third class is chosen. These are the rulers. The state, on completion, therefore, has three classes: the citizens, who are understood in terms of their being gratified and whose virtue is temperance (*sophrosone*); the warriors, who are understood in terms of their devotion to what is their own and whose virtue is courage; and finally the rulers, who are understood in terms of their recognition of the value of truth for its own sake. Their virtue is wisdom.

These three classes correspond to the three divisions of the human soul: appetite, spirit, and reason. When the state has all three classes ranked in the proper order, one has a just state. When an individual ranks the three parts of his soul in the proper order, appetite, spirit, and reason, one has a just man. The search for a definition of justice is complete.

But one almost overlooks the truly important discovery in this rush to finish off the state and grab the prize of justice. Socrates has recognized a tripartite soul, consisting of appetite, spirit, and reason. And the most important part of the soul is not the highest rank, not mind. No, it is spirit. And spirit here is seen as corresponding to the warrior's virtue of courage. The warrior, who enters the state alongside the poet, undergoes training which is unnatural and unpleasant. Even Glaucon protests that the life of the warrior is not enviable. But it is noble. And Glaucon recognizes that without this strange character the life of excellence is impossible.

A tripartite soul? For Plato, the division into three is critically important. Today we readily recognize appetite and mind. Why the third and middle part? Why spirit? Aristotle defines man with only two parts, animality and reason. Kant talks of inclinations and duty. Descartes talks of body and soul. Why then does Plato talk about *three* parts? Is it not possible to understand the human species merely by reference to the body and the mind? Socrates seems to take for granted the tripartite soul. His friends assent to the correspondence between the state and the individual quite without criticism or even comment. Of course, they had seen the development emerge from their dialectic, and each step seemed so natural and obvious that they assented with

the truths as they unfolded. But we, perforce, must look more
closely at this curious doctrine. Why must a soul have *three* parts?
Surely two is enough.

Spirit is a link between appetite and reason. Without spirit
there would be neither appetite nor reason. But links are not as
important as the things linked. A telephone links my voice with
that of my friend; the friendship is important, not the telephone. Body is real, mind is real. If we need some mysterious
'link' to connect them, perhaps we must make room for it, but it
cannot be as important as the two things that really matter, body
and mind. Is spirit, then, merely a formal requirement to satisfy
the need to establish a connection between mind and body? In
Descartes's dualism he found the need for a thing sharing both
substantial qualities, the pineal gland. Surely this is an unworthy
solution, almost comical in its naivete. Is not spirit deserving of
the same contempt?

But spirit is not merely or even fundamentally a link.
Rather, it is the origin of both appetite and reason in the sense
that only in understanding spirit can I understand appetite and
reason. If we consider the Platonic account more closely we will
see that the warrior class, which corresponds to spirit in the individual, is not just one of three, but is the central and focal
point of our understanding. For it is the warrior who first breaks
from the very *principle* that makes the citizens intelligible, namely
happiness. The warrior is trained to develop entirely unnatural
values. His entire education is designed to focus his attention not
on his own pleasure or delight, but on the good as such. Not on
his good, but *the* good. Furthermore, the ruling class is chosen
from the warriors; one must first be spirited in existence before
one can revere truth as a thing worthy in and of itself.

Or, if we may borrow even more from the Socratic *elenchus*,
by the central role it plays in the natural development of the
state, spirit not only explains both appetite and reason, but the
two extremities in turn provide us with an understanding of
spirit. Glaucon, after all, in shattering the pastoral tranquility of
the pig-state, at first simply asserts that he *wants* there to be
spices and couches and other luxuries. This makes the introduction of the new class a seeming desire not any different from the
more basic ones. But the dialectic proves more elusive than the

spirited Glaucon, for the youth raises his objection in anger and disgust, not in calculative speculation. Indeed, Socrates seems at first reluctant to introduce luxury. He knows it will upset the peace of the bucolic pig-state. Socrates is ever charmed by the young men he loves, and so, almost against his will, he yields to the outrage of his young beloved and finds the discourse revealing greater truths than any of them imagined. To be sure, Glaucon may merely *want* spices and silk and couches to lie on, but this development cannot be explained in terms of want, for it is obvious to all that no one would ever *want* to be a warrior. How, then, are we to understand its origin in the lively disgust of the noble boy, Glaucon? It soon becomes clear that Glaucon himself is a spirited young man, and the interests of the spirit are not the same as the interests of satisfaction. What, after all, do his requests amount to? What are spices, after all? Spices do not add to the nutrient value of food. Without spices, we eat to live; with spices we live to eat. This makes the pleasure we take in dining no longer in the service of our health, indeed it may be unhealthy. But what is the formal significance to this? By shifting our eating from a purely purposive enterprise to an endeavor which justifies itself, a new kind of thinking occurs.

We can make sense of everything the citizens do by understanding their actions as resulting in some benefit to them. But the new class, those who must exist if there is to be excellence in the state, cannot be understood in this way. But if we do not make reference to the benefit of the warriors, then what kind of reasoning are we using? Socrates makes an astonishing and even wry metaphor: the warrior, he says, and even the philosopher if it comes to that, can be compared to a faithful dog. Now this delights the many, for there are legions who would gladly compare the philosopher to the dog. But Socrates' analysis is, as always, awesome in its power. A dog, he points out, will be friendly to his master, even if his master is cruel; but he will bark and even try to bite a friendly stranger. These adjectives are too important to pass without comment. The master may well be harsh and severe, the stranger may indeed offer the dog far more pleasure and comfort. But the dog is loyal to his master. The dog knows his own. He attacks the would-be benefactor who is alien, not because he is harmful but simply because he is *other*. Socrates claims that the dog is like the warrior and the philosopher because he, like they, prefers knowledge to benefit; that is, they serve that which is their own, even though it may be painful, rather than serve that which is alien even though it may be pleasant.

The metaphor of the warrior-philosopher as dog reveals one of the essential ways in which we think about spirit. For the citizens, the interest is the "I"; they band together in the primitive state solely for their own benefit. But the warrior sees the good not in terms of his own private satisfaction, but in terms of the state just for its own sake. Just as spices make eating worthwhile in and of itself, without the purposive reasoning that food sustains health and life, so the state is no longer seen merely as a benefit to the citizen, but as something intrinsically worthwhile. The dog serves its master simply because it belongs to the master; the warrior serves the state simply because it is his. The "I" shifts to the "We." And this is, of course, the original meaning to spirit: that who I am is understood in terms of my belonging to a greater reality than my own private existence. I do not serve the state merely because it is greater than I, rather I myself become greater because I belong to it. Spirit is surely this, that "I" am now a part of "Us." To be spiritual is to recognize the greater reality which is a part of me but which is greater than I am by myself.

To say that the warriors are an essentially new kind of class is to say that we think about them with entirely new principles. The citizens are given benefits by belonging to the state; the warriors, however, are understood as serving the state. Consider their remarkable and demanding education. They are taught, in the education of beauty, to love what is their own. They become "We" not "I"; they are trained so as to sacrifice their private lives, even suffer death on the battlefield, because it is no longer the "I" that matters but the "We." In order to achieve this, the young men are trained to forego the natural instincts of satisfaction. Rather, they value sacrifice and service. If their training strikes the modern democrat as totalitarian, that is because such education is seen only from the perspective of the citizen. Who, then, is a spirited man? One who sacrifices his life, if need be, for the sake of the whole. He is one who is trained to focus his attention on goodness as such, not goodness for him. He is one who ranks courage and nobility above gratification and desire. To be sure, the just state cannot be achieved until from among these warriors are chosen those very few who also learn to serve truth for its own sake. But the warriors obey the laws and rules given by the rulers, not out of fear or out of blind obedience, but out of respect for the rules as constituting what makes them who they are.

Spirit, then, following this Socratic insight inspired by Glaucon's disgust, is all those things we find among the young and the valiant. It is courage, it is sacrifice, it is nobility, it is honor. It is grounded on the educated realization that who *we* are outranks who *I* am. Just as we cannot understand a state without these young warriors, so we cannot understand ourselves without seeing the autonomous worth of the spirit which makes up our soul. Indeed, spirit is necessary for the other two classes or 'parts' of the soul to exist. One should not forget that in the original pig-state, grounded on the principle of self-interest, there is not even yet the virtue of temperance or *sophrosone:* that virtue comes only after the other classes are introduced. The highest ranking virtue of wisdom is also impossible without spirit, for according to the Socratic dialectic, the wise men originate from the warrior class.

Why is this the case? Let us assume the possibility of a state in which only rulers and citizens exist. The rulers pass a law. Why should the citizens obey it? The rulers by themselves do not have the authority or power to enforce the law; their recognition of the law's rationality is not possible for the citizen class, since this group acts solely on the basis of self-interest. The warrior or guardian class is needed to make the laws obeyed. But, merely as strong and aggressive soldiers, they could enforce their *own* laws upon the citizenry. Why should the soldiers enforce a law given to them by the rulers? The answer is obvious: they have been trained to revere the laws passed by their rulers because they have affection and respect for what is their own. The warriors do not even know if the laws passed by the rulers are in fact the best, since their training is to revere the laws, not evaluate them. But if this is so, we must ask: Why is a wise law (assuming that the rulers, who are wise, would pass only wise laws) obeyed; why should the powerful and spirited youth who has the power, enforce such a law? The point is, a precept passed down from the wise rulers is not even a law unless it is enforced. This requires that those who enforce the laws (the warrior class, acting as guardians and hence protectors of the law) revere the laws as essential parts and commands of their own sacred state.

This political picture is, we are told, merely an easier model to follow; it corresponds to the personal soul of a man. So we ask also: Why not understand ourselves solely in terms of our mind and our bodies? What need do we have of spirit? Suppose our minds tell us what is right and wrong. Why should we obey such commands of reason unless we first already have developed a respect for what is reasonable? Spirit, then, is a prerequisite for rationality, for without spirit reason would be an empty formalism, an unheard and unrespected source of wisdom which is not revered and not followed. Surely Socrates is correct in pointing out the essential need to have spirit. On the one hand, it governs our lower appetites; on the other it is reverential of reason. To understand ourselves as beings with pure reason and base inclination in no way accounts for why we should ever heed the directives of our minds. Respect for the authority of mind is what is called spirit. Without it, neither the interests of the appetites nor the effectiveness of reason can ever be fulfilled.

This, then, is the meaning of Glaucon's outrage that the state, and by analogy, the human soul, can be understood solely by the satisfaction of wants and needs. In addition, one must have a genuine affection for what is one's own, and a lively sense of sacrifice to make what is one's own the controlling guidance to our conduct and our self-awareness. Glaucon's disgust with the picture drawn of men who live merely by instinct and want provokes the profound analysis of the Socratic notion that spirit lies at the very center of our self-understanding. Without spirit, men would remain as beasts, and that is disgusting. Glaucon, to be sure, is disgusted only because he is already a spirited and noble person, but that is not a weakness to the argument; indeed it shows the strength and power of the dialectic. Socrates has shown the necessity of spirit.

However, even if we provisionally accept the argumentation of the *Republic,* there is something deeply unsettling about this account. In the sketch of the argument we have seen spirit described in terms of the warrior's virtues: courage, loyalty, devotion, and self-sacrifice. But our modern term 'spiritual' does not seem to be the same thing at all. When one thinks of spirit one does not usually think of warriors. Rather, the spiritual seems to evoke pictures of saintly, gentle, and nonviolent men and women. One is far more likely to imagine someone on his knees than to picture someone with a drawn sword. What do the qualities of prayerfulness and worship, the normal predicates of the spiritual, have to do with Socrates' young men who are armed with aggressive splendor in defense of their state? Surely no two people are more dissimilar than a praying monk and a warring soldier. Even if we grant the soundness of Socrates' analysis, what has it told us about the spiritual?

We must, of course, make an important distinction here between the spirited and the spiritual. Their differences are so obvious we need not even list them here. But what is necessary is to focus our attention, not on the differences, but on the sameness. Granted that spirited and spiritual are different, the first question is: To what extent are they alike, or even, the same. Even the most casual glance reveals that both terms contain the same term, 'spirit.' And so, accepting the huge differences, let us rather consider the common element. What is shared in the spirited and the spiritual?

The spirited and the spiritual both share the common element of spirit. What does this mean? We have already seen, from our brief sketch of the argumentation of Socrates, that what is important about the spirited is the shift from personal interest to shared concern, the revolution of thought that centers no longer on the 'I' but the 'we'. The good replaces the principle of gratification. This is a fundamental change: it is no longer possible to explicate the good as the mere enlargement of the numbers gratified; there is no utilitarianism here. But what is the good, if not gratification or at least satisfaction of wants? From the *Republic* we learn that the good is that which, guided by reason, is revered because it establishes a noble meaningfulness to those who share in it. The good is now seen as that which befits the high calling of the human species.

But the same kind of thinking applies to the spiritual as well as the spirited. A spiritual being is one for whom the central concern and focus of his existence is a greater reality than the sum total of human wants and desires. To be spiritual means to think of oneself in terms of a reality which is beyond one's private limitations. Reverence is essential for both spirited and spiritual; a greater meaningfulness which is accomplished by a belonging to that which is both beyond one's private existence and yet which, by means of the belonging, enhances and ennobles our existence. In both spirited and spiritual the 'I' is replaced by the 'we', though in the spiritual the 'we' may not always be understood in terms of the state. For both the spirited and the spiritual, however, being itself is interpreted as belonging to what is greater. Indeed, this belonging may be, for both the spirited and the spiritual, not only that which is greater, but that which is absolutely great, i.e., the supreme source of value. Both the praying saint and the sacrificial warrior recognize the authority beyond themselves which makes them greater beings. Not necessarily greater in the satisfaction of wants but in the range of meaning. Both soldier and saint *matter* because of their allegiance to whatever this greater reality may be. Thus, the true shift that is common to both the spirited and the spiritual is in the way we think about what makes us matter.

For this reason neither spirited warriors nor spiritual saints can be persuaded to think of themselves by means of a hedonistic calculus of any sort. The true warrior does not merely believe that his bravery will win him greater pleasures, nor does the true saint believe his piety will merely result in some post-terrestrial paradise. There are some warriors and saints who might also believe in such things, but that is not what distinguishes them from ordinary citizens who understand their worth in terms of their opportunities for pleasure. The difference is a way of thinking about oneself, and in both the spirited and the spiritual, that way of thinking must entail some sense of belonging to a greater and more noble reality which is served solely because it is worthy of being served, not because of its promised benefits.

But the present inquiry is not yet concerned with describing that reality. Indeed, we may have already strayed too far ahead, which in an inquiry based upon the analysis of meaning is always a danger. At the present, our sole concern is with raising the question of spirit. The appeal to the *Republic* is not meant as any claim to authority, as if we must believe Plato simply because he is both wise and revered. Indeed, it was not Socrates but Glaucon who led us to the sketch in the *Republic*. The purpose of listening to the outrage of the young friend of Socrates was simply to show that, in this case at least, the fundamental disgust Glaucon feels when he considers the purely natural state of satisfied citizens—which he contemptuously calls the pig-state—seems inevitably to lead us to some appeal to spirit. Our primary concern is to understand spirit; and we have already seen that spirit has two manifestations, the spiritual and the spirited. We are not yet ready to examine these with any degree of profundity or detail. We have merely seen what an ancient thinker offers as a response to a young man's disgust.

Nevertheless, Plato's analysis of spirit has suggested a critical and fundamental point of great import. If Plato is correct, spirit is necessary to understand both the just state and the soul. Thus, spirit is an essential part of us and not a mere contingent possibility. We sometimes speak of the spiritual and the nonspiritual or secular, as if there were two kinds of people, those with spirit and those without. This is to see spirit as something we can accept or reject, or perhaps inherit, like the color of one's eyes. And indeed, our normal way of speaking seems to give this idea some support. We say of someone that they have a spiritual nature, or that someone is entirely secular. But if Plato is right, we all are spiritual. Those who appear to be lacking in spirit would be, under this persuasion, merely denying an important part of themselves; they would be disingenuous or even self-deceptive. But we must raise this question seriously and on its own merits: Are there genuinely spiritual people and are there others who are not? Is spirit like wealth, possessed by some but not by all? To answer this requires a deeper understanding of spirit than this preliminary question can provide. It is nonetheless proper that it be *asked* (though not answered) now, for the question already shows us some of the major difficulty one has in raising the question honestly. Surely I cannot answer the question whether spirit is universally shared by all until and unless I first consider deeply just what spirit means. The obvious evidence seems to support the notion that some people have spirit and others do not; our experience seems to show this is the case. But Plato's suggestion

opens another possibility: that those we think of as lacking in
spirit are merely untrue to themselves. For the moment this
question must rest until we have considered more deeply this
simple question of meaning.

But there is another advantage, possibly even more monumental than the first, which the tripartite soul suggested by
Socrates provides in our understanding of spirit. Let us suppose
that the soul is indeed merely of two parts, that of the appetite
and that of reason. We are considering, in this inquiry, the nature of the sacred. Is then, the sacred *sensed* (by means of the
senses), or is it *thought,* by means of reason? If the soul consists
only of appetite and reason, and if there is something sacred in
our world, then we must learn of it, or at least become aware of
it, either through our sense or through our mind. But both of
these faculties seem inadequate to account for our understanding of the sacred. We do not calculate or reason out the sacred as
we would a problem in logic; nor can we verify the sacred
through sense experience. If we were to *sense* the sacred, it
should be open to verification and falsification; believability in
the sacred could be tested by the same canons that we test other
questionable experiences; there could even be laboratorylike
conditions for verifying the nature of the sacred experience. But
none of these accounts seem adequate; indeed, they seem out-
landish.

However, if we suggest that perhaps the soul has three
rather than merely two parts, the difficulty is resolved. I neither
reason out the sacred nor sensually experience the sacred,
rather, through the faculty of spirit, I grasp the spiritual meaning of the sacred. This is not to deny that both reason and sense
may also play a role in our understanding of sacredness; but its
central and critical avenue to us is through the spirit only. I have
used the term 'grasp' to refer to the assimilation of the spirit
because of its dual usage. On the one hand, 'grasp' means to
seize with the hands, to make something one's own by possessing
it. On the other hand, 'grasp' is also used as a synonym for understanding, as when we say we grasp the solution to a puzzle. If
there is spirit, and if one of its functions is the assimilation of
that which is sacred, then surely 'grasping the meaning of it' is a
far better locution than any term which is overtly identified with

the other faculties of the mind, such as 'knowing' or 'experiencing'. In any event, I shall use the term 'grasp' in this special sense when I mean the power of the spirit to assimilate the meaning of what is holy or sacred.

This advantage, of course, has no persuasive or compelling conviction as regards the question whether there exists a spirit, or even a soul for that matter. It merely shows the wealth of the Platonic view and also serves as an excellent reason to initiate our inquiry into the nature of spirit by making reference to Plato's *Republic*.

We have attempted to raise the question of spirit by spotting the existential modality of disgust with flesh. The picture sketched at the opening of this chapter evokes a curious unease, a sense that something about our meaning and our natures has been left out; and this evokes a powerful rejection which we have recognized as existential disgust. By centering on the youthful Glaucon's disgust, we see the outlines of a general theory of spirit, that clarified in Plato's *Republic*. But spirit there is but the spirit of the warrior. To make the inquiry clearer, we distinguish the 'spirited' from the 'spiritual', recognizing both as characteristic of spirit itself. But this is merely an attempt to raise the question. We must now proceed to an even more difficult endeavor, and that is to see the philosophical barriers that lay before us.

2

The Paradoxes

In the very serious business of fighting forest fires, rangers will often resort to a most peculiar and counterintuitive procedure by actually setting a new fire to a part of the forest: this is called "fighting fire with fire." Counterintuitive though it may be, and even paradoxical as it may seem, the method is often successful. Of course, once the rationale behind the procedure is clear, the paradoxical character of the action vanishes entirely. For we realize that by burning a controlled fire, the threatening fire will have no fuel and will eventually burn out. It may still sound a little odd to say that the best way to extinguish a fire is to start another, but it is obvious that it works, and once understood, it is also rational. There are many endeavors or procedures which at first sound paradoxical or even contradictory, but which turn out to be quite effective and immanently rational. A brilliant statesman like Otto von Bismark, for example, was famous for accomplishing great achievements by doing nothing at all, so that the maxim "one does most by doing least" came to be a veritable truism in the field of nineteenth-century politics. Surgeons often have to rebreak a bone in order to set it straight. Silence is often louder than speech.

Seeming contradictions, or even genuine paradoxes, therefore, often lie at the basis of our deepest understanding. Contradictions of course are simply illogical, and we cannot accept them as parts of our explanations. Things that appear counterintuitive are often resolved by clearing up what amounts to ambiguities. But genuine paradoxes have this peculiarity that they persist in producing anguish and torment in our minds even as they illuminate the problem. Thus, tragedy is a paradox because even after we understand the need for the conflict, our sentiments remain in turmoil although we see that the greater truth requires the tension. War is a genuine paradox because no matter how deeply we affirm the right of a nation to defend itself, we lament the dreadful loss of life. Courage itself, obviously an admired virtue, is something of a paradox because in order for there to be courage there must be an unpleasantness or pain which must be endured. Indeed, we praise the virtue of courage just because we celebrate the endurance of a pain we would prefer not to have to encounter. So there is a paradox in the praise of courage: we want to have it, but would prefer not to have to endure what it entails.

The present inquiry into the meaning of spirituality is a genuine paradox. By a genuine paradox is meant that the truth we seek is possible only because of a conflict of some sort. Unlike a contradiction, which invalidates the entire rationality of the inquiry, and unlike a mere counterintuition, which completely disappears once the purpose or rationale is uncovered, a paradox continues, even after the resolution or confrontation is achieved, precisely because the paradox is essential for the understanding. The meaning of spirituality oddly enough can be grasped only when it is seen as a paradox. To try to remove the paradox by interpreting it either as a mere counterintuition, or to dismiss the inquiry because it is genuinely contradictory, removes the very source of our understanding. Paradoxes are not resolved or dismissed; they are absorbed or embraced, and only in so doing can the paradox become a source of illumination. This is especially true of the present inquiry into the nature of spirit.

What does it mean to be spirit? And by this we refer to either 'spiritual' or 'spirited' or both. The final response to this question requires extensive analysis and sympathetic inquiry, and certainly cannot be answered by some dictionary definition. In order to understand spirit, or the meaning of spirituality, it is necessary to expose the truly paradoxical nature of the inquiry. This may sound to some as a fairly irreligious thing to say. To others it may sound as if, from the very beginning, spirituality is fraught with deep and troubling conflicts, suggesting that 'spirit' is an illusive, perhaps even deluding, concept. Why, one may ask, is there anything paradoxical about being spiritual? Why is 'spirit' any more troublesome than 'mental' or 'coherent' or even 'scientific'?

Spirit itself, or perhaps one should say, 'what it means to be spiritual' or 'spirited' is essentially paradoxical for the simple reason that in order to understand the nature of spirit I must first recognize that I cannot understand. Spirit is that which is not understandable. However, this does not mean that spirit cannot be the object of a rational inquiry; nor does it even suggest that there is something 'irrational' about spirit. It merely means that a proper understanding of spirituality is the recognition that the notion must contain some sense of ignorance, some sense of accepting or belief. There are many things we believe, and we do not hesitate to deny that it is 'knowledge' in classifying it as belief. (Trust, for example, is a virtue precisely because there must always remain the possibility of treachery. I trust someone only when I recognize that it is possible for the trusted one to betray my trust. If I *knew* with absolute certainty that the entrusted one would not betray, there would be no virtue in trusting. It is the same with courage: if I were to know with absolute certainty that I would escape all injury from the day's battle, there would be no virtue of courage in entering into the fray.)

The very nature of spirituality, therefore, is profoundly paradoxical. It is something we grasp most profoundly precisely when we admit we do not understand it completely. (Is not love like this? Or loyalty? Or even philosophical inquiry itself?) To come to a deeper awareness of this paradox, however, it is necessary carefully and respectfully to explore the various notions and terms involved.

From the very beginning of Western thought, in the Socratic approach to inquiry, it has been maintained that the most important question one can ask is about one's self. "Know thyself!" is the command of the Delphic oracle, and Socrates repeats over and over again that this primary task is the most fundamental of all. But, with all due reverence to both the oracle and Socrates, surely this is a curious and even a mysterious beginning. For the question is not how or why I should know myself, the greater and even more primordial question is how on earth it is possible *not* to know myself. Surely I am often mistaken about persons and things other than myself. I am mistaken because of the distance between myself and the thing analyzed or asked about. I can easily understand John Locke's confusion about a square tower in the distance appearing round; I can rest easy with my own ignorance of the other side of the sun. Gentle and sensitive people can be understood in their ignorance of what inspires a violent or a cruel man. There is no problem in recognizing that Saint Therese may find Joseph Stalin somewhat difficult to comprehend. The reason is simple: the knower is other than the known. But I am I myself. I *am* what I seek to understand; hence it would seem impossible that I could make a mistake about myself. I may, to be sure, be confused about how I should fit into the universe, or what I should do with other agents in the world, but this is surely due to my ignorance about the universe or about others, not myself. Since my own existence is already bound up necessarily with my being conscious at all, it would seem, as Descartes apparently recognized, that there can be no doubt about myself. But if this is true, then to make the task of 'self-knowledge' the paramount issue seems ridiculous. How can I fail at all in understanding myself? Surely the one thing that is truly impossible is that I would not know myself, for to know at all already assumes my self as knower.

Is Socrates, then, guilty of a simple but profound mistake? It seems irreverent to say so. Socrates has achieved the status of being almost the patron saint of philosophy and one contradicts him with great reluctance. However, Socrates himself recognizes the value of this question: if self-knowledge is the goal of the philosopher, then surely we must first examine how self-ignorance is possible.

Yet, the paradox is even darker than this. For if we succeed in uncovering what makes us ignorant of ourselves, we will no longer be ignorant; and if an essential condition of spirituality is to remain self-ignorant, then its meaning would vanish upon successful analysis. If spirituality matters, then, it would seem that it depends upon a kind of self-ignorance which we would not want to change to knowledge, so that an inquiry into spirituality would make us unspiritual. Is it possible to inquire into what makes us

148,376

ignorant of ourselves without destroying the very essence of spirit? Perhaps, then, we should avoid such inquiry at all costs, lest in discovering what makes us ignorant we eclipse the very possibility of spirit itself.

This, however, is surely an unworthy position. Inquire we must. Curiosity, or perhaps a nobler sentiment, will not let us remain in such blind acceptance of so primordial a question. So, we must inquire into a kind of ignorance which, when understood, does not forfeit the ignorance. We must seek to understand without the understanding removing our ignorance. This is not irrationality raised to the level of mystery, for the paradox is precisely this, that the deeper we understand our spirituality, the more we understand our ignorance. Wouldn't we concede the greater the pain that is endured, the greater the courage? The greater the dubiety, the greater the trust? May it not also be that the more profoundly we grasp our natures as finite and unknowing, the greater the value of our understanding? Perhaps.

But for a philosopher, the paradoxical character of spirituality is a special burden; for philosophy seeks for clarity, and the present inquiry into the meaning of spirit is fruitless and empty if we cannot gain a deeper understanding. But this is a paradox and not a contradiction. To discover our ignorance is indeed a kind of wisdom. It is like the love of a parent for a growing, adult-becoming child; for a son to leave his family unsuns the sky, yet no parents would lovingly deny their child adulthood, even when that means the departure of the beloved. Is it a cruel love that attaches us to that which we must learn to leave? Perhaps; but if so, cruelty is a sacred virtue. In the search for the meaning of spirituality if we must confront a necessary ignorance, it may be like the cruelty of parental love: difficult, but not contradictory.

The paradoxical character of spirituality is not only the purely epistemic one of understanding our own ignorance, it is also the metaphysical paradox of finding the true meaning of one's self to be the nonself. I am most truly myself when I realize I am not myself: i.e., when what I am is greater than what I am. For any spiritual understanding, there is always a profound realization of belonging to something or someone which is far greater than our own private existence. Indeed, it is not merely that I *belong* to a being or reality greater than myself, but that I *am* this reality. Richard II, entombed in his tower prison, reflects on this same mystery:

> I have been studying how I may compare
> This prison where I live unto the world:
> And for because the world is populous,
> And here is not a creature but myself,
> I cannot do it; yet I'll hammer it out. . . .
>
> Thus play I in one person many people
> And none contented: sometimes am I king,
> Then treasons make me want to be a beggar,
> And so I am: Then crushing penury
> Persuades me I was better when a king;
> Then am I king'd again; and by and by
> Think that I am unking'd by Bolingbroke,
> And straight am nothing: but whate'er I be,
> Nor I nor any man that but man is
> With nothing shall be pleased, till he be eased
> With being nothing. . . .
>
> (5.4)

Surely the one characteristic which distinguishes a 'spiritual person' from one who is not spiritual is the sense or realization that one's existence is determined by a greater reality, whether a god or a force or a union with the entire world. We think of it as a kind of sympathy with the All, where nothing is alien, where one's utmost privacy is pervaded by Another. And yet the spiritual being may also be thought as among the loneliest of all human types. No matter where one turns in the asking of this question, there is paradox.

Well, then, perhaps the grasping of a paradox is the most profound form of human understanding. Perhaps sheer clarity, or knowledge conceived as a total absence of all doubt and uncertainty, is a myth. It may be that anything conceived with such direct apprehension is simply neither knowledge nor truth. Analytic propositions are said to bring no new knowledge; the predicate of such propositions is said to add nothing new; it is already contained in the subject. Is that knowledge? Surely it is not understanding in any meaningful sense. Thus we must consider carefully the suggestion that the deepest minds, the greatest sources of truth, lie not in the removal of uncertainties and doubt, but in the peculiar mode of comprehension that consists in grasping a paradox without loss of tension.

But even if grasping a paradox may be the most profound kind of understanding, surely the present paradox defies even that. How can I be that which I am not? I may well be said to be *in* the world, but I cannot be said to *be* the world. In the reach for mystical comprehension have we not simply violated the laws of syntax and grammar? Richard may *pretend* he is many people in his tower cell, but in fact we know he is there alone. He is Richard II, unkinged perhaps, but still *not* a beggar or a commoner. That is but fancy, or imagination; or worse, illusion. For, when all poetry is put aside and the wild soarings of the fevered brain have settled back on the safe perch of reason, the brute fact is that this huddled ex-monarch is the same child born of his mother's womb and no one else. Simple common sense and the fundamental law of logic demands that I am I; I am not anyone else, I am not the whole world. When I bleed the world does not suffer; when I sleep the world does not close its eyes. When I grow hungry, no one else feels the gnawing in my stomach save me. Unless we insist upon this, we lose all sense and reason. We lose *me;* for who and what I am is characterized by the qualities that distinguish me from others.

This protest is absolutely valid. I am not others; I am not 'more' than myself. Perhaps in some poetic metaphor we might allow someone to convince us that one man's hunger is all our hunger; because what we mean by that nice imagery is that all men somehow belong to the same species and that perhaps there is a moral law which requires me to care about the well-being of all those who suffer. Fine. *That* is intelligible. But certainly I cannot accept as literally true that I am more than what I am. That is not a paradox, it is a contradiction.

Nevertheless, Father Zossima, in Dostoyevsky's *The Brothers Karamazov* tells his fellow monks that he and they are responsible for all the wrongs and sins and faults of everyman. And he claims this because we share in the same mystical union with all men. Are we simply to reject this out of hand? Perhaps we must. Perhaps reason will demand that we forego such violations of sense and common understanding. But even if we do abandon it, the paradox still haunts us: by spirit we mean sharing existence with others, transcending the limits of our immediate and corporeal reality, and actually *existing* beyond the limits of our own particularity. At the very least, then, we must ask what this means.

In addition to the epistemic paradox of understanding spirit only when we accept our ignorance and the metaphysical paradox of being more than what we are, there is a final, and perhaps even fatal, paradox of spirit: the moral paradox. Surely there is no more dangerous belief than that some secret power or force directly informs us of our duties and obligations. A few years ago a man on board the Staten Island ferry drew a sword and began hacking, slicing, and killing his fellow passengers. When the police finally subdued him, he admitted that he had heard a voice from God telling him to do these things. Of course, we consider him crazy. He is no longer sane; we lock him up. Yet, Joan of Arc also heard voices, and in heeding them she convinced the king of France to put her in charge of a mighty army which drove the English army from French soil. Was she crazy, too? Perhaps she was. It may have been her good fortune to have used her secret voices to carry out a worthy endeavor, at least for the French; the man on the Staten Island ferry, however, is judged simply as insane and his acts outrageous and dastardly. But fundamentally, we must ask if there is any difference between Joan's private voices and those of the man who killed his fellow passengers aboard the ferry.

Spiritual union with God or some other powerful celestial force has this grim and terrible consequence, that we submit our will to a command which we ourselves admit we do not understand. Two things bother us about this. The first is the complete capitulation of all autonomy and hence all meaning. If I obey whatever voices sound in my ear, whether they come from God or from the devil or simply from psychological confusion, I am not a free being. On the other hand, if the voices tell me to do something which I then test by my own moral standard, what is the need for a voice at all? To be spiritual, then, *seems* to mean a capitulation of autonomy; but if that is the case, then we have no independent worth at all. It would be better not to be spiritual than to lose one's own worth.

It should be emphasized here that these examples are not meant to disprove the possibility that a divine voice might instruct some of us to act in certain ways. The question is: even if the voice *were* from God, as free agents, as moral responsible people, how could we ever obey the commands from this voice? If the commands are already in accord with moral acceptability (as Joan's seem to have been), then why do we need the spiritual at all? Perhaps Joan of Arc is simply a brilliant general who, through her natural gifts as military leader, led the French to victory. We can celebrate that. But if so, we do not need to hear of her voices to make her a champion of French history.

So the spiritual seems oddly inconsistent with the moral. Surely the moral law is followed just because we recognize its moral authority, not because it has some spiritual resource at its base. It would seem, then, that morality itself must shun the influence of the spiritual.

The three paradoxes of spirit then, the metaphysical, the epistemic, and the moral, must be seriously confronted if we are to make any sense at all of spirit. On the first level we have the paradox of mystery: how can I seek to understand that which by its very nature is mysterious and hence not understandable? On the second level is the paradox of meaning: how can I recognize my own meaning if it is grounded in that which is other than myself? To know myself would then be to know that which is not myself but which provides me with meaning. And finally the third paradox is the moral one: how can I be true to my own freedom and responsibility unless I am true to my own guilt and conscience; yet, spirituality places the authority of my responsibility and freedom beyond myself. These three paradoxes threaten to undermine the intelligibility of spirit, making it more rational to be unspiritual and less rational to be spiritual. And yet, these three paradoxes, when properly and deeply examined, will reveal that spirituality remains a noncontradictory modality; for they are all three genuine paradoxes and not irrational inconsistencies.

THE EPISTEMIC PARADOX (MYSTERY)

In a later and separate section 'mystery' will be analyzed as one of the essential predicates of spirit. Here our concern is not with mystery *per se* but with the paradox of inquiring into that which, in order to be understood, must be recognized as ineffable. How is it possible to inquire into spirit if spirit itself is essentially mystery?

In the first place it must be recognized that no inquiry, whether into spirit or science or everyday events is ever without some unexamined presupposition, some element that explains which itself is not explained. I can explain any natural phenomenon by pointing out the conditions and causes which precede it. Such an explanation means that whenever these conditions occur, the consequent will always take place, hence the phenomenon is the result of a natural law. But *why* that law is in effect at all times, or *why* the conditions were present cannot always be explained, indeed if one includes the entire series, such events can never be explained. This is not skepticism or even an attempt to belittle the authority of science. In the first place, science does not need to make such explanations, nor should it. But the point is made to remind the reader that in the phenomena of human explanations, total and absolute explanatory power is never the result. If it were, to know one thing completely would be to know everything.

Nevertheless, we still need to grasp how one can inquire into spirit if the fundamental core of spirit is ineffable. Is this not like shining one's light into a bottomless pit? The beam may penetrate into the darkness but not reach the end, and so the pit remains as unplumbed as before. Is it not a contradiction to ask about that which cannot be asked about?

In spite of this troubling paradox, if not contradiction, there can be no doubt that men of spirit do indeed maintain that the object of their adoration and worship is beyond their full comprehension. The ways of God are mysterious. This means we do not and cannot understand them. But we still obey them. One can only admire the depth of faith contained in such assertions, but such admiration is tinged with uncertainty and even scorn. Surely we ought *not* to obey that which we do not understand.

Or, if we interrogate a deeply religious mystic or contemplative monk, we are assured by him that he cannot express or even comprehend the magnificence of his spiritual union with the divine. We are told no words can express what it is like to be in the presence of God. But of course, there are no words that can express what it is like to taste an orange. If someone has never tasted citrus fruit, there is no way to explain what it is like to experience the explosion of tangy and succulent juices in the mouth, the counterpoint of sweetness and tartness which gives such exquisite pleasure to the taste buds and causes such irrepressible reactions in our saliva glands. Biting into a fresh, sun-ripened orange is simply indescribable. But have we, in comparing the sublime to the banal, reduced the analogy to insult? Perhaps, but there is too much truth in the comparison to leave it unexamined. What is the mystic worshiper saying when he attests that his God is ineffable? First, he is not saying that the experience is entirely unintelligible, for he at least characterizes it by such vague phrases as "being in the presence of God." By assuring us that it is unique we know that we are not supposed to compare it to other experiences—but then *no* two experiences are completely comparable.

Yet it is an almost universal quality of those who seek to explain their spirituality that they rely on terms like 'inexplicable' or 'ineffable'. As was noted, the same can be said for the taste of an orange, but somehow we sense that in the case of the spiritual experience, the mystery is not a *negative* quality but a *positive* quality. The point is not that the experience of spiritual union is difficult to explain—what isn't?—but that essential for its explanation is a grasp of the ineffable. But is not 'the ineffable' precisely what cannot be grasped? And that, of course, is what the spiritual consciousness seeks to deny.

We must remind ourselves here that we are not trying to explain what is infinite; we are merely trying to make sense of what it means to be confronted by the infinite, and those are two quite different things. To confuse these two notions is a mistake too often made by the spiritual writer and the skeptical secularist both. To be spiritual may imply being in some kind of relationship or belonging to a force or reality which is so great it cannot be fully comprehended; but here the pronoun 'it' refers to the greater reality, not to the relationship or the experience of belonging. Our task is not the impossible one of describing the undescribable, it is the more modest one of trying to make sense of what it means to confront that which is beyond our descriptive powers. Is there anything to guide us in this inquiry?

Immanuel Kant, in his *Critique of Judgment*, explains the experience of the sublime in exactly those terms. The sublime, according to Kant, causes us both intellectual pleasure and pain. It causes us pleasure because it is an aesthetic experience which thrills us, but it causes us pain because our faculties of understanding are simply exceeded by the enormity of what we confront. We are frustrated because we cannot contain the enormity of what we experience in the ordinary and common categories of our understanding; but we are also thrilled by this very incapacity to control our aesthetic response. One of the deepest reasons for this paradox is the mistaken plerophory that to control is always good, to comprehend always to be preferred to wonder. In many things we actually prefer to be conquered, as when a moving drama overwhelms our aplomb and we react to the emotions we no longer control, or when, in sexual ecstasy, we find ourselves submitting to a power which exceeds our capacity to master. By analogy, there is an epistemic delight beyond knowledge, when what we confront is so full of meaning that our faculties are inadequate to grasp them. This is, to be sure, a kind of ignorance, but it is, if you will, a 'good' ignorance, for its foundation is not deception or illusion but simply the magnitude of meaning not yet fully appreciated. As in the case of Kant's analysis of the sublime, there remains that pain and frustration in not being able to categorize and master the knowledge; but there is also affirmation in the realization that the confrontation with the ineffable sequesters a truth far greater than our capacity to understand it.

But, of course, that is the annoying question. Is it really *truth?* We must avoid accepting certain spiritual experiences merely because they are unintelligible. Not even the religious mystics would argue that any religious experience is necessarily correct, and the human mind is sufficiently critical, if not cynical, to want to know if that which looms largely beyond our comprehension is illusory or true. Few will deny, I think, there are truths which we may not understand, and we would not want to exclude them merely on that basis; but there are also many falsehoods lying behind that mystical veil of ignorance which we likewise do not want to accept merely because they are mysterious. Fortunately, our present concern is not with the impossible one of knowing in advance which mysteries to accept and which not to accept—for then they would not be mysteries—but simply to understand what it means to accept a mystery. The former is beyond our powers as philosophers, but the latter is not. It would be a methodological error to argue that because we *want* there to be great realms of truth which are nonetheless mysterious that therefore we should believe in them; that is to reduce this inquiry to mere psychology, which in the present case would be grossly condescending. The sole purpose of this section on the epistemic paradox of spirit is to show that one can indeed reflect upon the structure of spirit without having to know what is inexplicable.

It may be said, for example, that all religions are basically good, that it is important for the human soul to have some kind of belief in that which is greater than oneself. This may be true. But to say that all religions are good does not imply that all religions are *true*. The concern of philosophy is with truth and not merely the satisfaction of primeval wants which satisfy without being true. The seeming ubiquity of spiritual belief may indeed lead us, as philosophers, to consider what it *means* to be spiritual, and this analysis may well help us decide the kinds of beliefs to accept. But philosophy is neither theology nor psychology: it neither claims to know more than is possible for human understanding, nor does it reduce all such longing to mere psychic phenomena which have no truth value at all. By raising this inquiry in terms of the existential meaning of spirituality, both of these extremes can be avoided.

This concern for 'truth' as opposed to "what satisfies the psyche," however, is itself troublesome. We must avoid being seduced by the lure of the Cartesian longing for certainty. Descartes counsels that if you cannot prove it, you should deny it. In this way he hoped to establish a few undoubtable truths which would allow him to construct an edifice of metaphysical certainty which would be unassailable. What he succeeded in doing, of course, was to present a problem knottier than that of any sphynx, and his appeal to certainty probably does more damage to such beliefs than the snide harping of countless cynics. On the other hand, Augustine argues, "Credo, ut intellegam," which, though it sounds at first like the complete opposite of Descartes, nevertheless also contains the need for critical thinking. "I believe," Augustine says, "in order that I may understand." Of course, the simple Latin sentence does not say *what* he believes; but the point is nonetheless valid: surely it is impossible to inquire *critically* without some kind of belief. Perhaps the belief itself must ultimately be criticized, but to begin *ab novo* is to begin nowhere.

These two precepts of methodology seem totally inconsistent. Descartes says, "If you doubt it, deny it"; whereas Augustine says, "Accept it first, then you'll understand it." If not out and out contradictory, these two methodologies surely represent opposing instincts. And yet, perhaps they can be brought together in a way that satisfies the deep concerns of each. Surely with Descartes we do not want to affirm as true anything which may be illusory; but also, with Augustine, we do not want to discard so much as to have nothing to go on. Is it not somehow possible to accept some things as provisionally true, and perhaps even as holy, and still be critical enough to satisfy Descartes's skeptical concerns? To do this we must begin with a simple description of what it means to ask about the ineffable. What am I asking *for*? If I believe there is something infinite and ineffable, then it is surely madness to ask that it be described. But it is not madness to ask what it means to be confronted by such enormity. The only thing necessary is that we retain our sense of paradox.

As we have noted, the difference between a paradox and a contradiction or a counterintuition is that when the paradox is understood, the pain still remains; the mind cannot rest, the soul is still in turmoil. However, when the paradox is understood at least we know there is no contradiction; we know that it is possible to accept both prongs of the aching fork. It is that learning which is so philosophically crucial. In the present case the paradox is 'understood' when we realize that our unease with ignorance is balanced with the sweetness of a comprehension which does not forfeit doubt but thrives on it. How is this possible?

It is possible when we recognize that spirit has never been known as a faculty of *knowledge;* it is neither reason, which protects us from inconsistencies, nor is it sensation, which provides us with new information about the world. Spirit is rather that which turns upon itself and illumines the meaning of existence. It may well be that this spiritual excellence requires some kind of confrontation with what is ineffable, but our inquiry is not, at this moment, concerned with whether such things exist, but merely with what it means to confront them. The paradox remains: I cannot rest easy with spirituality; on the other hand neither can I rest easy with the complete dismissal of any and all spirituality. Of course, there is no doubt that I can adopt a mode of existence and behavior in which I simply stop thinking about such matters. Indifference is the greatest balm against the ache of uncertainty. It is not knowledge which satisfies the doubter, it is indifference; for knowledge always brings with it more problems and hence more uncertainty. But indifference is the death of spirit as well as of inquiry.

This first paradox, then, explains the format and methodology of the inquiry. It is essential first to describe as carefully as possible the various ways in which spirituality seems to manifest itself. This is the purpose of Part Two: The Predicates of Spirit. Then, having examined all of these external manifestations, taking care to include all dimensions of spirit lest by prejudice we exclude those which might reveal the greatest meaning, we seek to penetrate into the essence of spirit. This constitutes the concern of Part Three: The Essence of Spirit. And finally, we are able to step back from the inquiry, reflect upon what has been discovered, and critically evaluate what has been uncovered by the analysis; and so we call the Fourth Part: Reflections on Spirit.

Briefly, the paradox of seeking after the ineffable is eased by the realization that we seek not after what cannot be explained but simply what it means to be confronted with the unexplainable. This furthers our understanding by revealing the truth that not all ignorance is bad. Ignorance of that which can be known but is not, through indifference or miscalculation, is bad; but ignorance of that which by its very greatness transcends human comprehension yet makes it possible is a good ignorance. Furthermore, such ignorance is not the mere absence of knowledge; it is the indirect awareness of what makes inquiry possible. If we may once more borrow from the *Republic*, the man standing outside the cave, from whence he has just extricated himself from darkness, can see the shadows cast by the trees and the reflection of the sun in the water, but he does not turn his eyes directly to the sun, lest he be blinded. However, he knows the sun is there by its effects. If we can but see the effects of the ineffable by considering the existential modalities of those who confront it in spirituality, it will be enough to satisfy the discomfort of the paradox.

THE METAPHYSICAL PARADOX

The extremes of this paradox can be stated in the following way. One is either so very individual that no sharing with others is possible and no universality, save the most abstract conceptual kind, binds us as members of the same race; or one is so completely absorbed in the All or the spiritual union that every aspect of individual meaning is eclipsed. Put in this way, even the most sophomoric of minds can see that the answer must lie somewhere in between. But there may be no middle ground. And for the spiritual person the problem is even greater, since spirituality seems to intensify both extremes: I am supremely an individual only when I am spiritual, and I am completely absorbed in the Other as a spiritual being. Again, as with the epistemic paradox, the attempt is not to find out which of the two attitudes is preferable but to accomplish some kind of coexistence between these conflicting sentiments.

There can be no doubt that the spiritual person often speaks of his unity with the One or the All, even to the point of seeming to deny the value of individuality altogether. Buddhism especially seems inclined to deprecate the self or 'ego', a doctrine which causes Nietzsche to despise Buddhism as profoundly nihilistic. Yet, all of us sense something valuable in this desire for universality or felt companionship with all that happens.

> To see the world in a grain of sand
> And a Heaven in a wild flower,
> Hold Infinity in the palm of your hand,
> And eternity in an hour.

These immortal lines by Blake, which begin his "Auguries of Innocence," express the sentiment which most spiritual people seem to adopt almost naturally. We must break down the barriers that separate us from one another; we must establish a unity among men and indeed among all natural creatures; we must excise the principles of private importance and substitute them with a generous egalitarianism, so that all men are brothers.

But even as we express these egalitarian sentiments a sense of distinct unease and even horror overtakes us. We recall the outrage of Glaucon and the disgust that comes with a world populated by clones of a common mold. Egalitarianism is opposed to one of the most sacred principles of spirituality, that there are special, chosen, and blessed ones; that not all are equalled, that "many are called but few are chosen." When Cleopatra watches her beloved Antony die in her arms, she sighs:

> Young boys and girls
> Are level now with men; the odds is gone,
> And there is nothing left remarkable beneath the visiting moon.

Surely this matters! For her, there is no other man like Antony. Though she tries to ply her honored charms against Caesar, she has no heart for it, and the rare Egyptian fails. Notice carefully her lament. Now that her beloved is dead, boys and girls are level now with men. To level out is the depressing result of lovelessness. For lovers know that all men are not equal; loving makes them unequal. Will Rogers is famous for his quotation "I never met a man I didn't like." Imagine, if you will, someone saying, "Hey, Will Rogers *likes* me." To which Cleopatra would reply, "But he likes everyone. What value, what benefit, what good is there in being liked by someone who likes everyone?" But for her, there is *nothing* remarkable left beneath the moon. Nothing remarkable. Is that not the dread, unholy, suffocating horror that threatens to eclipse all excellence, all greatness? Is this not the nausea promised by utilitarianism and egalitarianism alike? When Antony goes, or even when his extraordinary lover goes, we feel that greatness is no longer with us. Something wonderful has past. Was it not Aristotle who said that he would rather be a cousin to someone in Athens than a brother to everyone in the whole world?

The spiritual claim that one can be so absorbed in the reality of the divine disturbs us because of this paradox. However, the tension is not reserved for mystics on their knees: it is a conflict for any thinking man who seeks to understand his place in the universe. The point here is not to achieve some kind of 'balance' between these two traditions, for that is unworthy of this paradox. Rather, we are seeking to understand how it is *possible to absorb* the extremes. For Cleopatra is not about to soften her judgment: Antony gone has removed the very possibility of the remarkable. Were she to relent and admit that perhaps all men were really equal and that she would soon find another Antony, she would not be Cleopatra, and we would not be who we are without that noble play. Yet, just as strongly we believe in the gentle wisdom of Blake and recognize that universality is a necessity for spiritual excellence no less so than uniqueness. And so, the paradox.

But whatever is the solution, the paradox cannot be eased by establishing some middle ground or compromise. The whole point of Blake's seeing the universe in a grain of sand is that he sees the *universe:* all of it, not part or some or even most of it, but all of it, including Antony. But Cleopatra refuses to see *any* of the universe as worthy of being seen now that Antony is dead. There is *nothing* remarkable beneath the visiting moon. Nothing. It is the very extremes of these two positions that make them powerful. It is their very uncompromising enormity that makes them candidates for spiritual meaning; but it is also their extremity that makes the paradox so cruel. We cannot weaken the paradox without undoing it altogether; and to undo it is to lose whatever truth is strung between the straining poles.

If I wish to matter, before God or before any tribunal, then why should I seek to be completely absorbed in anything, even God? Yet, unless I embrace the whole world in my being, can I matter at all, either to myself or any other? And it should perhaps be stressed here that merely because someone is indeed spiritual does not mean he is always right. Mistakes are made by those who struggle to achieve sanctity as well as wisdom. The struggle may well reveal much to us that is true, but only the naive would believe that all who struggle achieve.

This second paradox, then, is far crueler than the first. The passion for unity and the passion for uniqueness are both too precious to homogenize: we want both Blake's vision of the universe in a grain of sand, and we want to dismiss all possibly remarkable since Antony is gone. How is it possible to absorb these conflicting passions so as to avoid contradiction but not defuse the flame of anguish? They are not, of course, truly contradictory: Blake's universal vision is *not* egalitarian; no worthy thought can be. And Cleopatra's lament itself has universal qualities, else how could it mean so much to those of us who hear it? But avoiding contradiction does not ease the tension, for these are conflicting passions and both are necessary for spiritual meaning. The individual must matter so much that to lose him is to have nothing remarkable left beneath the sun and moon; the universal must matter so much that without it we are entirely sequestered from the world, incapable of love, passion or sharing.

The very confrontation of these two opposing passions, both so necessary for spiritual existence, serves at least to instruct us on how not to strive for spirituality. We may speak of "losing oneself totally in the All of the divine," but if this eclipses that which makes us matter—and it *can* if done foolishly—then we know we have erred. On the other hand, if our individuality is so intense we cannot share at all, we know this too is a mistake. But how can these mistakes be avoided when the very intensity of these passions is requisite for spirit to have meaning? In our existential description of the predicates of spirit it will be required that the analysis and interpretation is so carefully drawn and so precisely plumbed that the two passions will retain their autonomy and yet become as one. The point of the present chapter is merely to raise the paradox, to show that the conflict genuinely exists and is neither a contradiction, which would discredit the entire inquiry, nor a mere counterintuition which would trivialize it. This we have done. To understand spirit we must understand the paradox of self and All. Just to discover this tormented problem already serves the inquiry. We now see, at least, something of the topography of the terrain we must climb. It may not be easy, but the effort itself ennobles.

THE MORAL PARADOX

Søren Kierkegaard has pointed out to us the existential enormity of moral faith. Abraham is commanded by God to kill his only son, Isaac, as a sacrifice, yet God has promised Abraham he will be the sire of a great and noble race. Abraham obeys, and prepares to sacrifice his only son. An angel stops this murder and substitutes a lamb instead. But Abraham's decision had already been made. The last-minute substitute in no way deters us from the grim realization that Abraham, knowing it is wrong to kill his only son, is willing to do so anyway because he is told to do so by God. In Kierkegaard's *Fear and Trembling* there are many points made which are wondrous and awesome about this reflection, but there is no point in recapitulating them here. The simple, bald fact is enough. If there is spiritual union with God, what about our ordinary moral understanding? It cannot be the same, for that is an insult to the autonomy of the spiritual. Yet, if it is not the same, then the spiritual must be, at least at times, immoral. But if, in order to retain my morality, I dismiss my spirituality, then have I not rendered the moral a purely formal requirement?

It seems as though 'being spiritual' and 'being good' are not only different, they are in conflict. And again, this paradox cannot be defused by watering it down or explaining it away. The spiritual makes immoral demands on us. We cannot resolve this one as we did the first paradox, by showing that the inquiry is into the meaning of the confrontation and not the infinite itself. Nor can we ease the paradox as we did in the second case when we recognize the need to absorb and coexist, even though they conflict. No, in this third paradox there is a moral issue which cannot be avoided. Surely if the spiritual in any way undercuts the absolute authority of the moral law, it must be rejected.

Consider the story of the holy man named Francis. He was a good and pious man who endeavored to love God to the highest and purest extent possible. However, as a devout Christian, Francis also believed that every good act he did warranted some post-terrestrial reward in heaven. It bothered Francis that he could not remove from his mind that reward; no matter what good act he performed the idea that he would be rewarded for it fascinated him. He began to doubt if he was capable of doing anything merely for the love of God; perhaps he was always acting nobly or kindly merely because of the heavenly reward promised those who perform good acts. Soon he began to worry this notion like an unhealed sore. Was it at all possible to act solely for the love of God? Convinced that such purity of motive was not possible, Francis decided on a remarkable course of action. His theological belief taught him that if one commits a mortal sin, one must go to hell forever. Perhaps, he wondered, if he were to commit one mortal sin, thereby guaranteeing his own damnation, then whatever good he performed from henceforth would be done solely for the love of God, since he would have forfeited all possible benefit by assuring himself of damnation. The idea grew in his mind until finally he decided this was the only way he could guarantee to himself that the only true reason for doing good was for its own sake and because he loved God, and not for any heavenly reward. Believing absolutely in the theology that damned him forever if he sinned mortally, Francis committed one fatal, mortal sin against his God, thereby forever damning his soul to hell. Burdened with this unbearable torment on his soul, Francis then continued to live the saintly life filled with good works. He felt assured that his motives now were pure, for since he totally accepted that his soul was damned, he could not possibly be acting in hope of heavenly reward. Having sinned, his good acts were done solely for the sake of holiness. In this way, he felt he had finally achieved his goal of being able to love God for the pure and simple reason that God deserved to be served.

Was he foolish? Of course he was. Was he, in fact, mistaken about the theology? Probably. The story is not told to be emulated. Rather, the story is told to emphasize just how the spiritual and the moral are different. Was he courageous? Indeed, he was. Even sinners can be courageous, even fools can be noble in their motives. Whatever else we think of Francis, we are stunned by his self-sacrifice in order to achieve a purity of loving which he felt he could achieve in no other way. The story impresses, even fascinates us. But philosophically it is powerful because it forces us to recognize that what it means to be spiritual is not necessarily the same as what it means to be good. And this distinction is absolutely critical if we are to succeed in isolating the meaning of spirit.

The story of Francis may be distracting simply because it is so remarkable. The conflict between morality and spirituality is even more intense in the distinction between morality and forgiveness. How is it possible for God to forgive a sinner without sabotaging the authority of the moral law? If God forgives a sinner, and a sinner by definition is one who deserves to be punished, then God is unjust. There is no way in which sleight-of-hand or clever definitions will resolve this: to forgive is to violate justice. We do not even need God in this proposition: for anyone to forgive any person is to suspend justice and hence violate justice. In his great novel *The Brothers Karamazov*, Dostoyevsky has the intellectual brother, Ivan, tell of several horror stories in which innocent children are cruelly tortured and killed by fat landlords looking for distracting entertainments. A boy is stripped naked and chased down by ferocious dogs for the sport of hunting; his distraught mother is forced to watch this sacrilege. The landlord laughs at the sport and is hugely pleasured as he watches the distraught mother grieve at her only son's savage mutilation. Now, Ivan asks: Are you prepared to believe in a God who would *forgive* the landlord? He protests that for the love of mankind he will *not* forgive him. But he knows the Christian teaching is that God can forgive anyone. What does it mean to forgive the landlord? Is there any passion, any reason, any argument available that can be brought before the ravaged mother which would convince her the landlord should be forgiven? Would it, in fact, not be a sacrilege of the highest order to ask the mother to forgive? And yet, forgiveness of the most scarlet sins is seen as a quality of the divine, a noble, uplifting, lofty excellence that radiates forth holiness. But is *this* forgiveness holy? Does not this forgiveness catch in our throats like bile and make us want to vomit in disgust?

And yet it is so idly, even cavalierly, announced that forgiveness is a greater endeavor than justice. Ivan's story has made that claim difficult to maintain. Surely, in this case, justice is better than forgiveness. In fact, if we look deeply at each case, is not justice *always* better than forgiveness?

There can be no doubt that this too is a cruel paradox. On the one hand, we want there to be forgiveness; it smacks of nobility and divinity, and it seems to elevate the soul. On the other hand, we cannot forego justice. There is a dignity about justice which deserves our praise as well. Justice is not revenge, although the contemporary consciousness often seems to make it so. But the import of these little stories is to show that justice is *not* revenge, that the mind and heart cry out for what is right. And so we want conflicting things. Like a child demanding both, we want justice and pardon. But the cruel truth is the pardon forfeits justice; justice cancels out forgiveness. Yet both are valuable, both are precious, perhaps even, both are sacred. How can we think? How should we think?

It is important here simply to realize that there is no easy, calculated solution that can put these conflicting passions to rest. The praise of pardon is noble, but unjust; the passion for justice is holy, but unforgiving. It is impossible to have them both. Yet, both we must have, if spirit is to be made understandable and acceptable to the mind. Let every spiritual soul who would, put aside a single demand for justice out of a sense of loving forgiveness and lofty kindness and see whether the glare of outrage can be avoided. Justice matters. Unless we keep this in mind, all mercy becomes a mere softness of the will, unworthy of those who would strive for nobility and decency.

The third paradox threatens more than the other two to sabotage entirely the authenticity of spirit. All that we wish at this moment is to avoid any cheap or inauthentic elimination of the paradox. The final paradox assures us, at the very least, that the inquiry into the meaning of spirit is no gentle and pleasant affair. The inquiry is tough, the journey arduous, the examination brutal. The above stories, brief though they be, have purchased a harsh lesson for those who would embark upon this journey of discovery: the truths we must discover are savage, tough, and hard. Like all true philosophy, it is not an embarkation for the light of heart or the weak of spirit.

PART II
The Predicates of Spirit

3

Radiance and Importance

The next task of this inquiry is to carry out a description of spirit. This is accomplished in the present section by an analysis of what I call the ten existential predicates of spirit. To be precise, the question asked in the present section is this: What does it mean *to be spirit*? The indefinite article which seems to be demanded by normal English syntax is here deliberately excised in order to focus on existential meaning. Such syntax is not altogether prohibited by the rules of good language, for it is permitted to ask, for example, What does it mean to be king? To insert the indefinite article and ask about being *a* king is not at all the same question, for 'a king' is merely one among many possible kings, but 'being king' is to be the immediate and concrete regent of the realm that matters immediately—this one. It is this kind of question that is being asked of spirit. It is not a question of whether one *has* a thing which is called spirit, as if a person is one kind of entity which then possesses (or possibly does not possess) another kind of entity with characteristics or attributes. Nor is it even a question of being *a* spirit, which suggests a possible plurality of kinds of things. Rather, this formulation focuses upon the modality of being spirit, i.e., what it means to exist as spirit.

But how can one carry out an inquiry into existential modalities? The idea of a special kind of predication, not of entities but of meanings, is needed. The term 'predicate' is a grammatical one and as such is an entirely neutral notion without metaphysical or theological overtones. To avoid metaphysical instantiation as well as the fallacy of reifying abstractions, the inquiry focuses solely upon what being 'spirit' means, not what

47

kind of entity or thing a spirit is. Thus each of these ten existential predicates is a modality or way of existing as spirit. They are identified as 'existential' simply because they are used to describe the meaning of existence.

It would be possible, of course, to carry out an investigation by pointing out attributes or characteristics of an entity. One could assert, for example, "A human being has a mind." However, under the present methodology this formulation is replaced by the assertion: "To be human is to be able to think." Here the nouns 'human being' and 'mind' are replaced by the infinitives 'to be human' and 'to think'. In this way, being human and thinking are considered directly in terms of their meanings without first having to identify an entity that exists or even without having to refer to possible entities.

In the following discussion, therefore, the method produces the following provisional claims:

1. To be spirit is to be important.
2. To be spirit is to radiate with inner light.
3. To be spirit is to worship.
4. To be spirit is to suffer.
5. To be spirit is to acknowledge mystery.
6. To be spirit is to become enrapt.
7. To be spirit is to be redeemable.
8. To be spirit is to submit to adventure.
9. To be spirit is to be able to laugh.
10. To be spirit is to be noble.

Identifying these modes of being spirit as 'predicates' may seem a curious, though legitimate, stretching of syntactical rules. Normally the proper use of the term 'predicate' would be the assignment of some attribute, usually in the form of an adjective, to a substantive, by saying, for example, that a spiritual person is worshipful or worshipping. For worship is an activity; it is a noun, not an adjective. However, in the precise and rigorous formulation of this methodology, what is being predicated or characterized is not the spiritual or spirited person but simply being spirit. Indeed, if English were like German, it would be possible to make the noun 'spirit' into a verb, and the purer but inelegant result would be "to spirit is to worship." But this would be to *violate* the English language, not merely to stretch its syntax. It is indulgence enough to ask the reader to understand all existential predicates as infinitives, so that when the suggestion is made that 'worship' is a predicate of spirit, what is meant in simple English is that to be spirit is to worship. The following analyses are carried out with this presumed indulgence.

Rumination on the preceding chapter may suffice to deter any further effort in this Jovian inquiry. Faced with such formidable barriers in comprehending the meaning of spirit, it may be the better part of valor simply to shrug and leave the topic for those who embrace mysteries unexamined. The three paradoxes of spirit are so intimidating that to embark on the journey any further may seem to invite ridicule from all tough-minded critics. Perhaps the only lesson worthy of being taken from the above considerations is that inquiry into the meaning of spirit is simply too thorny and too confusing to straighten out by philosophical analysis. Perhaps unguided and irrational belief is the only way left to grasp the meaning of spirit.

Should our desire be to establish a perfect, deductive system of explanation, perhaps this gloomy assessment would be in order. But the inquirers have one enormous advantage, and that is that the question at hand is vast in its richness and scope, even though the possible approaches to the giant in question are ubiquitous. Like the Lilliputians who ultimately conquered the giant Gulliver simply because he was one and they were so many, so the approach to the thrice-girded puzzle of spirit offers many chinks simply because of its size, and the inquisitive, restless, and unending approaches of inquiry need not fell the behemoth in a single, telling blow of insight but like a million flies can drive the elephant into a stampede.

The original approach to our understanding of spirit will thus be small, subtle, and perhaps even quaint. But we must attack somewhere, and after the enormity of the speculative grandeur of the last chapter, perhaps the first step into the turmoil should be indirect and even innocent. Indeed, the first approach to the meaning of spirit shall not be one, but two minor and almost inconsequential questions. And the first of these will be to ask the painter a simple, direct question. In painting a picture, how do you represent a spiritual being? Does the pigment itself glow with recognition, assuring us that this one is holy, whereas the others are dull and secular? There is, of course, an ancient and honored iconography recognized as the mark of the saint, and that is the halo. If you want to paint a realist canvas on which saints and nonsaints both occur, it is possible to identify the holy ones by simply painting a halo around their heads. This iconographic device is wonderfully simple, for it allows the observer immediately to determine which are spiritual and which are not. But why do painters, at least realistic and classical painters, use the halo to spot saints and even the figure of Christ? The method suggests that the holy ones are radiating a simple and joyous light at being spiritual. There is no quarreling with the fact: for centuries European religious paintings have halos around the saints and especially elaborate ones around the figure of Christ. Why?

The iconography is an easy metaphor. Radiance, or light, is one of the basic ways in which we think about the spiritual. Not even the simplest peasant believed that in the flesh these figures actually wore golden rings hovering over their heads. They knew it was a way of telling us something about sanctity: it is like an inner radiance or light, which, if we were spiritually endowed we might be able to see, as the artist himself, through his gift, also sees. But such 'seeing' is not literal but metaphoric. Saints are radiant. Artistic license allows such radiance to be placed on the canvas. Not, as one might at first suspect, merely to inform us who is saintly and who not, but rather to show us something important about how we think about such spiritual people. Their being is like a light, an inner radiance which defeats the eclipsing darkness.

But, if the halo is a mere iconographic device, how are we to understand light and darkness? It is easy to say that the spiritual are radiant and the unholy not, but it is far more difficult to explain just what that means. In our opening chapter we saw ourselves depicted in a disgusting way, in which the very turning away was the beginning of understanding who we really are. The picture sketched on our first page is that who we are can be seen in the disgust with which we exist, and this disgust, a special kind of self-disgust, makes room for spirit. What does this have to do with inner radiance, which is symbolized by halos in sacred paintings? The suggestion is richly obvious. Radiance is not just light, it is *inner* light. In spirit we are not illuminated from some external light; rather we ourselves become a source of brightness. And the darkness is also easily recognized; it is the shadow of a disgusting, meaningless existence. What disgusts us about our first picture is not that pleasure is wrong or even leading to wrong, but that a life understood solely in terms of gratification is a dark picture, one in which there is no meaning. And of course, that is the true meaning of the halo: light is seen here as the source of meaning, just as the sources of light in Plato's myth of the cave are the origins of understanding who we are. Darkness, on the other hand, represents a meaningless, confused state in which we do not know who we are. To be spiritual is to be radiant. Of course, this is only a vague suggestion, a hint gleaned from an aesthetic device. It proves nothing, for the painters could be wrong. But it does provide a glimpse of what spirit *means*. It is a single, Lilliputian sting against a leviathan.

The second question also comes from the arts. Suppose a young but gifted writer visits a professor of literature whom he has provisionally adopted as a kind of mentor. The youth wants to write a great novel. What, he asks, should he write about? The mentor may smile at the arrogance of his young poet, but he recognizes true talent and perhaps even an emerging genius. And so they discuss the topics that deserve to be treated with total dedication. They draw up a provisional list of possible themes. As a young and virile man, the writer may feel the ache in his groin is a predominant and all-consuming passion, and so he suggests a story of sexual frenzy, culminating in conquest. Jack meets Jill, desires her; Jill plays hard to get, but is finally overcome. The story line provides much opportunity for seamy lust and compulsion; the resolution provides gratification. The young writer is unabashed about the intensity of his feeling and his disdain for censorship, but even he recognizes that perhaps the work should not degenerate into pornography.

The mentor admits that such a topic may provide the writer with an opportunity for some fairly vivid prose. But he asks: are we, in fact, riveted by a story line whose sole purpose is the ful-

fillment of a desire? No one denies that we all enjoy being reminded of such pleasures, and reading about these triumphs
often can cause some degree of pleasure. But the mentor's hesitation makes the young writer wonder, and so he suggests another topic. Perhaps instead of Jack merely desiring Jill and
finally getting her, he should reveal his intellectual powers as
well. Give him a problem to solve. So the second suggestion is
the theme celebrating intelligence and the joy of problem-
solving. Why not a mystery story?

Mysteries are the delight of civilization. Agatha Christie,
Rex Stout, Dick Francis, John Dickson Carr, and Dorothy Sayers
have all shown that the detective thriller can be well-written as
well as highly entertaining. Few pleasures equal sitting by the
fire, with a beer and sandwich, losing oneself entirely in the delightful escapism of a mystery story. Such hours probably are
more successful at relaxing the body and mind than all the yoga
and Transcendental Meditation in the world. Surely, if the characters are well developed and the plot sufficiently puzzling, such
a theme is worthy of a writer anxious to display his skills. But our
young writer still hesitates. He recognizes there may be more
dignified entertainment in Jack getting a murderer caught than
Jack getting into bed with Jill, if for no other reason than the
latter is a mere gratification of a want, whereas the former at
least makes us rejoice in justice done. Further, the intellectual
satisfaction taken in a puzzle well worked out is worthier stuff
than a hunger satisfied. But the youth wants something noble in
his writing.

They then suggest a third topic. Jack could perform a
rather heroic task, experiencing high adventure and bold daring.
This appeals to the young writer because it affords so much opportunity to explore the adventures of life. Yet, even as he considers with delight the high thrills which his hero would endure,
the author recognizes that, in such literature, made lofty by the
likes of Robert Louis Stevenson, Jack London, and Hammond
Innes, the rank of adventure story is scarcely more, perhaps even
less, than that of a mystery story. And so, feeling that the first
three suggestions are a bit light, he turns within and considers
the torments of a hero struggling, not with some external adver-
sary, but with his own psyche. The psychological novel has far

more range and meaning than either a sexually explicit conquest, a whodunnit, or even an adventure story. Surely this is the stuff which can give meaningful topics for the ready writer. His fingers ache to get at the typewriter, his hands twitch ready to hit the keys. All he need do is look within and expose those wondrous torments and internal agonies of the mind seeking to find peace. Furthermore, such a tale would allow elements of the other types dismissed: he could include sex and mystery and adventure, yet all would be seen in a far more serious light because it smacks of the reality of our own anguish.

His mentor seems pleased. The list has now approached a more serious level; perhaps this type of novel would indeed prove worthy material for his young protégé. But the would-be artist is a sensitive and high-minded youth, and he cannot escape the small lines of disappointment around his professor's mouth. Do we really enjoy reading the files in a psychiatrist's office? If the purpose of the novel is to go from mental illness to mental health—a noble enterprise, to be sure—is that not properly the realm of the therapist or counselor? When one is finished, one can celebrate mental health, but health is the kind of thing we forget about when well; we worry about it only when we have symptoms. Is mental health a sufficiently noble enterprise about which to write a great novel? Are there indeed even more lofty themes?

And so they go on in their search. Suppose the hero defeats, not a psychological illness but a moral weakness or even an ethical outrage. Write of a hero defeating the Nazis, or of desperate guerilla fighters overthrowing a cruel regime. Here at least the goal is noble. No one can deny that there is mental satisfaction of the highest order taken in the achievement of justice or honor. These are the issues which burn in the mind. These are the exploits that make for true heroes: not the passing adventurism of those who explore a lost continent or who discover a lost city, but the very real courage taken to defeat genuine evil. Can there be any nobler theme than that? The mentor reminds the youth that Melville once said: "If you seek to write a mighty book, you must choose a mighty theme!" The triumph of good over evil is among the mightiest themes available for the human pen.

Yet, if they were to go just one step further, they may discover what it is that has made all truly great literature worthy of its high and noble place in the libraries of the earth. Greater even than our defeat of evil is our confrontation with God. The struggle between doubt and belief, the triumph of our most profound battle of all: the clash between what is lofty within us and what is petty and small. These are the topics and themes that make up the epics: the *Iliad,* the *Aeneid, The Divine Comedy, King Lear, Paradise Lost, The Brothers Karamazov.* These epics not only confront the great issues, they do so greatly. There is truth in them, and honesty, and no little courage. They remain as masterpieces, not only because they are brilliantly written, but because they consider the loftiest theme of all: who we are. Should the mentor and his protégé decide upon this kind of theme, the topic will ever outrank the skill of the artist. The theme itself becomes a part of the art.

Now, lest we misplace our energy, we must be reminded that great artists have taken even the simplest themes and rendered them magnificent. If we rank the first suggestion, that Jack wants Jill, as the least worthy, we must not forget that Shakespeare wrote *Romeo and Juliet* and *Antony and Cleopatra.* But even the young writer recognizes that neither of these stories is merely about venereal satisfaction; they are not about lust but about love. And love is a great theme in itself. How do we turn a simple story of a boy's lust for a girl's beauty into something magnificent like *Romeo and Juliet?* First, the lust is quickly turned to love; the metaphysical reality of Fate becomes the central theme, not the mere union of two hot-blooded youngsters panting after a common bed. True, *Romeo and Juliet* is a love story, but it is also a play about Fate, and the inevitability of destiny. Their love only makes the fate all the more poignant. It is fate, and courage, and deep devotion which lifts the simple attraction of Romeo for Juliet to the level of greatness. If this can be grasped, the young writer will not be lacking in opting for a worthy theme for his eager art.

We can sketch the list to remind us of the development:

Jack desires Jill—sexual satisfaction.
Jack solves a puzzle—a mystery story.

Jack performs heroic deeds—an adventure story.
Jack struggles with his psyche—a psychological novel.
Jack defeats a moral evil—a moral drama.
Jack confronts the anguish of spirit; perhaps he even meets
    the reality of God—an epic.

This is an extremely modest endeavor. We have merely listed topics which make for interesting reading; furthermore it is speculative and somewhat arbitrary. The judgment of the ages and those who seem to know about literature may support this ranking, but honest and sensitive readers may disagree. And after we have made the list, then what? Does it tell us anything at all? I think it does. It may be fanciful and prejudicial for what is classical, but it does show us what serious-minded people consider to be worthy of being read. And in telling us what is worthy of being read, the list reveals something of considerable value in our attempt to understand spirit. For at the very least it shows us that we can make judgments about what is important; we can rank those topics which are more or less meaningful.

It might be argued that a list based upon what makes a literary work worthy of being revered need not coincide with what is really important. Perhaps not; but such a list does manifest some kind of concern for the spiritual significance of these issues, and that is enough to gain purchase upon this slippery mound of confusion that faces us. That we can make such a list at all shows that the ranking of these ideas is not entirely arbitrary, that we are not faced with mere subjectivity when it comes to assessing the importance of things.

But surely, the critic might protest, there is nothing more subjective than importance. What is important to me may not be important to you. Can 'importance' have any authority at all? Or, are we left forever with the purely subjectivist assertion that such judgments are only relative? Is not 'importance' the same as 'being of value'? And surely no one would deny that values are subjective.

But 'importance' does not mean the same as 'being of value'. It is possible to utilize the notion of importance in an *argument*, and thus provide it with rational persuasion. Consider for example the following argument. Suppose we entertain the classical punitive doctrine of Christian theism which asserts that sinners who have mortally offended God will be punished forever in hell. In our mind's eye we can imagine visiting such a suffering soul. On this earth he sinned by seducing his friend's wife and died before confessing his sin. We are visiting him fifty million years into his sentence of eternal damnation. He protests to us that his sin, which he admits was wrong, deserves punishment, but fifty million years is a remarkably long time to be punished by an avenging God. He says, "Neither I nor my sin is that important. After suffering fifty million years I have not even begun to serve the sentence of eternity. For me to be so punished makes me infinitely important. But I am not infinite, hence I am not infinitely important. To deserve eternal punishment implies that there is infinite importance both in the act and the agent."

This is a fascinating argument. And, of course, it works the other way: *not* to punish a wrongdoer implies he is completely without importance at all—unless, of course, he is forgiven. Thus, based on the argument of importance, eternal punishment for finite beings seems impossible, and complete indifference to justice implies a total lack of importance. Thus, if any finite being is important, he must be neither punished eternally nor left unpunished unless he is forgiven on independent grounds. Many theologians, however, disagree with this argument, for they maintain that eternal punishment is deserved because, as an offense against God it is an offense against an infinite being and hence deserves an infinite (or at least eternal) punishment. But degrees of punishment do not depend upon the worth of the offended but on the character of the offender. If there is such a thing as an infinite Being who is offended by what is called sin, it does not follow that the punishment for such sin be unremitting, any more than in human offense do we severely punish those who are incompetent to judge the severity of their acts. We do not severely punish children who mistakenly offend an important personage, nor do we hold those criminally insane responsible for harming presidents or kings. To deserve supreme punishment is not the result of the offended's rank, but the rank of the offense; and for a finite being with finite comprehension, created with weaknesses and frailties, it is impossible to have an *infinite* offense, i.e., one deserving of eternal punishment. For how can a mere finite being offend infinitely? But anything *less* than an infinite offense is undeserving of eternal damnation. Since, as finite, we cannot commit an infinite offense, it follows we cannot be infinitely (eternally) punished.

This appeal to the fantastic theology of medieval theism is made deliberately to show the validity of using 'importance' in an argument the premises of which may be highly dubious. But the emphasis is on the inference. We have made an inference based upon the operating notion of importance, and this shows that importance cannot be a mere subjectivist attitude.

But to return to our main concern, namely, the little list of possible themes for the would-be writer, the guiding principle in such ranking seems to be that of importance. Jack managing to get Jill into bed may be important to Jack, but as a theme it is not as important as struggling for dignity or justice. Perhaps the vernacular serves us better in this instance: it's what *matters* that counts. We want to matter. What we fear most in this life is not personal sorrow or suffering, not confusion about the world's great questions, or even the impending nothingness of death; what we fear above all, and indeed in the midst of all these other concerns, is that we do not matter. Not to matter is to be trivial, unworthy of existence. Nihilism is the doctrine that nothing matters, which is a difficult thing, logically, to say. It is embarrassing for the skeptic to say the sentence: "Human knowledge is impossible," since, if that sentence is true, it presumably conveys knowledge, but if it is true, it cannot be known. Likewise it is troublesome to say: "The world has no meaning," for in saying it the speaker achieves a kind of bold and defiant meaning in the face of the absurd.

But the self-refutation of nihilism is not the central concern of the present investigation; importance is. Or, if we stick to the richness of the vernacular, mattering matters.

It is one of the things we seem to notice about those who are spiritual or spirited. They are serious. Not necessarily solemn or morbid, but serious. If we take our fantastic visitation to the hapless sufferer in hell, we might recognize the reverse side of the argument. Let us assume for a moment that there actually are souls suffering forever in the torment of hell. Then we must assume that life is very important indeed; indeed it is ultimately and supremely important: 'ultimately' meaning there is no more fundamental concern, and 'supremely' meaning that nothing ranks as more important. It is, however, not only 'life' that is important if eternal damnation is possible; it is we who are supremely important. There simply cannot be anyone more important than I if my rewards and punishments are *eternal*. Everything I do is so very important, and matters so very much, that for an eternity a watchful and energetic torturer (God) will remember it. Eternality makes things matter.

But whether the spiritual person believes in eternality of personal punishment, there can be no doubt that such a person believes very much in the *modality* presupposed by the analysis— namely, that to be spiritual is a way of being important. It is a life in which things and oneself matter. There are no trivial saints or indifferent worshipers. The list of topics for the would-be writer shows that the more serious the theme, the worthier the reading, and the highest of such themes are spiritual. Is Hamlet's riotous torment about his moral obligation to a spiritual visitation anything but lofty? Is Ivan Karamazov's titanic struggle with atheism not also richly serious? Is not Faust's lament "Zwei Seelen wohnen in meinen Brust!" Goethe's contribution to the same splendid literature that lasts because it matters? Or is not Milton's account of Eve tortured by temptation in the ninth book of *Paradise Lost* remembered because it is so serious a matter? Or Wotan's anguish in Wagner's *Die Walküre?* Or, if we insist on more recent literature, what can compare to the struggle between the sacred and profane in Thomas Mann's *Death in Venice,* or the novels of Iris Murdoch? The point of this name-dropping is that we simply do in fact rank as among the world's greatest literature and art that which concerns itself with matters of spirit, flesh, fate, God, evil, and guilt: all terms which belong to the spiritual arena. I realize that in saying this I incur the wrath of the deconstructionists, but it cannot be seriously entertained that these authors and artists just happened to be skilled, and just happened to choose mighty themes.

If one were to play a parlor game of sorts, it might prove interesting to list all the authors of spiritual themes on one page, and list all the atheistic writers on another. The latter would certainly have some winners: Marx, possibly Nietzsche, Jean-Paul

Sartre, possibly Mark Twain. But on the other side not only would one have all the classics, but among the best of the contemporary writers: Evelyn Waugh, Graham Greene, Flannery O'Conner, Alexander Solzhenitsyn, Chaim Potok, etc. The evidence is overwhelming: those for whom the spiritual problems are meaningful and real seem to constitute our finest writers and gifted artists. The same list would not prove as overwhelming if one listed only philosophers: in such a list the atheists, cynics, disbelievers, and demythologizers would surely outrank the spiritual group, at least since the turn of the century.

But what does all this prove? Again, as in the case of the halo, it is not meant to prove anything but rather to show how we think about the subject. By these two techniques we have isolated two predicates that might provisionally be assigned to the spiritual: radiance and importance. By observing the techniques of artists we have discovered a small but possibly important beginning: that when we think about spirituality we think about inner radiance and importance. By suggestion, if not inference, then, the nonspiritual are dim or dull and trivial. But when these terms are directed toward the nonliterary meanings as sources of how we understand spirit, it is not enough to hint at vague significance. And so we must now ask: What does importance really mean? Why is spirit radiant? These hints have given us perhaps a foothold, but we must proceed further into the inquiry. If importance and radiance do indeed constitute fundamental predicates of spirit, we must now consider them directly.

Importance is a difficult notion to isolate, since it is one of those fundamental terms that we seem to use to describe other things, rather than ever describing them themselves. The Latin etymology suggests "to bring in" or "to carry into"; it suggests having weight, ranking above other things. In ordinary discourse, importance can, of course, be subjective, as when we speak of something being of importance to one person but not to another. On the other hand, the word is used in nonsubjectivistic ways. When Othello describes his misprizing Desdemona, he speaks "of the rude Indian,/ Who threw a pearl away,/ Richer than all his tribe." Here we distinguish the rude Indian's valuing the pearl as little or nothing, but its genuine worth being very great. The Indian does not recognize the true importance of the pearl. In this case, 'importance' means objective worth, something which only true understanding or knowledge reveals. In characterizing importance as a predicate of spirit, then, we mean that being spiritual is being true to one's genuine worth. Negatively, it means not squandering one's existence on what is trivial; knowing what the true meaning of existence is all about.

To be spiritual, then, is to exist in the realm of the important. This does not forfeit the ever-present possibility that one may still be in error in assessing one's true worth; it merely means that the spiritual person is concerned with the weighty, significant, and full significance of what it means to be. But what does it mean to say that we are important at all? Are we really important? Or is our existence purely fleeting, replaceable, insignificant? To say we are important is to say we matter, that we count, that we "have weight in the ultimate scheme of things." And it is this final phrase that seems to attach itself to the sentence almost by instinct that turns out to be so critical. For the notion of a nonsubjective importance can only mean that individuals somehow matter, not only to themselves, but to the whole. Importance simply means that who one is can be understood only by reference to a greater reality.

Surely, this is phenomenologically correct. The observation of holy or spiritual beings seems to reveal their own sense of belonging to a greater reality; but in addition their own particular existence matters very much. Their existence matters, not just to themselves, but to the greater reality. To be spiritual, then, means to be important for all of reality. (We recall that Glaucon's disgust with merely satisfied beings initiated the Platonic doctrine of spirit, which was a kind of importance for the whole.) To be important spiritually then is a metaphysical and not a merely psychological modality; it claims that the spiritual one matters to and for the ultimate reality of God. One is important ultimately; not because of what one does—though one's actions are also rendered important—but simply because of who one is.

I should perhaps take this opportunity to emphasize the methodology of the inquiry: We are not saying that the spiritually important person first decides that God exists and then infers he must matter; rather he is first existentially aware of his being important, and then articulates this importance in terms of there being a God or some ultimate reality which, by being shared, grounds the fundamental importance. Thus, strictly speaking, we could carry out this discussion without mentioning God, for we are describing what it means to be spiritually important, not what makes that importance possible.

Is this a genuine option? Can we, somehow, decide whether to be important or not? Is there a procedure for discovering if we are genuinely important or only think we are? To return to our opening paragraph, is that not in part what turns us away from what we have called 'the flesh,' i.e., that it is mindless, empty, and vain? Is it indeed an important question to be important or not? Or is it not the case that importance, like rationality, is always necessarily being begged? Is not this inquiry itself being carried out because it is important? And if so, then must we not be important in a way which only spirituality can sustain?

Let us consider the opposing view; that our importance is based solely upon our private interests: that we are important only to ourselves and perhaps to a few others who care for us. Then, importance always means only "importance for me"; i.e., I want it. But this is absurd, for I could easily desire to be trivial. (Certainly the unfortunate sufferer in an eternal hell wishes he were *not* so important; he would prefer peaceful triviality to painful importance.) Can the mind actually come to the conclusion that the greatest truth about our meaning and our existence is that we do not matter, that we are unimportant? Certainly it cannot come to that conclusion if it admits the possibility of there being a nonsubjective importance.

It should be stressed here that throughout this discussion the term 'important' is meant to imply some kind of spiritual meaning. There are, of course, hundreds of ways one can consider oneself important in nonspiritual terms: one can be economically, politically, or athletically important. But all of these uses are subjective: not everyone would agree that it is important to be wealthy or powerful or attractive. In this discussion we are using 'importance' in a purely nonsubjectivist sense, and that necessarily entails spirit, though it need not always be a *religious* spirituality. Nevertheless, to assert that one has autonomous, nonsubjective importance forfeits the possibility of explaining this importance in terms of private wants or individual goals.

One must assume some kind of world-plan, divine providence, world-significance, or even something as vague as the general scope of ultimate reality. To say one is nonsubjectively important therefore does imply *some* sense of belonging to a greater reality, even if that reality is the goddess Fortuna, the most fickle and least theistic of all gods.

The point that is critical in our investigation of this predicate is that when we think of a spiritual person we think of a nontrivial being who takes his own existence seriously and who recognizes this importance in terms of a reality which transcends the narrow limits of private interests. That may be vague, but it is enough. It is phenomenologically impossible for there to be a trivial and silly spirituality. It is possible for there to be a seriously misconceived, erroneous, and even immoral spirituality, but not a frivolous one. Thus, one of the determining predicates of spirit is importance.

The existential predicate of 'radiance' is closely connected to that of 'importance'. What importance is to the self, radiance is to others. By this I mean simply that the radiance of those who are spiritual is the illumination from within which guides others to recognize the importance that glows within the spiritual. Just as a candle's radiance glows not only for itself, but to illumine the way for others, so to say that the spiritual is predicated by radiance is to say that spirit is a guide or source by which seeing is made possible. Radiance, or light, allows us to see.

But the question here is: to see what? Certainly not merely to see that the spiritual is itself radiant. We can, of course, light a candle merely to see the candle glow; but we can also use the light of the candle to see our way in an otherwise darkened room. The spiritual radiates not only for its own sake but for the sake of those who would see. From the earliest of images in philosophical history, the metaphor of light has always been a symbol of truth. In Plato's *Republic*, for example, the great central metaphor of the light of the sun is used as the ground of truth. Even in poetic uses, light and truth are interchangeable. What, then, does this suggest? That the spirit is a source of our being true. The spiritual are not only important, they are also true.

The spiritual are therefore custodians of truth. This does not mean that every spiritual belief is true, for that is impossible, since many of them are contradictory; rather, it means that in being spiritual they are concerned about truth. This is an important realization, for one of the most frequently heard protests about the spiritual life is that of contentment and *belief.* Here, curiously, the term 'belief' is presented almost as antithetical to what is true. We say of a man that he lives by his beliefs, meaning that he has stopped inquiring, or even stopped caring whether his beliefs are *true;* he is merely concerned with retaining his beliefs just because they are his. There can be no doubt that the lives of many devout people are lived in an unquestioning way. Indeed, it is an essential and fundamental principle of all philosophical thought that we *must* distinguish what is true from what is believed. How, then, can the radiance of spirit in any way represent truth?

Does the sentence "I believe that x" imply "I believe that x is true"? Surely the correlate term suggests this, for if I say "I doubt that x" what I mean is that I am unconvinced that x is true. Since 'doubt' and 'belief' are contraries, the meanings of both must parallel. Thus it makes no sense to say that I believe in x or believe that x unless I hold x to be true. The lack of inquiry here is merely a manifestation of the depth of belief; they do not inquire, since they have no reason to do so: inquiry is sponsored only by doubt, not belief. Thus, radiance here is little more than the positive side to what the word 'belief' means: I hold what I believe to be true.

Beliefs are curious and troublesome things. It is often thought that in the repertory of epistemic states, one has either knowledge, belief, or doubt. That is, if what I maintain is now not only what I think is the case but is also true, this is called knowledge. Then there are those mental states which I maintain as true but which are not: these are called 'mere' beliefs. And finally there are doubts, which are beliefs which one admits may be true or false. If the doubt is strong, the belief is held to be likely false. The trouble with this threefold division is that it is not complete.

We can easily imagine a troubled thinker responding in the

following way. When asked if he believes in a soul, he may say he is not sure. But he may be reluctant to assert that he actually doubts he has a soul. He may admit a profound anguish and confess he neither believes nor doubts he has a soul.

How is it possible to have a soul and not know it? Surely if one has a soul it cannot be doubted. If I can see, can I doubt I have eyes? Something so important and fundamental as a soul could not be a part of us unless we were aware of it. To doubt I have a soul, then, seems to imply that I do not have one. Perhaps those who believe in souls have them and those who do not believe they have them in fact do not have them. This may seem highly unlikely from a metaphysical point of view, but epistemically the solution is amusing though oddly satisfying, since the very possession of a soul would seem to guarantee awareness of it. "I can accept having a soul," our tormented thinker might protest, "and I can accept not having a soul. What I cannot endure is not being sure whether I believe in a soul or not." To say that this tormented thinker doubts the existence of his soul seems too strong a claim. To doubt is an active verb, and this man is plagued by so many demands on his acceptance that he is rendered too numb to be active. He may not even know what he believes.

Consider if you will the enormity of our situation. On a crowded city street, thousands go about their business, all seemingly sharing the same species, humanity. Yet, of these thousands, let us assume that one-third devoutly believe in God. Another third are unsure of their beliefs but would never call themselves atheists; they are content to live in confusion and uncertainty. The final third are atheists. In each third are men and women of considerable intelligence, wit, and sensitivity. And yet they intercommunicate with each other almost as if these monumental and awesome beliefs *do not matter!* Indeed, two friends, one theist, the other atheist, could go through life together, sharing almost all the same joys, the same love of beauty and compassion for suffering, and even a mutual respect for the moral law. How is this even conceivable, that a belief so *ultimate* can be so cavalierly disregarded? For surely, if there is a God, then everything is completely changed. Down to the last movement of the tiniest molecule or even subatomic particle, to the lightest breeze, to the most ephemeral and errant thought, the entire world of all phenomena is simply and hugely different. How can intelligent members of the same species disagree so fundamentally about the most important question one can ask?

Or, is it the case that, in the last analysis, the question simply does *not* matter? If the atheist and the theist friends share so much, including the love of beauty, of morality, and of the things that make life worth living, then perhaps the fact that God exists or does not exist simply cannot matter at all. What is the *difference* in believing? Even within the same person who one year believes, the next year doubts, the third year disbelieves, aside from these purely formal things going on in his head, does anything else change? Is he not the same kindly or cruel person throughout this internal debate? Perhaps belief changes some people, but it surely does not change all, and very surely it does not change them that much. (I am speaking here of belief in God, *not* of a conversion to a particular religion: that *does* bring about serious change.) So, perhaps we might suggest that whether one believes in a soul or even in God is simply unimportant. In some sense, of course, this is true. Whether we believe in souls or in God does not change the rules of nature or the laws of society; and however human nature got to the stage it is, either through creation or evolution, belief or disbelief will not change that, either. And if this 'human nature'—developed either from purely evolutionary principles or from some spontaneous act of willful creation—necessarily includes within it the wonder of our origin and our nature, then the question is merely inevitable, not important. We seem to be able to live without answering it. We may even die not answering it.

Of course, the fact that atheist and theist may be friends and that belief or disbelief does not change our environment, or perhaps even our personality, has little to do with the seriousness of the problem. The point is that truth matters, regardless of its effects on other things. And so this question matters, hugely, just because we are concerned with truth. The remarks about our daily lives altering not one whit if we believe or disbelieve is merely a remark on the unimportance of our daily lives, not on the insignificance of the question as to whether we have souls or whether there is a God.

The beliefs and disbeliefs in these questions, however, are not quite as neutral as the above ruminations seem to suggest. One interesting thing about the opposing beliefs is this: those who believe in soul and a god consider the disbeliever simply to be *lacking* in something important; whereas those who disbelieve consider the believers to be *naive*. And so, those of us who are agonized in the torment and turmoil of this questioning must choose between two unacceptable modalities: either we must be judged naive fools, gullible and childish; or we must be judged as lacking in something fundamentally important, as one who has a deaf ear is pitied for his inability to realize that an entire world of delight in music is simply wanting in him. For there can be no mistake about it: even the two friends, one theistic and the other atheistic, see their friend as either naive or lacking. "How can you believe in all that silly nonsense?" "I only wish it were non-sense."—"I feel sorry for you, my friend. You have nothing ulti-mate to believe in." "I believe in myself, thank you."

Many honest inquirers may endure this agony throughout their lives, ever unsettled about this all-important question. Are such confused minds then unspiritual? Surely this is a harsh judgment. Thomas doubted, but he was still an apostle and saint. To doubt, or if that term is too active, to agonize in the thrall of uncertainty, is no disbarment from spirituality. How, then, can we say that a predicate of the spiritual is the radiance of truth? This would make the naive nonquestioner more spiritual than the ag-onized inquirer. Again we must return to the notion of impor-tance. Having a soul, whether that belief is fact or fiction, remains of high importance. To be spiritual is, as we have seen, to be important in a nonsubjectivist sense; to be spiritual is also to be radiant of truth. But truth here is determined by impor-tance, not correctness. The question remains, not what *exists* (for we might be in error or simply remain in suspended and ago-nized uncertainty), but simply what matters. I may not know if I have a soul, I may not even know for sure if I *believe* I have a soul, but having a soul *matters*. The manifestation of this impor-tance is truth lived rather than truth known, and in this way the existential predicate of radiance (of truth) remains a part of spirit even if the person is wrenched in the turmoil of agonized bewilderment. Even his own confusion may remain sacred to him, and his commitment to truth, even if not known, makes him important and radiant.

This first step of our inquiry may be so modest as to be called timid. We have asked a painter how he designates a saint on canvas, and we learn of the icon known as the halo. We ask a would-be writer what topics he would rank as being worthy of being read, and he places confrontations with evil and God above adventure, mystery, and satisfaction. From these delicate phenomenological inquiries we have circled hesitantly around the giant, making small thrusts to test the weakness of the armor. We must begin on such subtle strategy for the leviathan in question, The Meaning of Spirit, is thrice-girded with paradox. The three paradoxes are so formidable that a direct assault would simply confound us, and reduce us to the unenviable position of having to believe or disbelieve on no rational grounds whatsoever.

But our delicate probes have not been without some result, even if we perforce grant that they are as yet little more than hints and suggestions. But from them we have dared to assert our first two existential predicates of what it means to be spiritual: importance and radiance. We assert that there is a nonsubjectivist meaning to importance, and that those who are spiritual are important in this sense. We assert that truth matters, and that the spiritual radiate this awareness of the importance of truth. It is a truth lived rather than a truth known, for at the moment we are not prepared to penetrate the giant without first weakening his defenses. To weaken these defenses we are limiting our questioning now merely to the simple inquiry of what it means to be spiritual. We have suggested the spiritual are important and radiant. Whether the monster is weakened by these jabs, at least our own assault is now prepared to launch worthier and more revealing attacks.

4

Worship

In *Hamlet,* the king, Claudius, prays that he may repent:

> O wretched state! O bosom black as death!
> O limed soul, that struggling to be free
> Art more engaged! Help angels! Make assay;
> Bow stubborn knees; and heart with strings of steel,
> Be soft as sinews of the new-born babe.
> All may be well.

When Otto von Bismark, the great Prussian statesman, was still a young man he held religious belief in contempt. Then, the beautiful young girl whom he loved was stricken with a fatal disease. Standing at the foot of her bed, this unbeliever suddenly felt the overweening compulsion to fall to his knees and pray. It was a bootless endeavor, and the prince later admitted that he prayed not with hope of a miracle, but simply because of the enormity of meaning that surrounded the deathbed.

On one of the darkest days of human history, W. H. Auden wrote *September 1, 1939,* and ended this cry of outrage with timeless words:

> May I, composed like them
> Of Eros and of dust,
> Beleaguered by the same
> Negation and despair,
> Show an affirming flame.*

Bow, stubborn knees! But King Claudius' lament is a universal entreaty; whether we like it or not, it seems the human species is a worshiping class. Men seem to worship from some inner compulsion of their nature. Whether it be fractricidal kings, arrogant German statesmen, or outraged poets helpless in their awe, there is an instinct to fall upon our knees, whether we believe or not. In Schaeffer's play *Equus,* the psychiatrist Dysart seeks to cure a terribly troubled young boy who carries out his instinct to worship in grotesque and horrific ways. Yet, Dysart wonders which of them is really sane: he who worships perversely or he who worships not at all. What does it mean that we, in the enlightened twentieth century in the Western world, have excised the instinct for worship from the psyche—we dare not say 'soul'? And what is the meaning of worship? Is not worship degrading? Is it not naive? The sociologists and anthropologists among us assure us that worship stems from long-forgotten and primitive fears based on false cosmogonies. We pray and then worship out of fear, we are told, for the powers of nature are threatening and awesome for the aborigine. But as time goes on, the fear is replaced by science, yet the instinct somehow remains, like ashes from a once-glowing fire. And so to kneel is a regression back to instincts, the cause and nature of which we have forgotten. Nietzsche, ever the bold one, dares to ask: But how is such forgetting possible? (And no one ever seems to take time out to try to answer this madman; his questions are too peculiar.) But the anthropologists and sociologists are quite ready to tell us with remarkable surety just exactly what motives were in the minds of our ancestors two million years ago, yet their compatriots the psychologists refuse to admit that our present motives can scarcely be identified, they are so multiple and complex. It seems we know the motives of those removed by two million years better than we know our own motives. How else is explanation possible in such disciplines?

But whether a regression or a genuine existential predicate, worship seems to be an essential part of us. We worship, often

---

*W. H. Auden, *Collected Shorter Poems* (New York: Random House, 1967) and *The English Auden: Poems, Essays, and Dramatic Writings 1927–1939* (London: Faber & Faber); quoted with permission of the publishers.

against our will and even oftener against our instincts. What is it about us that makes us go down on our knees and raise our eyes upward, as if seeking what is low and what is high at the same moment?

Worship is not merely the genuflection before power. Though it should be said that infinite power does indeed deserve recognition, even if fear plays no role in the veneration at all. In worship we recognize absolute greatness, but we also yield to the awe and the wonder, one might even say the beauty, of what is worshiped. There is the concomitant passion that greatness deserves and demands our affection simply because of its majesty. In worship I am not dissevered from the great, I am brought near to it. In the same way that a loving populace will cheer a beloved monarch, a good soldier will salute an honored officer, a grateful audience will applaud a brilliant musician, it is inherent in the affirmation of what is true that we participate in it by revering it. For thoughtful beings, to be is to worship.

What does it mean not to worship? It is to accept an egalitarianism which demands nothing outstanding, nothing remarkable. To remind ourselves of the prior chapter, like Cleopatra, to be without worship is to see boys and girls made even with men and nothing remarkable is left beneath the visiting moon. But what is so wrong with that? Can we not all enjoy our little pleasures and our fleeting lives all the more greatly and gracefully if there is nothing to worship? Or, like the psychiatrist Dysart in *Equus*, we can take vicarious and nostalgic memory of a time forever gone, when worship no longer threatens our safety and our tranquil nothingness. Perhaps, however, that is where true worship belongs: in a fondly remembered past we no longer hold as valid. We can look at cathedrals built by mistaken believers in the past and recognize that, though wrong, they really knew how to build magnificent churches. Of course, the churches are magnificent only because of the belief, and so we find ourselves in the inauthentic position of rejoicing in their previous error: glad, because in their belief they built St. Peter's, but also glad because we need not believe in such things. We see these wonderful buildings merely as monuments to a past that no longer represents our values. We no longer admire the truth, but the sheer loveliness the error wrought.

It is a curious situation to stand beneath the dome of a great cathedral and admire its beauty, without reflecting on the belief that made the structure possible. Rather like deconstructionism in literature, we deliberately bracket the truth and meaning of the piece, and focus solely on style, charming turns of phrase, and the sheer entertainment of reading what is no longer seriously believed but is read for fun. This brings about an inauthentic separation between seeing the world and belonging to it. To be without worship is to see grandeur and never participate in what is grand. This bifurcation of seeing and being is celebrated by the pure aesthetes. They maintain it is better to walk down the corridors of great art museums insulated from the very passion toward the truth that made the paintings possible. These critics not only admit this divorce, they celebrate it. They seek to expunge all worship, for worship makes things matter too much and thus destroys the recollection in tranquility which is, for them, the highest art. And there is no denying that theirs is an attractive aesthetics. It is decisively attractive, but it is inauthentic.

There can be no doubt of the ubiquity of worship. From the hundreds of thousands who jam into St. Peter's square to receive the blessing of the pope to the countless pilgrims who kneel prostrate on the holy ground of Mecca, wherever the modern electronic eyes of TV cameras turn, they focus on the humble worshipers throughout the world and amuse the armchair observers without awakening any sense of piety or respect at all. Is this a mere comment on the gullibility of the human species in believing in fantasy, or is it a testament of the human urgency to bow down before that which is wonderful? But, indeed, one must ask in all seriousness: Is there really anything truly wonderful at all? Psychologically, of course, individual viewers may be struck with a passing feeling of awe, but can we not render an acceptable account of such phenomena merely by pointing out that wonder is nothing else but that reaction?

To be spiritual is to believe that wonder and greatness are objective realities, not mere feelings we have of ordinary things. And this is what is so important about worship: it cannot be accounted for merely as a psychological phenomenon. In order to worship, truly worship, *acknowledgment* of the ultimate validity of the worshiped is essential. For it must be stressed: to acknowledge is to grant as *true*. This cannot mean all worship truly, for Odin and Wotan and Allah and God the Father are different. But it does mean that to worship abstractly is impossible. It is truer to worship a false god than to worship an abstraction. Thus, Alexander Pope's attempt to universalize his prayer is deeply misguided:

> Father of All, in every Age
> In every Clime adored,
> By Saint, by Savage, and by Sage,
> Jehovah, Jove, or Lord!

How can we worship when we don't know who it is we are worshiping? To be indifferent whether one worships Jehovah, Jove, or Lord is to deny the all-important *acknowledgment* of who the worshiped is. Yet, many of us would worship but confess our own confusion about the metaphysical reality. Does this mean a confused person cannot worship? Surely not; it merely means that when one worships one intends the object of worship to be the true god, not just any god.

But the truth and the greatness of the worshiped are not enough to understand the phenomenon of worship so essential in understanding spirit. Surely it is possible to realize an all-powerful being, perhaps even see it, and not worship it. I do not worship the eighteen-wheeler Mack truck that is booming down behind my small compact on the highway, even though it is so huge it could simply drive over me and smash me without the driver even knowing it. Worship seems to entail some kind of reverence for the worshiped, as well as a willingness to submit to it in some way. How are we to grasp this?

Perhaps, once more, we should approach the predicate modestly and indirectly first. Worship. Whom do we worship? Perhaps we ought not do so, but sometimes we worship that which is less than the divine, or at least we approximate worship in such cases. A young lover may be so overwhelmed by her beauty, that he loves his beloved to the point of worship. He feels a happy enslavement, a willingness to subjugate himself, perhaps even denigrate himself, before his beloved. Shakespeare, in one of his rarer, self-revealing moments, confesses in Sonnet 57:

Being your slave, what should I do but tend
Upon the hours and times of your desires?

In a way, the reader does not like to hear this. The noble poet is castigating himself unworthily before an undeserving beloved, and the insight embarrasses us. The sonnets are too naked, too revealing, to be enjoyed without pain. But they nevertheless give us a profound hint about the true nature of worship. For in worship we do accept a kind of loving slavery, a submission to the power—in this case the power of beauty—of the worshiped. So, it can happen that in ordinary human love, the lover worships his beloved. We may not approve of this, but it happens. But since it is a human worship of a human beloved, perhaps it is more approachable. What is meant by love-grounded worship? Again, as in the slave sonnet, there is a submission of wills, indeed almost an eclipse of self, an absorption in the other even when that other is undeserving. We let ourselves become slaves, not because we approve of slavery, but quite to the contrary, because, while we hate slavery, we embrace it to show the extent of our devotion. We say: I do not matter, you alone matter. But this is paradoxical, because the lover matters very much, in loving. And of course, this insight is the true point: in letting ourselves be absorbed in the worshiped one, we achieve not only an importance but a reality we cannot achieve independent of that worship. Of course, in the love-grounded worship it is easy to see why we revere and submit to it: simply because we love the worshiped. But not all worship is of a lover. Nevertheless, this visit to mortal worship has elicited a provocative notion: submission. In all worship, whether of mortals or of a divinity, worship seems to imply submission of some kind.

Now, I submit often in my ordinary world. I submit to the demands of my children simply because they are mine, and my love for them makes room for their claim upon me, even if the submission is not earned or even prudent. I submit to my family and friends, often merely to keep the peace. I submit to the legal authorities mainly out of fear, but there can also be simple respect for the law. But in all of these cases, the submission is willed, i.e., whether gladly or begrudgingly; it is chosen by a free act. However, in the face of the majestic, whether it be a mortal beauty which has enthralled my soul or a divine reality that instills both fear and total reverence, the submission is not so much granted as torn from me. Submission is demanded. Now, when submission is demanded or required by force, there are two options as to its meaning. On the one hand, it can mean mere loss of dignity. When a powerful enemy has disarmed me and forces me to degrading acts, I must submit to his will or face greater torment. This degrades. Yet, the power of the majestic can also demand my submission without degradation: it can also aggrandize. Why should there be shame in submitting my own power to a being more powerful than I? Unless I am God himself, surely there are others who will be more powerful. It is not insulting to recognize this and to acknowledge it. As long as my submission is not achieved without struggle, there is no dishonor. The only way bowing before the infinite implies indignity is if I myself ought to be infinite. But, in submitting to that which is majestic, my very submission can be seen as a celebration of a power so great that, submitting perforce, I am lifted up to the absolute dignity of my own will, since it is now measured against the splendid and the magnificent. It is something like this, I believe, that provokes even proud and arrogant men to bow their knees before that which is sublime and great. In the phenomenon of worship, submission is not degrading, because the worth of that worshiped supports the dignity of the worshiper, even if his submission is forced.

Nevertheless, these ruminations force us to consider the seriousness of possible indignity in worship. The case can be stated simply: A human being has intrinsic worth, and to bow before another, even a god, or to kneel before a magnificent power is simply inconsistent with an autonomous will. As long as we maintain that the human person possesses true dignity and intrinsic worth, is it not always a violation of that nobility to kneel, to prostrate ourselves on the ground, to crawl before any power, no matter how worthy? Surely it is nobler to stand up to whomever we honor, and submit our devotion with self-respect! Let the undignified worship; we who care about our own dignity will remain upright. Even if I admit a creating, fatherly God, surely he would not want his beloved creations to crawl on the ground like dogs. But we have shown that essential in our understanding of worship is submission and even self-debasement, an embracing of slavery, all the more heinous because it is self-induced.

This is an important protest and needs to be considered carefully. Of course, the true worshiper denies that he debases himself in worship, but our question is: Can it truly be avoided? There must be something to worship that keeps the kneeling from becoming debasing. Mere submission is not enough. And so, we ask why to bow or kneel does not forfeit our dignity.

There is first a fact to be noted. Some of the greatest men and women in our history, the true citadels of majesty, from the towering poets and the mighty musicians to the conquering heroes and mighty kings, have indeed worshiped. During his triumphal entry into Rome, the mighty Caesar suspended the march to the Forum and actually got upon the ground and literally crawled before the temple of his favorite divinity, Fortuna. Mozart worshiped, Shakespeare worshiped, Michelangelo worshiped. Even the most arrogant men in history worshiped, men like Caesar, Bismark, Washington, Wagner, and Louis XIV. Their worshiping did not seem to degrade their images either to us or to themselves. So it is not merely an abstraction, but a historical fact that greatness and dignity are not always or even usually disjoined from worship. But why? The facts are not in dispute; the explanation alone is wanting.

Caesar crawling on the dirt before his goddess is not merely a manifestation of his submission, essential though that is, it is also a revelation of something much simpler, yet perhaps something more profound. Caesar was also grateful.

Why must our critical instincts always be so base? The worshiper is not only submitting his will before what is magnificent, he is also showing his gratitude for what is spendid and wonderful. To be grateful is not to be ignoble; on the contrary, to thank is to elevate the soul. To worship is to thank; to kneel before what is magnificent is to be grateful. For the moment I shall delay the question, grateful for what? First, it is important to understand existentially just what it means to be grateful.

Again it is perhaps the wisest course to approach this question of the meaning of gratitude indirectly through an appreciation of an artwork. In what is surely one of the world's finest pieces of literature, *King Lear,* Shakespeare shows us the story of three daughters, each of whom, including the relatively innocent Cordelia, fails to recognize her duty to be grateful. At the beginning of the play the wicked daughters, Goneril and Regan, are bad enough, but they are not yet true villains. The play is about what happens when we forget to be grateful. Lear is led to call his daughters ungrateful wretches. Why should ingratitude make us wretched? There can be no doubt that the author of the play firmly believes that their ingratitude not only offends the king, but actually turns the two thankless daughters into little more than beasts. Theirs is a deterioration, a rapid descent from unkindliness to thorough wickedness, fed by the consuming flames not of hatred or malice or cruelty but simply ingratitude. Why? Why does mere *ingratitude*, a seemingly small fault, turn out to be such an enormous force of malice and menace? The theme is also revealed conversely in the character of Edgar, later disguised as Mad Tom. Edgar is also ungrateful, though in an innocent, careless, and thoughtless way of the favored son, not in the rancid, malignant self-destruction of the two daughters of the king. Nevertheless, Edgar, as Mad Tom, learns through his suffering to be grateful and in the end is presented as noble and dignified. So why is his discovery of gratitude and the sisters' loss of it so very important? Why does this quality make the noblest tragedy of them all? A brief reflection will suffice.

For what am I grateful? For that which is not earned or deserved. I am not grateful for the wages I earn by hard labor, for I have, by dint of my work, a right to them. Rather, I am grateful only for what is bestowed as a gift. And for what reasons are gifts given? Again, not because they are earned: a wage is not a gift. What is bestowed as a gift is given not because of what I have done but simply because of who I am. A father gives a reward to a child for a deed well done: we understand that as earned. But the same father gives a gift to the same child not because of what the child has done but simply because the child is his. Or because the father loves the child as his own. Thus, gratitude is a response to the existential worth manifested in the giving. Being grateful celebrates the *existential*, not the moral, worth of the recipient. To take a bestowal and treat it as a right does discredit not only to the giver but also to the recipient. The two ungrateful daughters insist that their dower is theirs by *right*, not by grace. This confusion of meanings is the single, fatal cause of their downfall. They become the "pelican daughters" because they have lost their capacity to be grateful. In doing so they have lost their capacity to matter as existentially meaningful beings, people to whom gifts are given simply because of who they are, not because they deserve or have earned anything. (This is the real reason for the difficult first act in which the king, quite rightly from an existential point of view, asks the three daughters to announce their love for him; for in distributing his lands on the basis of love rather than merit, an entirely different kind of meaning is given to the endowment.) Thus, to be ungrateful is to forfeit one's existential worth; it is to say: Give me only what I earn or have a right to; do not bestow any gift, which is always given only because of who one is. But these women were not just potentially good rulers of the state, they were the king's beloved daughters, and hence were given the power to rule just because of who they were. Lear wanted to give them the various parts of the kingdom because he loved them.

To be grateful is thus to affirm the existential worth of one's own existence; to be ungrateful is to deny such worth. Little wonder that Goneril and Regan, already fairly snappish and waspish, in evaluating their dowers as *rights* begin the fearsome tumble down into the lowest levels of human existence. They become as beasts. The play, after the first act, abounds in low and bestial imagery, constantly comparing the human situation to that of the base animals. If I refuse to accept anything as a gift and demand only what is mine by right, I completely excise all possibility of being valued merely because of who I am. That is what thanklessness does to the human soul. It makes us like the lowest beast. Thus, it is not thankfulness manifested in worship that degrades, but rather thanklessness, which is manifested in the orgulous refusal to bow down or kneel in gratitude before the magnaminity of a gracious bestower.

We have spotted four essential elements that make worship intelligible. The first is *fear;* there can be no doubt that the mighty instills a fearsome respect, but such fear is not necessarily degrading. It is degrading only if it is undeserved. The second element essential for worship is *acknowledgment* of the truth of the worshiped. I cannot worship a possible being or an abstract being; though I may admit ignorance of ultimate things, when I worship I acknowledge that what is worshiped—though I may be vague about what it is—is true. The third element is *submission.* This is a yielding of one's will to the interests and even magnificence of the worshiped. It is the one element of the four which disturbs those who are fearful of losing their dignity. But the fourth element, *gratitude,* restores that dignity by revealing that what is bestowed as a gift can only be given to one who has existential worth, i.e., they matter simply because of who they are and not because of what they have done. These four elements allow us to proffer a provisional understanding of worship as a fearful acknowledgment of greatness before which we submit our will and for which we are grateful.

When King Claudius cries out, "bow, stubborn knees!" he is asking for repentence and forgiveness: that he may repent and God may forgive. His stubbornness is not based on a misplaced conception of his own dignity but on his psychological inability to relent his kingdom and his queen. He realizes that in kneeling before the divinity his own existential worth is celebrated; but to ask forgiveness on the basis of who one is and yet retain the advantages of his crime is duplistic and inauthentic: hence his agony. When the disbelieving young prince falls to his knees at the bedside of his beloved, he is impelled to acknowledge a greatness which alone could ground the meaning of his grief and his realization of the finitude of human nature. When Auden finds in the September night a single ray of hope in the midst of gloom, he too attests to the greatness which is necessary if we are to make sense of what is happening about us.

But where, in these events, is there any gratitude? Surely, King Claudius is not grateful for his misery, nor is Bismark thankful his beloved is dying, nor Auden for the start of a terrible war. No, they are all grateful simply for the awesome truth that a divinity is there is give them meaning. This is the stumbling block for all who would seek to explicate worship solely from what the worshiper expects or hopes for from certain forms of worshiping such as fear, supplication, obsequious ingratiation, or theological bribery. The essence of worship cannot be found in the seeking of any benefit which could be bestowed on the worshiper, but in the simple, human phenomenon of gratitude. It is a gratitude grounded on a spectacular acknowledgment, a surrender to a truth far greater in its meaning than all possible doubt. And because it is a gratitude grounded on acknowledgment, it entails a submission. This, surely, is the proper understanding of Claudius and Bismarck and Auden. They worship, not because they expect any reward, but simply because they must. This necessity is a part of one's existential makeup and thus is self-affirming rather than self-denying.

In the opening chapter a comparison was made between a humble farmer who takes off his cap when the Angelus is rung from the village church and the farmer's wife who tosses salt over her shoulder for good luck. It was suggested at that early stage of the inquiry that there may be a difference between *how we think of* spirituality and simple superstition. In the present analysis of worship, which is one of the predicates of spirituality, this difference can now be seen more clearly. Both the farmer and his wife may be mistaken in their simplistic view of the universe, but the farmer's devotion is contrasted to his wife's gullibility: the latter expects some reward, whereas the former acts out of a sense of grateful acknowledgment. Again it must be stressed that the difference is *not* that the wife's superstition is false whereas the farmer's beliefs are true. Such metaphysical judgments are simply suspended in an existential inquiry into meaning. We sense the dignity in the farmer bowing his head to respond to the Angelus, but can have only gentle contempt for the superstition of the housewife.

Heretofore we have examined the phenomenon of worship directly. But to comprehend the phenomenon fully it is necessary to consider ancillary phenomena as well; those events which are similar to, or close to, that of worship and which may also throw light on worship itself.

Often when a sensitive listener or observer witnesses a mighty work of art there is an internal response which is very similar to actual worship: it may indeed even be a subclass of worship. A truly monumental work of art, like the Ninth Symphony of Beethoven, the *Ring* of Wagner, the *David* statue of Michelangelo, a well-acted performance of Shakespeare's *Hamlet*, or Saint Peter's Cathedral may present us with an experience of the sublime which lifts our consciousness to the level of sheer wonderment. Such an experience, though not directly religious, may induce a strong sense of humility and gratitude, which is nevertheless uplifting. Many religious people have expressed that such an experience of high art is so similar to the religious phenomenon of worship that they think of the two kinds of experience as belonging to the same impulse. There are those who, listening to the *Messiah* or Bach's Mass in B-Minor simply identify their experience as a form of prayer or worship.

This may provoke a critical thinker to wonder if perhaps worship itself is little more than an extension of such artistic response. Great art is so lofty an experience that one may feel an urge to transfer this same sentiment to the metaphysical world, so that worship becomes a mere artistic response to the masterpiece of nature. God is thus adored as the supreme artist, and in thus demythologizing worship, we have rendered it accessible to the ordinary understanding of aesthetic appreciation. But even if we identify worship as an aesthetic response, the philosophical question still remains: Why is it that these works make us respond in such a worshipful way?

Appreciation of genius, especially in the arts, is a deeply disturbing phenomenon. Someone aware of the vast amount of mediocre music may find his appreciation of Beethoven's Third Symphony so overwhelming that he is confronted by the incontrovertible fact of genius. What is it that makes the *Eroica* so absolutely great? It is, after all, merely music, made by man, played by dedicated human musicians, formally no different from any organized sound designed by the ever-reaching spirit of the human species. But, though we may believe this intellectually, we cannot accept it spiritually, or in this case, aesthetically. The *Eroica* is a work of genius: it does not merely entertain; it lifts us up to lofty heights of self-awareness. At the very least, we are forced to recognize that men are not equal. Beethoven had a genius that simply transcends most ordinary understanding. We cannot help but ask: Why? Why was this tortured man so driven to achieve things which were simply not even possible before him? It is tempting to suggest that such genius is simply the gift of God. This temptation is exacerbated when we reflect upon the

nonaesthetic qualities of the composers. Were it not for his music, would Beethoven be anything other than a pestiferous and
obnoxious bore? Would Mozart be anything but a spoiled brat
who deserves a public spanking? Would not Wagner simply deserve to be shot? If we are to believe the legends, many great
artists, particularly in the world of music, are unhappy, grumpy,
nasty, ugly, cruel, and objectionable men who are harshly insen-
sitive to the feelings of others and who live the most wretched
and undesirable of lives. Yet. Ah, yes, there's always that 'yet'.
The 'yet' is their music or their poetry or their art. It is their art
that forces us to yield to the inevitable: all men are not alike;
there are, in this world, a few geniuses. Now we can explain these
men away by all kinds of psychological accounts, some of which
may even be partially true. But their impact, their *gift* to us, remains a source of awe and wonder. Why? Not how, but why?
There can be no doubt that the beneficiaries of their genius are
not themselves but us. It is almost impossible to resist the passion
of gratitude when we contemplate what they have done *to* the
world, not merely for the world. They have changed it forever
and we can only be grateful. Knowing of their own wretchedness
and misery, we cannot even be envious. (Who would want to be
Beethoven: deaf, alone, admired by millions but loved intimately
by none?) Yet their art has made our world infinitely more
worthwhile. How are we to think about this? It is not enough
merely to be glad they lived, to consider ourselves fortunate to
have their art. To feel fortunate is not to feel grateful. Most of us
smilingly surrender and yield to the impulse and acknowledge
our gratitude. But *why* are we so favored? Is it because there is a
divinity bestowing upon us the fruits of genius? We *feel* this sentiment even if we intellectually doubt its soundness. Yet how else
are we to make sense of this submission and acknowledgment of
a greatness beyond ourselves for which we must be grateful? Is it
sacrilegious to suggest that we actually worship truly great art?
At least we can admit that the appreciation of such magnificence
reveals our existential propensity to recognize a greatness of
meaning which transcends our animal and even our ordinary human modalities.

Still, great art may be beautiful, indeed it may even be sublime, but can it truly be considered *sacred*? If by the sacred we

mean that which evokes worship and reverence beyond the worldly understanding of ourselves, then surely great art is sacred. But this is to say that great art is sacred, or at least participates in sacredness; it does *not* say that the sacred is merely a certain kind of artistic awareness. We do know the difference. In other words, I can explain the magnificence of art by appealing to the sacred, but I cannot reduce the sacred to the mere aesthetic response to art.

One of the characteristics of worship, whether of the divine, the human beloved, or the artistically great, is the insatiable desire of the worshiper to be in the presence of the beloved and to know as much about them as possible. Yet the means taken to achieve this nearness as well as this knowledge are often bizarre and rarely respectable. Of course, a devotee of Beethoven may read countless biographies; a lover may seek to find out as much as possible about the beloved from any source available; a worshiper may study the holy texts over and over, seeking for inspiration. These are acceptable means, but there are also the more fantastic means: the lover's keeping a lock of the beloved's hair, the music-lover's fascination with the paraphernalia and trivia which surround the hero; the worshiper's quiet and constant association with one's god through strange rituals and private prayers. Such behavior is not an indication of madness or silliness but simply evidences the intensity of the worshiper's awe and respect. And of course, this observation prompts our recognition that people can and do worship totally unworthy things: misers worship money with as much devotion as pilgrims who trek to the holy places; drug users worship the powders that keep their brains befuddled with happy numbness; and, perhaps worst of all, fanatics kill, pillage, rape, and destroy the enemies of their god in the execution of holy wars. That many worship falsely or even badly does not annul the authenticity of worship any more than inept lovers undermine the institutions of human love. To worship falsely is still to worship; and as inquirers into the meaning of the phenomenon we cannot excise the undesirable without sabotage of the truth.

In the realm of spirit, however, worship is usually directed toward a god or God, and for many religions this entails not only the worship of a power or even a truth but of a person. To complete this picture of worship, then, it would be deficient to omit mention of that special kind of love which humans seem to have for their objects of worship. For some love is essential for worship—not just the human worship of young lovers, but the loving worship of a saint for his or her God. Surely this quality belongs as a provisional part of our account. Even so, it is a strange doctrine indeed: that we should love the God we worship. Love, even in the most stretched and bizarre of senses, usually seems to entail some kind of intimacy and sharing. But is not worship exactly opposed to sharing? When we worship someone or something do we not elevate it beyond intimacy? In love, we approach, we draw near, we grasp to ourselves, and intimately identify and share the beloved as our own. Can this ever be a kind of worship? Apparently, in the case of great saints, it is not only possible but actually happens. When this does occur, however, the worshiped must be understood as a *person*. But since some religions, though not all, maintain a personal God, to worship the beloved is not a violation of the laws of reason. Such a love, for a God and by a worshiper, is itself a special theme deserving of independent analysis, but in a theological text, not in a purely philosophical one. It is enough for our interests to point out that some people do include in their notion of worship the idea of love. But even in such theological worship, the four essential qualities remain and are necessary: fear, acknowledgment, submission, and gratitude. If one insists upon adding love, that requires an act of specific faith and the establishment of a precise, theistic religion.

To conclude this sketch of the predicate worship, a thought experiment may prove beneficial. Suppose we are in a field where there is a cheetah. Instinctively, we want to see the animal run. The cheetah is the fastest mammal in the world, and simply looking at the beast at rest suggests not only power but grace. But why have a cheetah if it cannot run? That is why we go to see cheetahs in the first place. Running fulfills the meaning of a cheetah. If we place an average man before a truly beautiful woman, we expect a fairly universal response. There may be a sexual attraction, but if she is splendid enough the mind is also lifted, and he is moved to love. We say that a beautiful woman fills him with thoughts of love and not merely sex. If I were to place a sensitive patron of the arts in the same room with a Rembrant, there is little doubt what would be expected of the art-lover: he or she would want to look at the painting. That is what a great painting is supposed to do: it awakens in us a sense of the very reverence of looking. Beauty makes us want to see.

Assume it is possible to find a purely tradition-free but intelligent and sensitive person who heretofore had been unaware of the actual existence of an absolutely perfect being. The question is: would this person instinctively know what to do? If they had no previous tradition to tell them, would they nonetheless instinctively know they ought to kneel down and worship? Is that not what an all-powerful being suggests, as the cheetah suggests speed, and the Rembrant looking? One might want to suggest that, confronted for the first time, with a truly magnificent being, worship would be a natural response. The question, however, is this: Is the instinct for worship, even of lesser or even unworthy things, existentially a priori? Do we worship because we believe that there is a God, or do we wonder about God because we are beings who worship? By this little thought-experiment I have tried to *suggest*—nothing stronger—that the existential modality of worship comes before the theological belief in God. But even prior to that I have also suggested that, after all, what do you *do* with a truly magnificent being? Is there anything you *can* do except worship it, in fear, submission, acknowledgment, and gratitude? If this is correct, then these three modalities wait upon a mere possibility. Is something magnificent possible?

5

Suffering

About suffering they were never wrong, the old
masters.

Auden, "Musee des Beaux Arts"

To the uninitiated, or even to the uninformed, the nature and
amount of suffering brought about by spirit is awesome and horrific. I am not here speaking of quite ordinary suffering brought
about by the vagaries of fate or the nature inherent in a sensible
body but about spiritual suffering, which includes gruesome pain
endured for the sake of spirit. Read an account of the child
Therese Martin, and you will see a representation of suffering
and pain so overwhelming it borders on the perverse. With the
decline of monasteries and convents of the stricter orders, such
practices are likewise receding, and many an honest soul sighs
with relief at their passing. It is one thing to accept occasional
misfortunes stoically, it is quite another to focus upon them as a
source of elevation or holiness. We have convenient psychological
labels to affix to these unseemly practices. The centuries of hair-
shirts and flagellations may have gone the way of the horse-
drawn buggy, but there are still a few seeking holiness who look
to suffering itself as some kind of radiance. Regardless of one's
persuasion, such revelations are deeply disturbing if not down-
right disgusting. Surely suffering endured is noble, but suffering
embraced for its own sake is inhuman.

Before we turn to the subject of spiritual suffering, which is
always a form of sacrifice, a few preparatory words should first
be made concerning the phenomenon itself. We suffer. I can account for pain, which is a part of suffering, on purely physiological grounds. The same nerve endings which provide pleasure

are, by their very nature, equally well equipped for pain. One can even see pain purposively: it is used, in nature, as a form of signal or alarm. When the fire is so hot that it hurts, move away. The pain is necessary for this lesson, and thus should not be despised. Suffering, including not only the experience of pain but the acceptance of its meaning, whether mental pain or physical pain, is usually seen as a problem only for theists. How could a good and powerful God allow suffering? Either God is not strong enough or good enough to stop it, hence a theistic God cannot exist.

I admit the theist has a special problem, but it is absurd to think suffering is no problem at all for the nontheist. Anyone who thinks must confront the seeming assault on our reason when great and undeserved anguish and torment wrack the innocent victim. At the very least we are forced, in the face of such seeming unfairness, to wonder about the purpose and meaning of it all. To explain suffering by causal explanations—physical trauma and agitated nerve endings—may satisfy our knowledge but not our understanding. This is a problem for all thinkers, not merely theodicists, and it is exacerbated by the uneasy realization that perhaps we would hesitate to prefer a world in which no suffering were possible at all. These uneasy sentiments may well disturb us because we are not absolutely sure just what it means to suffer. Perhaps we may even realize, without full analysis, that in some way suffering belongs to us merely because we are human beings, that our humanity depends, in part, on our capacity to endure, though not to desire, our torment. At the very least, many nontheistic thinkers are aware that they do not yet fully understand the meaning of suffering, and that is sufficient grounds for raising this question as a possible source of illumination on what it means to be spirit.

Consider the perverseness of nonphilosophical folk who behave exactly opposite to the way the academicians say they should. We are told by the professors that nothing uproots the foundations of belief more readily than the existence of evil; that a person more readily drops faith in God because of evil seen in the world than for more refined doubts. In some sense, this may be true. Yet, surely as many are brought to some belief, however nebulous, by evil as are distracted from it. Kant points out, for example, that the sight of justice unfulfilled on earth fills the average mind with a longing for something to even it all out. (He calls this "the postulate of immortality.") Yet, both of these arguments are impressive: (1) If God is good and powerful, he should not allow evil, but it exists, so he doesn't; and (2) There is no justice in this world, hence we must assume there is another world beyond to find a place to establish what is deserving. Many are persuaded by each of them. But in actual places of abject misery, as in the 'Gulags', the Nazi concentration camps, the cancer wards of hospitals one does not find wholesale abandonment of faith; rather one finds some attracted to faith by the failure of this world, and one also finds a smaller number whose anger and anguish simply extinguish both God and hope.

These references are made not to persuade the reader, but simply to show that the problem of suffering does not seem to have an overly persuasive influence one way or the other. It is not as though the believer were disarmed before the problem of evil; but neither is the doubter persuaded by foxhole conversions. Indeed, it would be surprising if such arguments were overwhelmingly successful, partly because abstract reasoning does not persuade many people, but above all because in the phenomenon of suffering the theme itself is so bewildering. We all suffer, and most of us know the proximate causes of most of our pains. Unless we are masochists we do not like to endure pain, and we would avoid suffering if we could. Yet we would not universally condemn all suffering as unworthy of the species; we might even admit that people are stronger or wiser or nobler because they have suffered; we might hesitate to push a button which would remove all suffering from the world. Furthermore, though suffering is often intense and frightening, it is not always seen as an evil and even less frequently seen as morally wrong. Suffering also seems to attract us in a peculiar way: we may seek out the presence of those who have suffered greatly; we respect those who have endured a great deal; we honor the sufferer as one who is somehow special. Above all, the notion of suffering seems to evoke a strong sense of humanity, as if suffering is our nature. Like death, suffering is so integrally identified with our own humanity that we think it inauthentic to pretend we shall never suffer and never die.

Aside from the purely physical reaction of nerve endings, how are we to understand suffering? There can be no doubt that the spiritual is the proper realm for understanding it: to be spiritual is to suffer. Indeed, one might even suggest converting the proposition: to suffer is to be spiritual. Suffering, unlike radiance and importance and worship, seems almost an initiatory rite, a necessary condition for spirituality rather than a true existential predicate. But true predicate it must be, for the entire edifice of our understanding of spirit would collapse without this fundamental prop known as human suffering. Unless we suffer, we cannot be spirit.

The etymology is suggestive. The term is an ancient one, and it means to bear or endure, or even to allow. The strict analysis seems to be: sub-fere, to bear beneath or carry under. What is striking about this origin is that it still seems to operate in revealing the fundamental way we think about the term. It is not the same as pain, for the word contains no sense of hurt or ache or sting; rather it suggests endurance. And whatever else we think when we think of suffering we think of endurance, a strengthening under a burden. It also emphasizes that not all pain is suffering, for in order for there to be true suffering there must be an awareness of its meaning: a painful distraction or stubbed foot may hurt enormously, but suffering seems almost to demand a nobler and more intense form of endurance. Further, although the parallel is not exact, the term 'suffering' is usually used when referring to spiritual or mental anguish as well as the endurance of great physical pain, with emphasis on the former. Pain, however, seems to refer more exclusively to mere physical discomfort. A woman suffering the grief of her husband's death or a nation suffering from shock at the loss of their king, for example, show us that 'suffering' more often than not evokes a sense of continual and persistent agonizing due to one's modality in the world. Partly due to its etymological source, and partly due to ordinary modern English usage, to *suffer* has also come to connote achieving, as if to have suffered is somehow to have made the grade of humanity—which perhaps it is.

But there is more to the term than this. When someone says "I have suffered," they do not mean merely that they have felt pain. They mean that they are now fundamentally changed, they are not who they were. "I have suffered" is often spoken as an accomplishment, rarely as an invitation to pity. (Indeed, it is curious, but except in cases of young children, one does not usually pity one who suffers: there is too much nobility for that.) "To have suffered" may include the forfeiture of natural innocence and bubbly happiness, but they are supplanted with wisdom, depth, and compassion.

There is a curious drawing into one's self in the phenomenon of suffering, a closure of all openings from without, a focus upon one's inmost being, as if for solace, or perhaps even strength. Why do we crawl up into little balls of wretchedness when we suffer? Perhaps it is because what we fear is the loss of our own privacy, the threat of what is our own being denied. We hunker around the knot of our distress and misery in order to keep ourselves intact. It is exactly the opposite of joy, in which the instinct is to spread the light around, to share with others our innate happiness. But suffering we not only cannot share with anyone, we do not want to. It is as if to share the wretchedness is to spread it, and like some contagious disease to open our arms wide to those around us would infect them with the unbearable as well. And so suffering drives us in upon ourselves, perhaps reveals our own nakedness to ourselves which had hitherto been decently covered. There is, even, a kind of fierce pride in suffering, a recognition of one's superiority due to the agonies one has endured. None of this is meant to imply any masochistic perversion, but the simple recognition that suffering, especially great suffering, tempers the steel of our souls, alerts us to the hitherto hidden cracks and crevices of our inner selves, rejects pity, and defies the utilitarian conviction that all suffering is morally evil.

Nevertheless, suffering is primarily undesirable. No one, perhaps with the single exception of the inveterate sacrificer, wants to suffer; and even the sacrificer can embrace the pangs of suffering only through enormous and perhaps unnatural acts of the will. But to say suffering is undesirable is not to say that it is bad, even less that it is evil. The first premise of the argument against God's existence based on the existence of evil is that suffering is inconsistent with the goodness of God; this is simply false. No one seriously believes that suffering is wicked merely because it is undesirable. (Unless, of course, goodness is equated with the satisfaction of all human wants and desires, a notion even sillier than the first.) It should perhaps be pointed out that the following words do *not* mean the same thing: unfortunate, undesirable, painful, bad, criminal, wicked, sinful, evil, sacrilegious, and malicious. They each have different meanings and different presuppositions.

But if suffering is not necessarily morally wrong, and surely not wicked, it is nevertheless both painful and undesirable. Yet, even in this recognition, there is a caveat. It seems there are, in fact, at least four instances of suffering in which the normal mind would find not only begrudging acceptance but actual affirmation and approval. Thus, merely because suffering by definition and meaning must always be undesirable and instinctively avoided, it does not follow that one cannot actually affirm certain cases of suffering and assert that suffering, in these cases, is actually a good and an acceptable thing. The first two of these four 'acceptable' modes of suffering are found in common life; the second two are to be found in art, but they are so revealing and so powerful in their art form that they seem to tell us about ourselves in the real world as well. These four acceptable modalities of suffering are: (1) punishment, (2) sacrifice, (3) tragedy, and (4) self-realization through rebellion. Since the second of these, sacrifice, constitutes the major emphasis of the entire next section, I shall here briefly sketch out an explanation of the remaining three.

Those who believe in justice (apparently a shrinking number) must recognize that otherwise noble and honest people would accept punishment for their misdeeds not only as a right but as a privilege to redeem the wrong they have committed. There may be few such noble people around, but they are certainly possible; and even if they do not exist, we as society do not hesitate to punish criminals. I do not say that we rehabilitate them, or that we isolate them from society, but we actually punish them; for if we did not punish them there would be no justice. And here, by 'punish' we mean to do actual physical restraint, the imposition of pain, and the gross violation of another's preferences and wants. The criminal, we hope, suffers. And we think this is a good and right thing. Why? Because justice demands it. If a man has raped my child, the utter anguish, shame, and pain he brings both on the child and myself remains unanswered until or unless the state enters in and tries to even out this imbalance by bringing the criminal enough suffering to compensate or at least offset to some degree the enormity of our grief and misery. This account makes sense; and because of it many people are assured that the suffering of the convicted criminal is deserved, and hence ought to be carried out. Indeed, were the criminal *not* punished, society would feel cheated of justice, and the *absence* of suffering would be seen as an affront to reason and spirit. Thus, in justice we see at least one example in which the mind can rejoice that there is suffering in the world.

The second case is the most spectacular of all: we are glad there is suffering because without it we could not sacrifice. On this we defer to the later section.

We now turn to the arts. In the form known as tragedy, great men and women are hugely tortured by fickle fate, and from their high and lofty seats are brought low in ignominy and death. To be sure, some thinkers, such as Aristotle, interpret this phenomenon in exactly the same manner as the criminal's suffering is explained in the above paragraph; the tragic hero is thought to *deserve* his inglorious end. But we have come some distance in our thinking about tragedy, and ever since Hegel and Nietzsche, this moralistic interpretation no longer satisfies the philosophical mind. Why, then, do we seem to rejoice or at least enjoy the witness of a noble character's fall? Artistic tragedy can be seen as the triumph of the noble over the good: i.e., we recognize their greatness simply because it does not depend upon good fortune. Antigone and her uncle Creon in Sophocles' great play are not seen as having done something wicked for which they are then punished; rather, their greatness expands our awareness beyond the earlier judgment that the worth of a person's existence is determined solely by happiness. In spite of the miseries that accompany Lear and Antigone and Othello, the audience is made aware of the *autonomy* of their greatness from the goodness of their deeds and hence the independence of their existential worth. By this interpretation, the miseries endured by the heroes focus our attention away from fortune and happiness and direct it rather on the sheer magnificence of who they are. Thus, by dint of their suffering, their existential greatness is revealed, and the audience can celebrate their suffering as a means of illuminating their meaning. Under this interpretation, once again suffering becomes something we actually want to see, for by it one is set free from the ignominy of having to be judged as worthwhile only when fortunate. To be sure, this suffering is on the stage only, it is a purely aesthetic sense of suffering. But the communicative power of tragic art is so enormous it is difficult to believe that the meaning is a purely aesthetic one. Somehow we feel that the dramatic message on stage is grounded within our deeper selves, that tragedy reveals something about the human species as such. In witnessing such a tragedy, the audience is enabled to feel the dignity of suffering and recognize that this Dionysian art form has succeeded in separating the meaning of our existence (and not just the heroes on the stage) from the grim requirement that only happy people can be appreciated as being worthwhile. In tragedy, it is precisely because we still revere, and even love, the Lears and Antigones and Othellos, even after they have suffered, that their misery does not cancel out their worth. This is a great discovery, and its awareness lifts our minds to higher levels of truth. But we need suffering in order to make this happen; it cannot happen without suffering, since in the absence of such anguish the worth would not be *autonomous*. Tragedy, then, may well be a mere aesthetic experience, but its truth transcends the art form. If this is true, then we have a third reason for accepting the idea that suffering can actually be acknowledged and approved without rendering it masochistically perverse.

From tragedy to the epic we turn our attention to discover the fourth of these curious ways in which suffering is actually condoned and embraced. Here we are speaking of those epic heroes who, by deliberately removing themselves from the friendliness and comfort of the godhead, achieve suffering as a price paid for freedom or autonomous meaning. There are several such epic works in the repertoire, but the one which best suits the present discussion is Milton's *Paradise Lost*. Especially in Book IX, in which Eve yields to the temptations to eat of the fruit of knowledge of good and evil, we can see that the acceptance of the Mother of Mankind of her own meaning brings enormous suffering both to herself and Adam, but also to the entire human race. This work can be interpreted as showing that Eve, in opting to eat of the fruit, has chosen to be herself. It is almost as if the incomplete and unfinished work of creation needs a free act which necessarily offends the God who made her in order to separate herself from too much happiness where her own independent meaning is eclipsed. Milton's Adam himself admits that:

> Full of doubt I stand,
> Whether I should repent me now of sin
> By me done and occasioned, or rejoice
> Much more that much more good thereof shall spring—
>
> (473, Bk. XII)

Adam admits this confusion because now, as free beings, severed from God by sin, he is capable of greater worship and even greater thanks. This rebellion by Eve is fraught with enormous suffering, chief of which is death; men must now earn their bread by the sweat of their brow, and women must bear children in pain. Yet, the mind is not entirely destroyed by this grief or this loss. There is something gained through this suffering: a greater capacity for worship. Satan himself echoes this sentiment earlier in Book I:

> To reign is worth ambition, though in Hell;
> Better to reign in Hell than serve in Heaven.

These words strike a resonant chord in every rebellious spirit, and perhaps there simply is no spirit unless there is rebellion. A few lines earlier, Satan also says of his own mind, now free from a necessary servility in heaven:

> The mind is its own place, and in itself
> Can make a Heaven of a Hell, a Hell of Heaven.

We can see the same anguish in Wotan's mind as he struggles with the enormity of creating a free spirit: he finds himself actually wishing his son to violate his own law, simply to be truly free. There are many early images of man in which this triumph of rebellion seems to be equated with freedom, and so here too one can rejoice in a kind of suffering, the suffering that deprives us of our paradise, but puts us on the path of greater meaning.

Both the tragic hero's triumph of his own meaning above that of fortune, and the epic hero's rebellion against an all-powerful God in order to create enough room for what is his own and no one else's—even if that single ownness is nothing else but sin—are invocations against a world of simple delight. They are both triumphs of a meaningful suffering, a suffering which, though painful, is embraced as one's own. In suffering, then, we find our true selves.

But suffering hurts. No matter what the poets or saints say, we do not want to suffer; it is built into the very meaning of the term. Why, then, do we turn to these four instances—and there may be more—in which we affirm suffering? Because, in seeking to understand the nature of spirit, we have seen that suffering is essential for our comprehension of it. But unless I can render suffering acceptable, at least in some senses, I cannot affirm spirit. Thus, we turn to these instances in which suffering is praised in order to learn what it means.

However, the three examples just sketched: punishment, tragedy, and rebellion for the sake of freedom, suggestive and powerful as they are in themselves, are not complete until we have examined the true meaning of spiritual suffering: sacrifice.

In the final chapter of Charles Dicken's novel *A Tale of Two Cities*, Sydney Carton, pretending to be his friend Evremonde who had been sentenced to die, is led to the guillotine to be executed. As the revolutionary terrorists prepare this mistaken victim for the public spectacle, Carton, who could have saved his own life by simply identifying himself, nevertheless sacrifices his life, speaking one of the finest lines in nineteenth-century English literature: "It is a far, far better thing that I do now, than I have ever done; it is a far, far better rest that I go to, than I have ever known." This sacrifice is usually considered a noble and virtuous act. The words of Christ found in the Gospel of Saint John, 15:13, seem to bear this out: "Greater love than this no man hath, that a man lay down his life for his friends." Thus sacrifice seems to be supported not only by Scripture but by honored literature as not merely justifiable but among the greatest of virtues.

By 'sacrifice' one often means simply the willingness of someone to endure personal loss, even death, for the sake of another, and as such it seems almost the paradigm of what is morally good. The etymology of the term also seems to elevate it highly, for the Latin from which the English term 'sacrifice' is derived means that which makes something holy. This further meaning seems not only to imply that sacrifice is virtuous but sacred as well. Certainly the willingness of Sydney Carton to sacrifice his life for his friend strikes us as both noble and good, perhaps it is even holy or sacred.

But 'sacrifice' bears with it another meaning, not altogether lost even when applied to Sydney Carton's courageous and bold act, which, when analyzed, reveals certain aspects of sacrifice that are not virtuous but horrific and primitive. This is the meaning understood by the term when it refers to the shedding of innocent blood as a ritual or sacred rite to please the divine in atonement or expiation. Anthropologists and theologians have studied the phenomenon of sacrifice and sought to give it various explanations, many of which are highly speculative and dubious, but most of which nevertheless indict the practice as primitive, selfish, and often cruel. Certainly there is something disturbing about judging the spillage of innocent blood, no matter for what reason, as an entirely noble and commendable act. Even Carton was innocent, and although we cannot but admire his courage, his love for his friend, and his boldness, it is not obvious that the notion of sacrifice adds anything to these established and recognizable virtues; perhaps indeed the purely sacrificial aspect of his execution is something which should be censured rather than praised. On this second interpretation, then, sacrifice is seen not as a virtue at all, but as a vice.

To put the question in more precise philosophical terms, we might all agree that Carton's willingness to die in order to let his friend live is simply noble and good. But if sacrifice is a *value*, it should not be seen as something which can be *endured* for the sake of something else that is good—the life of Evremonde—but that it should be seen as something which is in itself worthwhile. I may willingly endure many ills for the sake of greater effects, but that does not make those ills themselves good. In order for sacrifice *per se* to be worthwhile, it must not only be willed or endured, but actually desired. And this may seem almost approaching the vice of perversion. Nevertheless, I argue that sacrifice, when properly understood, is indeed worthwhile; and here I must insist that by 'properly' I mean 'philosophically'.

It seems, then, that the single term 'sacrifice' has three distinct meanings: to endure suffering for the sake of another, to make something holy, and to spill blood in a religious ritual. These variant meanings seem so different that one might be inclined simply to distinguish them and separate them, treating them as three quite different words altogether. But this would be a mistake. To comprehend fully the meaning of the term 'sacrifice', all three of these meanings must be thought together, or at least understood as overlapping concepts from which the single notion of sacrifice takes its essential meaning. It is part of the task of the inquiry to show that the three variants, which I designate the 'endurance variant', the 'etymological variant', and the 'ritualistic variant', all come together into a single meaning.

The first two variants, that men endure suffering for others and that something is made holy, may seem innocent enough and may perhaps evoke our readiness to classify them as virtues. But the third variant, that of the ritualistic spillage of blood, seems inimical to virtue, and possibly should even be censured. But, as I shall argue, the first two variants in fact include the third variant, as long as all three are seen in a philosophical way. However, most work done on the ritualistic sense of sacrifice is carried out not by philosophers but by anthropologists and scientists of religion.

These attempts to explain sacrifice are at best meager lights thrown upon primitive *motives*, which are always highly questionable, and not on *meanings*. I may indeed kill a calf in order to expiate for wrongs committed against a deity, but this does not explain the meaning of expiation in the first place. What is so remarkable in the reading of these various accounts is that each differing theory sounds quite plausible, but they all assume that we know more about primitive motives than we know about our own.

But these references to the scientists of religion are not intended as put-downs, for their inquiries do reveal a great deal. However, the philosophical question is not one of motives but of meanings, and even if we accept much of the scientific data (while suspending, perforce, their theories since they contradict) we still need to dig more deeply into the phenomenon of sacrifice. Besides, these writers have focused only upon the third variant of the meaning of sacrifice. What do their observations tell us about the other variants? Does Carton really *sacrifice* his life for his friend? And if he does, can we call it virtuous? In order to answer this question, the nature of sacrifice itself must be more deeply probed.

Let us suppose that I give a man something of value that belongs to me originally. On purely speculative considerations, it seems there are but six basic and fundamentally different ways in which we can understand this transference of ownership from me to him: (1) I give it to him to expiate a wrong I have done him, either out of fear of reprisal or out of a genuine sense of moral retribution; (2) I give it to him to ingratiate myself before him, since he is more powerful than I; (3) I give it to him in exchange for something else; (4) I give it to him in response for something that he has done that deserves praise, as a reward; (5) I give it to him simply because of who he is: I have affection or admiration for him; and finally (6) I give it to him because it causes me pain or suffering to surrender what is precious. In each of these six cases I give something that belongs to me to someone else, but in each case the *meaning* of the giving is radically different. I maintain that these six are the major interpretations to giving, and that if there are others which one might speculate upon they will fall as subdivisions within these major groups.

In the first case, my giving is understood in terms of fear and perhaps a sense of punitive justice. Not wanting to be punished more severely, I give the valuable object as a kind of payment. Although fear may be the original emotion, there may be, after much cultivation of the sensibility, a concurrent sense of rightness about the act, so that I also feel that it is right and good that I surrender the valuable object. (2) The second is an extension of the first, except that it focuses upon the future rather than the past. If he is powerful he may feel paid off from any threat he might make to me. This is the kind of thing that school children must undergo when in the ghetto districts: they pay 'protection money' as a form of extortion to avoid getting beaten up. In both (1) and (2) fear is the basis of the transference of the valued object; in the first case it may be accompanied by a primitive sense of justice, but in the second case it is merely prudence.

In the third case, however, a slightly different kind of presupposition is made. Here I exchange something valuable for something else. This is the basis of contractual justice. It is what we do every time we buy something at a store. The exchange, unlike the first two cases, is without fear; and the ensuing sense of obligation or justice is contractual: i.e., we assume that both of us will benefit if the exchange is relatively egalitarian. The underlying emotion here is not fear but the expectation of mutual benefit. Not only does this case cover the exchanges of commerce, it also covers service. Thus, if a man works for me, I pay him an honest wage, and both of us benefit.

In the fourth case, I give it to him because of what he has done, but in this case the understanding is noncontractual. If he has saved a life, I may give him a reward. (Thus I distinguish a *wage* which is deserved and contractual, from a *reward* which is deserved but noncontractual.) The very concept of a reward implies that there is no contractual prearrangement, but that it is nonetheless deserved. A telling example may be the father who, seeing that his daughter has received an 'A' on her first arithmetic test, may feel impelled to reward his child by giving her a toy. I would strongly distinguish this kind of giving from the payment the father might give his daughter for doing some household chore. They both are earned, but the reward transcends the mere contractual character of the wage. It is of extreme importance to recognize in this difference that justice or obligation is contractual in the third case but transcendent of mere contract in the fourth, so that a meaningful sense of noncontractual obligation is revealed.

In the fifth case, there is no sense of earning involved at all. The father gives the valuable object to his daughter simply because she *is* his daughter: he loves her, not because of the things she has done, but simply because she is *his* daughter. (To emphasize this, the father may well recognize that there are many more deserving children on the block, more attractive little girls, and even perhaps a few he thinks would appreciate the valuable object more than his own daughter; but he still gives it to her simply because she *is his* daughter.) This kind of giving is called a gift, and should never be confused with reward. A reward is given because of what one has done, a gift is given because of who one is. The recipient in this case is given the gift simply because of who she is, the man's daughter. The point is, when this is pointed out to us, we understand it completely. Of course, we say, it is understandable that a man would give a gift to his daughter rather than to more deserving other children. The child neither earns the gift as she would a wage, nor does she deserve the object as she would a reward; rather, she is *bestowed* with the gift, and the basis for her receiving it is simply who she is, or what it means for her to exist as a daughter. There is a noncontractual sense of rightness in giving a reward for a deed well done, but there is no moral obligation at all in the giving of gifts. The support is not moral but *existential,* that is, the recipient is honored by the bestowal of the gift because of her *existence* (that she is the donor's daughter), whereas the moral givings are based upon what she has *done.*

We now turn to the remarkable sixth case. It may at first sound perverse: to give simply because the very giving *hurts.* This is sacrifice. A sacrifice is indeed a gift, so its value too lies in the existential worth involved and not in the moral worth of action. However, whereas the simple gift is understandable because of the worth of the recipient, the sacrifice is a gift in which what is affirmed is the worth of the donor as well as the recipient. A sacrifice is that gift (hence, unearned and existentially meaningful) which in giving establishes the worth of the giver and the recipient simply in terms of who they are, not in terms of what they have done. But how is that possible? How can I give a gift in which my own worth as well as the worth of the recipient is manifested? Surely when what I give is of myself. But, in order for a gift to be 'of myself' the value of myself must in some way be transferred to the recipient. I must give of myself, but that is simply what suffering or pain means: to lose that which is valuable, either an object dearly held or my own pleasure, lost in the pain of giving. It is, if you will, a gift that works both ways: it celebrates the meaning of the existence of both the recipient and the donor. In the case of the gift, the valuable object celebrates independent worth of the recipient (which is why friends, lovers, and family are the usual givers of gifts), but a sacrifice, in addition to celebrating the autonomous worth of the recipient, also celebrates the independent worth of the donor. Some amount of pain or loss is thus logically required in a sacrifice, otherwise the focus is solely on the gift and the recipient. Sacrifice is a deliberate rejection of the pragmatic interests of the first five kinds of giving in which the donor is benefited.

It must be noted, however, that in sketching out these six instances of giving, there is no historical guesswork about what some primitive felt, thought, or believed. All six of these kinds of giving are available to us as a part of our own meaning: we need not reach to some mystical or mythical past, nor do we need to speculate as to how men, ignorant of science and technology, must have thought about the world. With these six instances of giving we are reflecting simply upon what giving means as we understand it today and probably have always understood it, even in times of primitive peoples. We may not always be aware of these six differences, indeed it may well be that only when presently pointed out are we alert to the obvious meanings, but that is simply to distinguish what is formally precise from what is vaguely understood. Hence the advantage.

Sacrifice is indeed a gift and not a reward, a wage, a payment in exchange for something else, or an expiation for either the past or the future. Thus, to explain sacrifice in terms of the first four kinds of giving, which is what so many anthropological and psychological explanations do, is to overlook the logic of giving as has been sketched out above. This is not a mere 'list' of various meanings to giving, it is a hierarchy which builds on itself and expands. As we proceed in the analysis of the *development* of giving, we notice ever increasing sophistication of meaning and presupposition. The first three cases are essentially *commerce*, and the ensuing morality which supports them is contractual, with the third case being on a higher plane than the first two, since they require fear. The fourth case seems to recognize a broader understanding of what is *deserved* than what is merely *earned*, and with this a further advance in our moral understanding is made. But it is with the fifth case that the hierarchy truly reveals its significance, for in going from what a man deserves to what he may inspire as a recipient of a gift, the mind undergoes a radical transformation of values. Here the value is no longer a moral one but an existential one. We discover that we can hold as dear and precious not only what is right and proper but that which is loved. There is a difference between goodness and beauty: the first four cases focus on the worth of goodness, the fifth and sixth on the worth of beauty, at least in the Greek sense in which 'beauty' simply means that which is loved.

But fascinating as the existential meaning of gift-giving may be, this essay is concerned not with gifts only but with sacrifice. And, although sacrifice is a kind of gift, it transcends the concept of gift by focusing on the existential worth of both donor and recipient. And here we must take a few moments to test this account as grounded in ordinary experience. In fact, for some strange reason, we do seem to value gifts which cost or hurt the donor more than gifts which do not, even though the market price of the latter are superior to the former. A youngster gives his mother a gift: this pleases the parent, for it is a manifestation of the child's love. But when a parent receives a gift which has cost the youngster considerable effort, suffering, and even physical pain, a different evaluation is placed upon the giving. We value the sacrifice more than the gift. But *why?* Surely this is but a carryover of more perverse times. Why should I want my child to suffer? Or, to put it more precisely, why should a gift given to me by my own child which cost him suffering rank more highly than a gift given simply out of pure impulse for love? It is to throw light on this 'why' that the present inquiry is being carried out in the way that it is, but for the moment I wish to focus merely upon this fairly universal fact among those fortunate enough to have friends and families: we seem to value the gift that hurts more than the gift that was easily bestowed. Why? I believe my analysis of the six different meanings of giving explains this 'why?'

Earlier I insisted that any adequate account of sacrifice must include the three variants of its meaning, the 'endurance' of a sacrifice, the 'etymology' of the term, and the 'ritual' of its occurrence. I argue that all three of these variants can be seen in the six-tiered hierarchy of giving which alone explains the meaning of sacrifice. The hierarchy develops from simple economics, to contractual justice, to noncontractual obligation, to existential value, and finally to the concept of the sacred. This implies that the hierarchy is not only ranked, but inclusive; that is, the higher ranks include the worth of the lower ranks.

But this reliance on the six-tiered hierarchy of giving merely tells us where sacrifice is located in the structure of transferring things of value from one person to the next. It tells us that sacrifice is on the top of this ranking, and it tells us that essentially sacrifice must be seen as a kind of gift, rather than a moral or even prudential undertaking. These are all advantages in our quest, but as yet the inquiry has only circled the concept: it has not yet penetrated into the source. The analysis has prepared us for this now.

There seems to be a curious hiatus in our understanding of the term 'sacrifice' with regard to the etymological meaning and the ritual meaning. If the term means "to make something holy," and to perform a sacrificial rite is to kill a living thing, then it would suggest that we make something holy by killing it. This may seem counterintuitive. It may further seem that neither the etymological nor the ritualistic meaning of the term truly fits the analysis of the six levels of giving. Why does the shedding of blood make something sacred? Why does the willingness to endure suffering for another necessarily entail some sense of the holy? Cannot atheists or agnostics sacrifice their lives for the loved ones without any sense of the sacred at all?

Of course, we are not here examining what goes on in the minds of those who sacrifice, for that would be empirical sociology or psychology; we are trying to find out the true meaning of the term 'sacrifice' and testing whether it is justifiable. What we must now explore is the connection between the spillage of blood and the understanding of what is holy or sacred. First it must be emphasized that not every shedding of blood is necessarily sacred, indeed perhaps most such acts are quite profane. The shedding of blood is sacred only when it is seen in light of the six-fold hierarchy of giving; i.e., when the blood is let as a gift which reveals the worth of both donor and recipient. But even under this restriction it may seem odd to equate such violence with the notion of the holy.

Two notions must be kept in mind if we are to make the connection between the sacred and the violent. The first point is that the ritualistic act is not so much a *taking* of life but a *giving* of life. This is far more obvious when the donor is himself the victim, as in self-sacrifice. We speak of a young warrior who throws himself on the live grenade to save his friends as *giving* his life for them, as *sacrificing* himself for them. It must be remembered that the substitute victims in ritualistic sacrifice are always dear and precious, from calves to virgins. One does not 'sacrifice' an old crone or hag, just because that might be misinterpreted as social engineering. The loss of these lovely young maidens is grievous and severe for a primitive group, not only because they represent a continuation of the species, but again simply because they are loved.

The second point to be kept in mind is that the notion of the sacred is itself intelligible only in terms of what makes gift-giving understandable, namely gratitude. But here we are not speaking of gratitude for a specific boon or bonus, we are talking of gratitude for existence itself. Indeed, it is perhaps essential for the religious consciousness that it be gratitudinous. The argument for this is as follows. I am aware that my own existence is contingent. Hence, I am not a necessary being. But if I nevertheless exist, I must either be indifferent to my existence, disappointed with it, or grateful for it. To be indifferent to one's existence seems nihilistic, to be regretful seems suicidal. Thus, I am grateful for my existence. To whom am I grateful? Possibly my parents, of course; but if I think of myself in a spiritual way, or as having a soul, I must be grateful to God. Perhaps the essence of religious spirituality is a gratitudinous existence.

Of course, it is quite possible to argue that one might feel merely lucky that the peculiar occurrence of the sperm and the egg of one's parents just happened to meet, and let the laws of biology explain the rest. And this is not only possibly but probably predominant in the modern age. That, however, is exactly the point. The above paragraph explains what it means to be spiritual or even religious; the present paragraph explains what it means to be secular or nonspiritual. The purpose of all rites and rituals, aside from their specific rubric, is to instill and enhance a sense of the spirituality in existence. Since the one dominant sense that every thinking man has is an awareness of the contingency of his existence, to be *grateful* for that existence is to affirm the meaning of his existence in a manner and way which evokes that sense of gratitude: the act or meaning of gift-giving.

For a religious or spiritual person, to be is to be grateful. Existence itself is a gift. But gifts, unlike wages, rewards, and commercial exchanges, are intelligible only in terms of the worth of existence, not the worth of action. Thus, not only is my raw existence given, but so is its worth. Not to be grateful is therefore not to recognize one's worth. To be grateful is to be worthy of existence. If we define the 'holy' or the 'sacred' in terms of gratitudinous existence, the relationship between ordinary sacrifice and a sense of the holy or sacred is obvious.

In Shakespeare's *King Lear,* as we have earlier seen, this point is the theme of the play. In the absence of gratitude (spirituality) a human being will simply degenerate into a life whose meaning is little more than the base animals. For the religious mind the world of the holy is meaningful, for the secular mind it is absent. But in the absence of the holy we become barbarians.

Thus it is a gratitudinous existence that inspires a sacred world, not a fear of nonexistence. Of course, to be grateful for existence and to be fearful of nonexistence are not completely disjoined: fear, particularly in the early stages of consciousness, may be the more vivid emotion; but it does not follow that it is the more explanative reason or meaning. To overcome a mere fear of death (the dread of nonexistence) in a courageous act of sacrifice is thus mirrored in the more positive image of a gratitude for existence, in an act of sacredness. Thus, the original sense of sacrifice as one willing to forfeit one's life becomes identified in the language of the sacred as a sacrifice in its etymological sense.

But why the violence? Even if we accept the idea that religiosity consists of gratitude and gift-giving, why must the gift be bloody? Why must murder lay at the heart of sacrifice, if the etymology means to make sacred? The point here is one of proper methodology: scientists have indeed shown us that religion is extremely violent, but they have not revealed what this means. As a philosopher, the question is one of meaning and not of motive; it is a question of how one thinks about something rather than how one feels about something. So how are we to understand the slaughter of innocent lives as sacred? (It might be pointed out that the slaughter of noninnocent lives would, of course, cause us no trouble, since that would simply be the virtue of justice.) First, we must understand that the model of such slaughter is not murder but suicide: that is, the victim is not an unwilling unfortunate who is killed for some external benefit; rather, the sacrifice is always, to some extent, a self-sacrifice even if surrogate. What is destroyed is what is precious to us, though not because it is essential or necessary for the continuation of the society. Thus a young virgin might be slaughtered because she is loved and beautiful and precious, but an old sage whose wisdom guides the councils would not be sacrificed since he is not loved but needed for survival.

In *The Myth of Sisyphus*, Albert Camus writes, "There is but one truly serious philosophical problem, and that is suicide. Judging whether life is or is not worth living amounts to answering the fundamental question of philosophy." Camus's point in this famous essay is that philosophy, after the existentialist revolution has realized that the question: "What is the meaning of existence?" is the proper concern of the fundamental speculative discipline. Nietzsche had raised the question before him, and perhaps even Hegel before that. But what is important in this awareness is the realization that this question is *autonomous:* that is, whatever principles, insights, intuitions, or even answers we may discover, cannot be derived from other disciplines, such as ethics or metaphysics. And this is the point of the six-tiered hierarchy of giving which is sketched out above: the later stages cannot be explicated or analyzed by the principles which explain the lower stages. Thus, the discovery that a gift presupposes the worth of one's existence rather than the worth of one's action, as does a reward, is an important step in the realization of how we think about ultimate and fundamental *meanings.*

However, in *The Myth of Sisyphus*, Camus seems to suggest that it is the speculative philosopher who discovers the poignancy and ultimacy of the importance of suicide. (Suicide here is taken as the concrete confrontation with the worth of one's existence. If life is worthy of existence, suicide should be avoided; if not, it should be carried out.) But surely Camus's insight is backwards. It is not speculative thinking which makes for the possibility of suicide; it is the possibility of suicide that makes existential thinking possible. In the act of sacrifice, the dreadful question is raised: what is the worth of human existence? But what foists the question with such dreadful impact upon our consciousness is not the consideration of abstract possibility, but the concrete realization that we can and do murder others and ourselves! That is, we have the power to end our own lives. There is nothing in our simple existence that can withstand our decision to forfeit our own lives, for whatever reason. Existence itself is hostage to our will. If we will to kill, the mere fact of life is insufficient to protect us. What does this dreadful realization tell us about ourselves?

The realization that we can indeed terminate our own existence informs us of two things at once: that such a possibility is of supreme significance, and that, though we can terminate our life, we cannot initiate it. This makes life curiously ours and not ours, both awesome in its independence of our calculations and ultimately vulnerable to our will. But such awareness does not first come from speculation; it comes from the realization that follows hard upon our looking at the bloody knife in our hands and the now lifeless corpse at our feet. The question we must raise is this: granted that men kill, and more particularly, that men kill themselves, what does this reveal about our natures? Not that we are savage or violent, for we are *not* talking about man the hunter or man the warrior, we are talking about man the sacrificer, in which the killing of either ourselves or a surrogate which represents ourselves is meaningful and thought about.

It is not when man kills that he learns anything about himself; it is when he kills and then reflects upon what it means that he learns about himself. And what does this remarkable and even awesome capacity reveal? It reveals several things at once: (1) that our life is fleeting; (2) that we ourselves control its possible ending; but (3) that we have no control over its beginning, and (4) that we control, in our ability to commit suicide, an absolutely final and complete destiny. I have tried to show that this awareness is neither commercial (i.e., self-advantageous) nor moral, but existential. But the phenomenon of gift-giving has already revealed the autonomy of existential thought; what is added to this thought by the possibility of sacrifice? The answer is: the significance of religious or at least spiritual consciousness.

The shedding of blood is therefore of supreme importance in this dialectic of giving because through it the ability to let oneself supremely matter is concretized, and hence made possible. In giving a gift to one I love, I say: this giving is made solely on the basis of your worth, not on what you have done. In the act of sacrifice, what is bestowed is the realization that I matter in who I am, not in what I do. Blood represents the finality of life, the end of what is valuable; but this is achieved through an act of thoughtful will, and hence establishes reverence for the meaning of our own existence.

Human sacrifice is rightly seen as a practice which must be eliminated, but for purely *moral* reasons. The continuation of the *meaningfulness* of that existential value, however, can be achieved through surrogates or ritual. Thus, when the brave soldier throws his body on the grenade to save his friends, the act is no longer merely a good and noble one, it is a *holy* one. This has nothing to do with what the soldier was thinking at the time, for it may have been an act inspired by mere instinct or a misguided desire for glory. The meaning of the act thus does not depend upon the attitude of the agent, for that is empirical and random, but upon the meaning as discovered in the hierarchy of giving.

Let us turn this analysis to a particular problem in the history of sacrifice. For those in the Judaeo-Christian tradition, the first sacrifice is that revealed in Genesis of the first two brothers, Cain and Abel. Unfortunately, this remarkable tale is often and usually interpreted as the story of the first murder and indeed the first fratricide. But what is truly telling about this fascinating event is what is revealed about the nature of sacrifice itself. We are told that both Cain and Abel sacrifice to the Lord; Cain, the elder, offering up fruit and grain, and Abel offering up a living animal from his flock. Apparently, God rejects the offering of Cain, an event which so fills the older brother with envy and venom that he slays his younger sibling. Now, this gives us pause. Why was Cain so upset? He must have been awfully hot-headed to kill his brother merely because his own sacrifice had not been accepted. If the point of the story is that only flesh sacrifices are acceptable, why then did not Cain simply borrow a calf from his brother and kill it? Or buy a calf with an exchange for grain? And *if* the point of the story is that only blood-letting is acceptable, then why was not Cain informed of this beforehand? How could he be held responsible for something he did not know? In fact, why did the two brothers sacrifice at all? We are not told who informed them it would be a good idea.

Furthermore, the later part of the story is not what it usually seems. Granted that God punished Cain for killing Abel, but very mildly indeed. The 'mark of Cain' was put on the elder brother, not as a punishment, but as a *protection* from others who might slay Cain. (Are we to understand by this that murdering a murderer is worse than murdering a brother? Surely not.) Cain is punished simply by the fact that his fields will no longer yield their fruit, so he goes off and marries a woman from another tribe (and where *they* came from is theologically mystifying: they certainly weren't the children of Adam); Cain's offspring, by the way, are those who first make music. So Cain's punishment is curiously mild for such a savage period. (Or are we to understand that in killing Abel Cain *sacrificed* his brother? It seems not.) Too much is spent, I think, on the murder of Abel and not enough on the weird story of the sacrifices. After all, it was after Cain's sacrifice was rejected but *before* Cain slew Abel that God appeared to Cain and asked him why he should be so upset. Now one must be careful about timing in these ancient texts, but the point is clear that God warns Cain about resisting sin *after* the sacrifice but *before* the murder, so Cain was not punished by God because of the inadequate sacrifice.

Light can be thrown on this bewildering puzzle, though not perfect clarification, if we bear in mind what the sixfold hierarchy of giving reveals: each step produces an entirely new set of principles by which we understand ourselves as givers. Sacrifice is the giving of one's self; if it is rejected, then *we* are rejected. Cain was outraged, not because his offerings were rejected, but because *he* was rejected. His worth as an existing being was denied and that of his brother accepted. That realization might induce murder, for what is at stake is the worth of our meaning altogether. And why was Cain's offering rejected? Because it was not a true sacrifice: i.e., it was not a shedding of blood.

This importance of the shedding of blood is thus not based upon any emotional sense of blood-lust, or a naive sense of propitiation, but rather the realization that what it means to be *as religious* matters. In offering grain, Cain was offering a gift—the penultimate rank of giving. But Abel offered a sacrifice: he offered himself. The irony of the murder is often missed: it is Cain who completes the sacrifice of Abel. Cain, however, is not unduly punished or even severely reprimanded, because he was, quite simply, not a religious being. It is the shedding of blood, or the surrogate's blood, which raises a mere gift to a sacrifice, and only those who can offer sacrifice are spiritual. The converse is also true: those who can sacrifice are understood, not merely in terms of what is moral or virtuous, but in terms of what is sacred.

But this brings us full circle. Suffering, especially sacrifice, becomes an essential part of our understanding of spirit just because it is intelligible only when spirit suffers. If pleasure alone justifies existence, then a suffering existence becomes irrational. (And since all of us suffer, unless I can ground suffering in the rationality of spirit, my existence becomes irrational as well.) But, in suffering, as we huddle in our fetal curves, wrapping ourselves protectively about our pain, we find ourselves seeking to justify even our pain-filled existence, and only the notion of spirit can fulfill this demand. If through the special courage of spirit we can reach out from our self-pity and self-protection and actually *offer* the suffering, we become illuminated from within: that is, we become the basis of our own meaning. This is sacrifice. Just as in tragedy we find justification for an existence which is not pleasant, indeed tormented, by affirming the worth or greatness of the hero, so in spiritual suffering we find autonomous worth in a person wrenched in the deepest agony.

One might object that our existence is worthwhile whether in pain or pleasure, and the endurance of the former is merely an intensification of that awareness. Such an account would not favor suffering, but it would deny it the right to veto our worth. But this is where sacrifice becomes such a remarkable form of suffering; for in sacrifice we bestow ourselves through our pain, we embrace our capacity to suffer just because it allows us to give—as in the bestowal of a gift—of ourselves. Suffering, especially sacrificial suffering, then, manifests itself as an existential predicate of spirit.

6

Mystery

It is in mystery that we are most familiar to ourselves, it is in the sharp glare of pristine clarity that we are most opaque. Of all things known only we are so; our truths are shadows, our deceptions are light. Whatever else we search for, the physical structure of the universe, the beguiling ways of the squirrels and the wolves, the scudding clouds overhead, they all are *knowable;* they are ours to look at and study and wonder about, and since we are an enterprising species, their secrets soon yield to the probing intensity of our lamps; we know they must, sooner or later. After all, that is what it means for a thing to be in the universe: to be thought about, to be known. And even the members of our own group, the human species, eventually are uncovered by the probers, the scientists, the examiners, the counters, the pollsters and the judges. Eventually they have us pinned on their charts and atomized in their laboratories. They know how the tiny drums in the inner ear give us sound, they know how to bypass our arteries and excise our tumors and balance our diets. Eventually they will know it all, every hair follicle, every sweat gland and DNA molecule; they will know it all and be able to tell us exactly how the thing works. And then we will be even more mysterious than we are now, for the bright lights of science simply cast sharper shadows and make it more difficult to discern into the dark corners where our essence lurks.

There is no single mark of maturity, no sign of wisdom more telling than the slightly wearied, but secretly thrilled sigh that comes over us when we finally must accept the strangest truth of all, that truth itself is mysterious. We are not knowable. To the cynic this is a curious ache, for as cynic he would laugh and say he told us so; yet even he recognizes a truth, an understanding in such realization that may bring him mild distress. For, this recognition is not a negative abandonment of inquiry nor an empty collapse into mindless nihilism.

Anti-thinkers, of whom there are legion and who wear infinite masks, would hurry to grab their gummed labels or tags and tacks to affix their identificatory adjectives: irrationalist! skeptic! faith-leaper! relativist! believer! (Yes, 'believer' is as scorned as 'irrationalist', for they would scorn us if we believe for naivité, yet scorn us in disbelief for skepticism.) But the understanding that we knowers cannot know ourselves is logically necessary, it is the result of reasoning and weighty thinking. Nor is it a despairing realization; indeed hope, that curious quickener, resides only in the folds of the drapery of mystery. How can I, or any writer, seek to communicate the ephemeral truth that this mystery is not the absence of reason but the product of it; that to affirm our own mystery is an accomplishment of years of thoughtful toil and not the abandonment of undertakings beyond our ken? Perhaps it may help to point out the care taken in this description. I do not say that in mystery we come to know who we are; the first sentence says that in mystery we are most familiar to ourselves. Need we repeat that 'to be familiar with' is not the same as 'to know'? To say we cannot know ourselves has been recognized for hundreds, perhaps thousands, of years. For to know is to objectify, and the knower is not an object but a subject. Is this a leap into mystic nonsense, or a wild embrace of irrationalism? Nor does this realization cease the digging, for it is a doctrine held by those who have dug the deepest: it is held by Socrates and Kant and Nietzsche and countless others whose names are honored among the deepest thinkers in our tradition. It may sound somewhat misological at first reading, to be sure, but that is because of the mistaken prejudice that what is mysterious is nothing else but what is unintelligible and unknown. Mystery can be neared or approached, it can even be learned, though the term requires some fine-tuning for this to be true. On the other hand, mystery is not contradictory, it is not irrational or even unexamined bias. Mystery can even be the final goal of supreme mental effort and concentration, as when a genius accomplishes the hitherto impossible.

However, this above all must be emphasized: mystery is not belief. Among the myriad beliefs within our species, many are strange and fantastic, perhaps the oddest found in the very citadels of high learning, and many who defend these conflicting creeds may appeal to mystery to support their irrationality. But this is to confuse unsupportable belief with mystery. If anything, disbelief is probably closer to mystery than belief, for beliefs are as easy as opinions, a penny apiece, and mystery is as dear as the rarest jewel. Beliefs are often taken to be little more than the residue of opinions which cannot qualify as knowledge due to lack of verification or universal acceptance. Thus, I have many opinions, some of which can be verified as true: these constitute knowledge (knowledge is verified true belief); the remaining opinions, which may be true or false, but which are nevertheless accepted and perhaps used as guides to life and a way of thinking, are called 'beliefs' in the narrower or more precise sense. However, this rather common way of speaking has nothing at all to do with the predicate of spirit known as mystery: by mystery is not meant those opinions or beliefs left over after the testing of verification has found them wanting. Mystery is rather that positive sense of being beyond the limits of my comprehension, but is nonarbitrary and true. I cannot prove it true; indeed I cannot even completely understand it directly, but I do acknowledge as true and accept its greatness as exceeding my capacity to understand. We should perhaps reflect that the etymology of 'mystery' has at its root the Greek verb *muein*, which means "to close" (one's lips or eyes). In Greek mythology a mystery was what was revealed to the few who had been initiated into the sect by rite or ritual. Hence, in its original meaning 'mystery' means anything but that which is unknown; rather it means that which *is* known, but only to the initiated. Even in the early biblical texts, the notion of 'mystery' was that of a privileged access to a secret truth revealed by God to one or a few special people. Thus, in the original sense, mystery was not the same as the ineffable; rather, it was simply that which was kept from us, but was certainly available to us if we were to go through whatever ritual permitted us the privilege or if God chose us as special recipients of this wisdom. Today, however, the term suggests not something that I can achieve through initiation or rite, but something which is so magnificent (though still true) that the human faculties of understanding are incapable of knowing it.

Mystery should probably not be identified with any 'leap of faith,' as that suggested by Søren Kierkegaard, for example. One of the reasons the critical mind feels so uneasy about such 'leaps' is that there seems to be no limit or guide as to where this leap might take us, or how many kinds of leaps there are. Can I 'leap' into a belief in magic, or racism, or reincarnation, or moral elitism which allows me to deny rights to my enemies? And even if we restrict this 'leap' to organized and traditional Christian belief, then does this not strongly suggest that such beliefs simply cannot be true, because they are contradictory? To accept a belief *because* it is contradictory may thrill the heart of a romantic, but it has no place in philosophy, nor even in serious romanticism. To argue that the truths of religions can be achieved only through a leap of faith makes it arbitrary and dangerously relativistic. It is also circular: I am inspired to make the leap only if I already feel the impact of the truth urging me to do so. Those who do not make the leap are seen as unprivileged, unenlightened ones who can see only if they forego their criticism and leap in with the believers. I do not deny that there are many who do this, and that many feel it is entirely meaningful and satisfying. I am merely saying that such Kierkegaardian leaps do not mean the same as 'mystery' as I am exploring it as a part of spirit. Mystery is far less random and less psychologically arbitrary than leaps of faith. The critical mind must be cautious of leaps, but need not reject mystery. For, mystery, conceived in this existential sense, is nothing more than the awareness that our knowing must be incomplete, that there is a greater source or ground to our meaning and our existence than we are capable of rendering intelligible by the faculties of knowing. To grasp the *truth* of this greater reality is the acceptance that I cannot know but must *acknowledge* a truth which illumines without being explained.

From our everyday experience of things (in the sense of the German *Erlebnis* and not *Erfahrung*) we have many concrete confrontations of mystery which we accept as being worthwhile just because they are mysterious. There is a mystery about persons,

of course, and individuals can rejoice in the mystery of their differences. There is mystery in great art, which is undermined by
the modernist reductionist to nonaesthetic and conceptual art.
But who can deny that when we are led to expect the clash of two
approaching melodies in a fugue and witness instead a remarkable resolve, it defies our comprehension? We may study the score
over and over, we may even be able to play the notes which Mozart
has written; but we do not understand how he has blended what
seemed unmixable, and the thrill of it adds to its worth. It is
beautiful to us just because it seems magical. There are no rules
which can account for it, and we would not have it otherwise.
Genius, as Schopenhauer points out, is precisely that which
achieves the greatness of the experience by bypassing the 'principle of sufficient reason', i.e., the steps necessary to understand.

However, the greatest of our ordinary, everyday encounters
of mystery is within ourselves, the human person. Two things
about us that assure some sense of mystery are first, the thought
of our future, and secondly, our unpredictable wills. The first,
that we have a future, is formally beyond the range of knowledge: one simply cannot *know* the future. We do assume the future will be like the past as regards the laws of nature, else
science and even coherent living would not be possible. But we
do not assume that the future will be identical to the past, not
even in nature. The weather differs from year to year, unexpected events such as earthquakes and famines are unpredictable, at least for now. And if they become predictable, and hence
within the range of science, that too makes the future *different*.
Thus, the very progress of technology assures us of the unknowable; we cannot know in advance what the advances of science
and technology will bring. If the future were just like the past we
could have no adventure, and adventure is essential for a meaningful existence. Nothing would be more boring than a determinable future, and so once again we prefer to be uninformed, if
for no other reason than to allow ourselves to be surprised with
what is coming next.

But it is our wills which make us ultimately mysterious,
even to ourselves. What we are capable of, in confronting dangers or challenges not yet met must always remain unknown. Am
I courageous enough to meet this difficulty with dignity? Will I

be able to sustain the anguish of a failed love, or even worse, will I have strength enough to endure a successful love? Can I know in advance why I shall fail in this moral situation, or succeed in that one? We can hope, of course, and, based on past experience, we can estimate the likelihood of our powers, but we surely cannot be said to *know* them. Human beings have free wills, at least in some sense and in some cases, so they are not determinable and hence not knowable. But do we lament this lack of knowledge? Most of us would prefer to be ignorant, for such ignorance gives meaning to our own existence. Nothing is more unfathomable than the puzzling, cantankerous, stubborn, occasionally wonderful creativity of the human spirit. And in this mystery we can celebrate our ignorance. We also mature. There is no way a youth, with all his wonderful idealism, spirit, and high energy, can anticipate the wonders of his learning, the wealth of his maturing which lies hidden in the darkness of the future. So, as human beings, we too are mysterious, and we want to remain so.

But these are merely observations that assure us that the idea of mystery in our daily lives is not something foolish or silly. When we turn our attention to the range of the spiritual, which as we have seen contains both sacrifice and worship, we must consider, not only the mystery of our daily lives, wonderful though that be, we must also confront the mystery of the absolutely ineffable. We worship, in part, because what we worship is mysterious. It is hard to kneel down before that which is completely knowable to us, like the machine we ourselves have created to move dirt or wash our clothes. The awe and the sense of the sublime necessary for true existential worship requires mystery. And since our own personality, our being a person, is itself mysterious, even to the probing psychologists, it is easy to see why people have thought of the supreme reality not as simple blind forces or as inevitable powers that function at random, but as persons. Surely the early anthropomorphism of the illiterate ancestors of the race imagined their gods as persons simply because they had no other model than themselves. An angry god was an explanation of thunder, because we understand anger as a part of being a person. No one pictures a rock becoming angry, but since the gods obviously do get angry—why else do the skies rumble so in discontent?—we can at least understand it.

But the personhood of the gods or of God is not so anthropologically naive. When the great pre-Socratic thinker Xenophanes wandered about the then-known narrow world, he
writes, in Fragment 16 (Clement, Strom. VII, 22, I): "The Ethi-
opians say that their gods are snub-nosed and black, the Thra-
cians theirs have light blue eyes and red hair." This man, born
approximately 570 years before the birth of Christ, recognized
that men, in their religions, obviously anthropomorphized their
gods. He knew that the true gods could not be both black and
fair, brown-eyed and blue-eyed, red-haired and black-haired. He
sensed that our understanding of the gods was characterized by
our own traditions. On this basis, he argued that there must be
only one god, and all anthropomorphism, save one, was illegitimate: namely, his mind. This one God had a mind. But that is
the essence of our personhood for Xenophanes. Even for a dis-
criminating and shrewd thinker like Xenophanes, it is necessary
to conclude that God, in the final analysis, is like us, having a
mind, because he remains a mystery. The point is, the personhood of God is not a naive and primitive belief based upon our
fear of natural events, but it is postulated because without personhood God cannot be worshiped. Other pre-Socratics, to be
sure, denied personhood to God, and made God instead pure
and rational, like an inevitable, unchanging force; but then they
insisted that if this were the case, worship was senseless. You cannot worship necessity. Milton himself saw this, and expresses the
thought wondrously in Book III, 102:

> Freely they stood who stood, and fell who fell.
> Not free, what proof could they have given sincere
> Of true allegiance, constant faith or love,
> Where only what they needs must do appeared,
> Not what they would? What praise could they receive?
> What pleasure I, from such obedience paid,
> When Will and Reason (Reason also is Choice),
> Useless and vain, of freedom both despoiled,
> Made passive both, had served Necessity,
> Not me? . . .

What is impressive in this passage is not the freedom of the created men and the created angels, but that God himself, the
speaker of these words in the poem, disassociates himself from

being identified as Necessity. We cannot think of a God who is to be *worshiped* who is mere necessity! But this makes God not a principle, but a person; and the essence of this personhood is mystery. In Milton's epic, it is clear that the poet wants us to accept the notion that God is not the same thing as necessity.

But is not our own most popular, if not problematic, 'proof' for the existence of God the ontological argument, which makes God identical with necessity? The argument in its simplest form is elegant in its directness: I can think of a necessary being; this makes a necessary being possible. But if a necessary being (i.e., one which *must* be) is possible (it *can* be), then, it is. So, a necessary being, God, exists. It is an awesome argument, the validity of which I shall not consider at the moment; but it should not be understood merely as a proof for necessity *per se*. (God can still be *necessary*, he simply cannot be *necessity*.)

It is easy, of course, to assume this 'mystery' as an excuse for anything that is incomprehensible, or even that we do not want to think about. "God works in mysterious ways" may be true, if there is a God, but in either event the remark is irritating because it covers everything. We may as well go back to Necessity for all the good it does. The mystery of God is not meant as an excuse to stop thinking. The mystery surely surrounds that ineffable quality found in our own souls, freedom. How can God create a free being? Is that not a contradiction, since freedom is the one thing which cannot be necessary or brought about by another?

This is a mysterious truth which we grasp and acknowledge, but do not understand. Necessity cannot produce freedom. Yet, if we are to believe that there is a personal God who creates free beings, the purely rational mind is offended by seeming inconsistency, or at least the darkness of the mystery. It deserves our reflection, for it is a wonderful mystery. We have seen the artistry of Milton's poetry attempt to throw light on it; another artistic source is to be found in Wagner's great opera *Die Walküre*, in which Wotan, the Chief of the Tuetonic gods, bewails his great misery:

> O heilige Schmach! O schmälicher Harm!
> Götternot! Götternot!
>
> O sacred disgrace, shameful pain!
> Godly lack! Godly lack!

Brünnhilde, his loving daughter, is distressed by this seeming impossibility: how could a god *be* a god and lack? What can a god not do? And how is it possible to have a 'sacred disgrace'? Wotan tries to tell her. He needs to create a being who is free from Wotan's own treaties since he, as a god, cannot violate his own word. But, for there to be a being who is free from god, that being must actually *defy* the gods. He says that a free man can only create himself. What Wotan desires, he tells his daughter, is

> ein Held, dem helfend nie ich mich neigte;
> der fremd dem Gotte, frei seiner Gunst,
> unbewusst, ohne Geheiss . . .
> Der entgegen dem Gott, für mich föchte,
> den freundlichen Feind, wie fände ich ihn?

> A hero whom I have never helped,
> A stranger to god, free from him,
> Unwitting and unprompted . . .
> This opposer to God, who will act for me,
> This friendly enemy, where can I find him?

Of course, the music is not here to help us understand this magnificent anguish, and my translations are inadequate, as all translations must be. But Wagner has created an awareness of the greatest mystery of all, and his music even more than his poetry reveals to us how we think and feel about this enormous truth. For when we speak of the 'mystery' of God behind any worship, what we really mean by mystery is the darkness that must be true: a god creating a sinner, whose sinning alone sets free the soul from the chains of necessity. Yet, even as this deeply puzzling enigma is presented, there is a powerful awareness that this is truth.

And so, the 'mysteries' of the worship of what is divine, the mystery which is necessary for spirit to exist, is not the mere ignorance of as-yet undiscovered physical laws which future scientists will isolate and determine. This mystery is built into the very nature of the spirit. Being spiritual means being a part of the mystery. The mystery is revealed in various ways: reflection on the creation of a free being is one of them, but not the only one. There is also the mystery of a just god forgiving, which is inconsistent but somehow necessary; there is the mystery of love, either human, or in the case of the spiritual, divine. That these are 'mysteries' in the spiritual sense does not mean that we do not understand them; rather it means that we understand them too well, or that we grasp them as necessarily belonging to our fate and our givenness.

It was Immanuel Kant who most profoundly showed us that the principles that explain things that occur in the world, what he calls 'phenomena', are simply different but no less rational than the principles which reveal, not the existence, but the reality of what he calls 'noumena', the world of spirit. I can make sense neither of mathematics nor of science unless I first distinguish between phenomena and noumena; of course, this distinction also allows for the reality of such things as spirit and freedom. Kant's arguments are deep and torturous, but they are certainly not arbitrary or silly. Kant may be the greatest thinker of the modern period, and his dominant conviction, indeed his central task, was to *limit* knowledge, to show what reason *cannot* do. We need only reflect on the titles of his great trilogy: the *Critiques* of pure reason, practical (or moral) reason, and of judgment. By titling these works *critiques* Kant meant us to understand that these faculties were limited: there is more to this world than can be known, there is more to our worth than can be achieved by mere obedience to the moral law; there is more to what we enjoy than what gives our minds pleasure. What this suggests is that mystery is no longer outside the realm of respectable thought; it belongs as an essential part of it.

It was Kant, after all, who solved Xenophanes' problem with anthropomorphism. That early Greek thinker is quite right in recognizing that different cultures depict their gods according to their own traditions, and that hence these depictions cannot be truly asserted of the one true God. But Kant teaches us the distinction between dogmatic anthropomorphism, which claims as true all the characteristics ascribed to our perception of the gods or God, and *symbolic* anthropomorphism, which he claims, is quite valid and legitimate. In order to grasp the personhood of the gods, I must be able to have symbolic representations of them in order to assure that what I worship is not without content. But symbols are a function of the aesthetic consciousness, not the constitutive authority of determinative judgments found in science.

But if symbolic anthropomorphism is essential for the study of religion and belief, then are we not back to relativism, with each culture merely manifesting its own peculiar prejudice? Not if the anthropomorphism is recognized as a *symbol*, which remains a symbol because what is worshiped is mysterious. The literal stories of the various religions may be doubted, but the meaning of these stories is surely true. Thus one may well doubt that Adam and Eve were real people in an actual place on earth which we have lost called Eden and that they ate of the fruit of the tree of knowledge of good and evil, thereby losing their innocence but gaining their freedom. But there is no reason to doubt the wisdom and even truth of the story's *meaning*. The story reveals so much about how we think of our own spiritual reality that it can be called a true story. We recognize, or if you will, *acknowledge* the truth that man as a mere creation of a god or God cannot be understood as he is, for man as he is is sinful and unhappy and unblessed. But he is also free. Does it make sense to suggest that the price for freedom is this acceptance of our own responsibility and hence an abandonment of Eden-like happiness? The story may not be believed as literally true in order for it to accomplish its greater purpose, to reveal something so profound that it can be communicated only by symbolic myths. The human mind simply does not mind being told myths which are true in this deeper sense even if fictional on the surface, partly because the mind itself knows that it cannot grasp the ineffable directly.

But all this merely shows that acceptance of mystery is honorable for rational and intelligent human beings. It does not show the positive side of mystery; why we actually prefer the greatest truths to be mysterious rather than scientifically clear and open. First and foremost the reason for a positive meaning to mystery is the simple truth that we, as human, are more than merely knowing beings. We not only know, we also wonder. We not only dominate, we are also controlled by mysterious factors beyond our ken. Men not only know that there is a woman, they may also love her; we not only know there is a mountain, we also react to its splendor and majesty. In short, we not only observe this universe, we also live in it, and the idea of the absolutely great is as necessary to our own reality as the precisions of a limited science. We not only see the world, we also care within it and about it. And to acknowledge a magnificent greatness which by definition cannot be known may well be a necessary supposition without which our very meaning ceases to be thinkable.

This is not an argument that God exists. It is merely a phenomenological realization that mystery is necessary for spirit. It *may* be an argument that a spiritual or spirited existence is more meaningful than one without spirit. It is more meaningful because we, as human beings, know our own limitations and therefore are not intimidated by the suggestion that there are greater things beyond our ken which nevertheless affect us and are relevant to us.

But what, we must now ask, is this mystery, if by asking this question we do not forfeit the mysteriousness of the magnificent? To respond to this we should go back to the etymological origins. A mystery, as was noted above, really means that which is known through an initiation or a secret ritual. This is something we sense in the presence of spiritual people, an awareness that they know something, or realize a deeper meaning to things, than ordinary people. It is, in fact, what attracts many younger people to try to become 'spiritual', that in being spiritual there is a special awareness, perhaps even a secret insight into the wonders of the universe. Even as we admit that this seems to be the aura or the mystique around the spiritual types, we may also question its authority and wonder if, in fact, such an attitude is nothing but a feeling, possibly built on self-deception or accomplished air. This skepticism is enhanced if the spiritual person in question assures us that the only way to perceive what he or she sees is by joining a particular sect or religion, and that of course is the 'mystic's fallacy' which is circular and unworthy of thought. Nevertheless, the etymological meaning of 'mystery' as a secret truth and not an unknowable one need not be cavalierly dismissed. If we return briefly to our sketch from Plato's *Republic*, we will be reminded that the warrior class shifts its concerns from the private 'I' to the broader 'we'. It is now necessary to examine this shift more deeply. The 'we' which replaces the 'I' as the central concern for the warrior is, first of all, accomplished through that special initiation known as education. Secondly, it must be emphasized that the term 'we' here does not simply mean a plurality or greater number of 'I's; rather, the 'we' now has an autonomous meaning. One cannot achieve a 'we' merely by adding up many 'I's. The plurality of 'I's constitutes a group or a mere collection, not necessarily a unified we. In order to have a true 'we', one must both acknowledge and identify the 'we' as a source of meaning and value. The 'we' must be sacred, i.e., given a special status of being worthy of our dedication and our suffering. Curiously, the 'we' does not forfeit the 'I', but enhances it. This sense of 'we' is, of course, better expressed by an analysis of the warrior (the spirited) rather than the saint (the spiritual), simply because the warrior is a defender of what is *ours*, whereas the saint seems to have a more private or personal relationship with the greater range of meaning provided by 'we'. Nevertheless, the warrior and the holy are not always disjoined, as when we recognize that the warrior is fighting for the sacredness of what is our own, the motherland. To be nonmysterious, such a commitment would have to show that each individual, personal warrior is benefited by his suffering and sacrifice; and of course that simply is inconsistent with the 'initiation' or training of the warrior, who is taught to revere the good as such rather than what is good *for him*. To shift from 'what is beneficial to me' to what is good in itself is to pass from clarity and knowledge to mystery. For mystery in *this* sense refers to the original meaning of sharing in a secret truth which is achieved by initiation or ritual.

There is a further meaning to mystery which needs to be explored if this predicate of the spirit is to be fully grasped. In popular talk 'mystery' seems to suggest the otherworld, the 'ghostly' or even the 'spooky', like the mists that hang around a dark castle or a graveyard. Few would deny that the term 'spiritual' implies some sense of the 'otherworldy', however vague and uncertain that might be. This sense of mystery suggests both comfort and unease at what is alien. Especially to one who is jaded by too much worldly experience or who has seen too much of human misery and human weakness, the allure behind some mysterious force which offers more than what is clear and knowable can be powerful and even dangerous. But, for some, it is the very danger that attracts: it is precisely because the mysterious *is* alien, ghostly, and ephemeral that one finds it attractive. The promise is there of new delights, secret sources of deep satisfaction and even wisdom. It is, of course, a preference for the dark over the light; but when the light merely presents the jejeune and commonplace, the dark opens up the possibility of adventure. It is adventure precisely because we *want* there to be unexplained and new things, else our daily lives become burdened by the dreadful yoke of sameness.

This aspect of spirit needs to be more thoroughly examined. The descent into darkness, away from light, the preference for night over day that is assumed in such an attitude, is doubtless tinged with a sense of the impish, the unseemly, perhaps even, the slightly wicked. Ghosts after all, in the minds of children, are not always friendly; but they are always exciting. This reveals once again that the spiritual, especially from the predicate of mystery, is not the same as the morally proper. Just as forgiveness transcends the purely moral order, so mystery as that which conveys a sentiment of the licentious, and hence of privilege, finds its proper realm in the world of the dark and the sinister. There is a great danger in this dimension of spirit, for anything that conflicts with the good is always dangerous. But beauty itself is autonomous of the good, indeed it often threatens to attract one away from duty.

Mystery, then, is obviously akin to the aesthetic consciousness rather than the strictly moral consciousness, and as such provides a serious problem to the thinker who must, perforce, respect both. However, this discussion leads us to the role that the aesthetic plays in spirit, and I prefer to discuss that under its own separate heading.

Yet, when all these dimensions of mystery are considered, the fundamental attraction found in the mysterious is power, a power which in part possesses its strength in being hidden. By participating in this hidden source of power, the spiritual person inherits greater meaning and even security. God may be ineffable and mysterious, but he is certainly powerful, and if he favors us, we sense the security just because we do not understand. If this power is mysterious, then perhaps I possess something of value which the nonmysterious does not appreciate; to worship what is powerful and mysterious is to open up possibilities which are all the more attractive for being secret. An empty lighted room offers us nothing for our imagination, but turn out the light and suddenly the sinister and ephemeral possibilities are there. It is this reach for broader possibilities, itself an advantage, which surely is the central reason for the attraction which mystery has for the spirit.

But, in the final analysis, it is not psychological advantages one must seek in penetrating the phenomenon of spiritual mystery. Rather, it is awe and wonder. Let us consider some specific 'mysteries' of the major religions. According to Islam, Mohammed did not go to the mountain, the mountain came to Mohammed. According to Jewish belief, Moses parted the Red Sea. According to Christianity, God actually became Man (the Incarnation). It is remarkable that all the technical problems that immediately besiege the mind when these events are described to the faithful are somehow disregarded. What happened to the place where the mountain was when it was on its way to Mohammed? What did people think when they saw it flying through the air? In the case of Moses, where on earth did all that extra water go? What physical elements were holding back the two walls of water? Could the escaping Hebrews look in through the walls of water like windows and see the fish? Or with the Incarnation, the strangest mystery of them all, if Christ were a real man but with a godly father, then what were those genetic codes like? Would the divinity be noticeable in his DNA? If the normal man shares inheritance from both parents, which were those inherited from his father? The color of his hair, the cast of his chin, the slope of his brow, all had to come from somewhere: the laws of genetics won't allow all of them to come from Mary. Furthermore, what does it mean to say this man is God? Does he *know* he is God? (How could he not?) But if he knows he is God, then he knows the future. Can he suffer, and can he doubt if he is God? When he was three years old did he play? But then he could not fully be God. These questions do not seem to bother the believers at all; if anything they shrug their shoulders and dismiss the questions as being heathen. Is this naivité?

No, what is believed in these mysteries is the magnificence of their meaning. It is not *how* God becomes man that interests the believer, it is the *wonder* of it; it is not *how* Moses parted the sea, it is the significance of God protecting his chosen, but undeserving, people that is so awesome. It is not how a mountain managed to move, but what this tells us of the sacred importance of the figure of Mohammed. For humanity itself becomes hugely altered in its very essence if an incarnation of divinity is possible. It changes who we are so enormously, so spectacularly that questions as to how seem almost impertinent. And, of course, within the various traditions, there are theological scientists who go about explaining these troubling details, some quite cleverly, but such explanations are of little interest to the vast hordes of believers who appreciate the true importance of the mysteries: what they *mean*. If God can visit our species and become one of us (and not merely: *like* one of us), then, although I cannot understand *how* it happened, I cannot escape thinking about who I am in a totally different way. Indeed, upon reflection, it is not even necessary that it actually happened; just that it is possible is enough to send a reflective mind to the highest reaches of dizzy speculation and wonder. Where did such an *idea* come from? What does it tell us about ourselves?

One thing these three stories tell us about ourselves is this: we do not understand our own existence solely by reference to what is determined by physical laws. Whatever is not determined by physical laws is a mystery, and so, in order to be true to one's nature, one must embrace and accept all the implications of mystery. To an honest inquirer, to accept mystery is fraught with the agony of doubt, uncertainty, and even the dread of being beguiled by what is, in the last analysis, supremely silly. But the awe, the honesty of recognizing one's own mysterious nature, the acceptance of the fact that we do not know ourselves in toto and never will, that I am, as a human being, not merely a knower but also a living, acting, hating, loving being *in* the world, not merely outside the world looking in: this is what mystery celebrates.

In the previous sections on the paradoxes of spirit, we discussed briefly this question of how it is possible for a rational man to accept that which in principle cannot be explained. We saw then that the paradox must remain but is not contradictory. (How can anything mysterious be contradictory? I have to know what x is before I can say it is contradicted by non-x.) What we have seen is that the essence of mystery lies in the subtle but powerful distinction between *acknowledgment* and *knowing*. I know what is true and I acknowledge what is true. Acknowledgment, however, is not belief. Beliefs can be true or false. But acknowledgment is the acceptance of something being true without evidence, but not without reason. One may be persuaded to acknowledge truths by nonepistemic conditions, such as aesthetic, spiritual, or existential awe, wonder, and gratitude. Thus, we can accept mystery; indeed, if we are to understand spirit, we must.

The purely formal considerations behind these distinctions need to be clarified. There is first, a *knowledge claim,* such as "I know that Chicago is north of St. Louis." Knowledge claims, independent of how one arrives at them, must imply the truth of the claim. I cannot meaningfully say I know that St. Louis is north of Chicago because the claim is false; so whatever is known is true. Then there are *belief claims,* in which one asserts a preference for one of two or more conflicting opinions but with the recognition that such belief may indeed be false. Thus, to say "I believe there is life on other planets" is an opinion which is either true or false. The point is, the logical possibility of the falseness of the belief is inherent in such claims, even though the believer may have powerful psychological persuasion. Now, however, we consider *acknowledgments.* These, like knowledge claims, imply the truth of that which is acknowledged, yet they are not the same as knowledge claims because what supports them are not epistemic principles or verifiable external evidence. But when we hear someone say: "I acknowledge my guilt," we do not equate such a claim with: "In my opinion I believe I am guilty." The latter must permit the possibility of the claim being false; the former cannot. The belief claims are essentially about the person having the belief; the knowledge claims are essentially about the world, but acknowledgments are about truth itself.

These analyses are not metaphysical verifications. It is quite possible someone can make a knowledge claim: "Capetown is further south than Tierra del Fuego," and be wrong. The sentence is false. But the claim as such is that it is true and not merely possibly true. If he were to say he *believed* Capetown is further south than Tierra del Fuego, *what* he believes is false, but it is still true that he believes it. But if one should acknowledge another's suffering, even though there is no verifiability as there is in the knowledge claim, it is still an assertion which demands the truth; though this does not protect one from acknowledging falsely. When I acknowledge something that turns out to be false, I was in error in acknowledging; but I would not have been in error in saying I believed it, since belief implies the judgment is either true *or* false. Strictly speaking, I cannot acknowledge what is false any more than I can know what is false, but in both cases I may be deceived; but what is then said is simply that I have misused terms, I did not *really* know that Capetown was further south than Tierra del Fuego, since that claim is false. Similarly, if I acknowledge the dignity of this man's suffering and it turns out he was deceiving everyone, the error lies in the improper use of the term 'acknowledge'.

It is important to recognize that 'acknowledge' is most often, though not always, about the self. I acknowledge my guilt, my love, my obligations, etc., and this may lead one to suspect that acknowledgements are subjective, but this would be an invalid inference. Thus, if one were to say "I know that God exists," such a claim would be a knowledge claim, and the validity of it *as* a knowledge claim would depend on whether God in fact exists or not. It seems the only people who could honestly say such a thing are those who have had a vision and witnessed an event that has some external testability, such as God appearing in some visual form and performing an act which altered the environment and was such that, after the vision, the change remained permanent and openly testable. Either that, or someone who discovers that the ontological argument can avoid any debilitating problems arising out of the de-re/dicto distinction and can demonstrate the existence of God. In any event, whether such claims are possible, at least we know what they mean: that God exists. If one merely states one believes in God, that sentence is simply about his own psychological state, and is true or false depending upon how deceitful he is about his own beliefs. But to say that one acknowledges God is not to establish his existence, but simply asserts the reality. To acknowledge God is to affirm God as real; to claim that one knows that God exists is to assert God exists.

But if we 'accept' or 'acknowledge' mystery, then seemingly we have completely submitted to the claims of irrationalism. For the very persuasion of this way of thinking suggests a capitulation of the critical and rational faculties. To acknowledge, independently of epistemic grounds, is an act of faith, regardless of whether we like the subjectivist sound to this or not. This, however, raises a most serious question: Is 'reason' limited to the business of acquiring knowledge supported by evidence? This, however, is obviously untrue. Kant argues, for example, that reason itself is the originator of the categorical imperative, the moral law. Thus, reason can function without giving knowledge: the moral law does not tell us anything about the world, yet it is rational and hence nonarbitrary and thus cannot be assessed as either belief or opinion. Unless one wishes to define reason solely as a faculty (Kant defines the faculty of reason as that which is the originator of all laws; it is the law-giving faculty and nothing else), one must recognize that reason is never an isolated concept. We are always being reasonable in certain ways, or we are being reasonable *about* different things or different ways of being. There is no such thing as 'reason' just by itself; it is always in tandem with what can be reasonable; i.e., when we think about reason, we think about being rational with regards to . . . something. It appears that there are six realms of reason, or ways of being reasonable:

Reason and Certainty (Doubt)
Reason and Ideality
Reason and Action (Morality)
Reason and Trust (Wagers)
Reason and Mystery
Reason and Existence

In the first of these six ways of being reasonable, one contemplates the absolute necessity of logical inferences and the complete and total necessity about such understanding. It is the one time in all of human reflection when certainty is assured. There are few things as awesome as to watch unfold the development of the laws of logic, with all their pristine elegance and absolute authority. Even the dullest student appreciates the inevitability and hence power that comes from the supreme self-recognition that is the use of the logical apparatus which assures us beyond all doubt that the inference is sound. If A then B, and A, therefore B. This outdistances even skepticism, for the skeptics use it too, in order to make us doubt what we have accepted without sufficient evidence or warrant. Thus Reason and Certainty becomes Reason and Doubt: the constant testing, weighing, and evaluating of inferences and their presuppositions. This is the stuff of mathematics, and some scientific speculation, and rationalistic epistemology and metaphysics. What do I know for certain? What can I doubt, and what *must* I doubt? What cannot be accepted as true? The very fact that we have any canons at all for determining such inevitable and powerful assertions remains forever a source of wonder to those who reflect upon the mind. But reason is by no means limited to logic.

Reason also idealizes. The schoolchild knows the figures drawn on the page are not perfect circles, and only perfect circles and perfect triangles can provide the ways of geometry. Nor are there any perfectly just governments on earth, but we know we can reason about what ought to be, and what perfect justice means. In fact, we can *only* reason about perfect justice. We cannot reason about imperfect justice; that comes from experience and an awareness of our limits. But being aware of our limits and at the same time being able to project what things must be in order to be thought, is Ideality. Lovers also idealize their beloveds, but this does not make reason an emotional or sensual faculty. Thinkers as profound as Plato, Kant, and Schopenhauer have all argued that reason is dialectical and can continue probing backwards from what we know to what is presupposed. This is Ideality, and it is rational, but it is not logic.

Reason and Action reveals that we can and do govern our actions by the dictates of our mind. There is the moral law, and although we can dispute its application and even its fundamental meaning, there is no doubt that one can expect reason to illuminate the dark problems of right and wrong. In this case, reason directly informs us of what we ought to do, at least in some cases, and this is neither logic nor ideality, but it is reasonable. It is a way of being reasonable, and hence it must be distinguished from Certainty and Ideality.

Reason and Trust assures us that it is reasonable to act without certain assurance of fidelity, either of persons or probabilities. With persons, the very virtue of trust is possible only because it is possible to be betrayed. The willingness to undergo that danger makes an act of trust a rational one, for we would consider it *irrational* never to trust at all, to demand certainty of character in all human dealings. There are internal canons even to trusting: the reliability and character of the trusted one, the degree to which devotion and affection for the trusted one makes it seemly to allow the possible violation, the importance of the endeavor weighed against the past performance of the trusted one. These canons reveal that we can and do distinguish rational from irrational trust.

But, we trust, not only in people and our own minds, we also trust in the odds. It is rational to wager; in fact, we are constantly assessing and wagering, making 'bets' on probabilities. I know it is logically possible that the oncoming auto may suddenly veer into my lane, perhaps because the driver has a heart attack. But the odds against this happening are so vast that we consider it *rational* to drive on the same road as the oncoming traffic. Indeed, we consider one who would refrain from ever driving or being driven because of the sheer possibility of this event taking place, to be *irrational*. So, we are continually making evaluations of this sort, trusting in the assurance of probabilities. The fact that there is a certain amount of trust does not make our actions irrational; we consider it irrational *not* to trust the odds. Thus, rationality in this sense is possible only *because* I am not certain, or even because I do not critically doubt the laws of probability. (Pascal's 'Wager', is, in this sense, rational.) Nevertheless, we do not hesitate to designate such trusting, either in persons or in the odds of probability, rational.

The next tandem, Reason and Mystery, rather than implying some fuzzyheaded mysticism, is the recognition that our whole reality, not just our faculties of knowledge, is a part of being rational. Thus I can *reasonably* accept mystery, for the simple reason that the faculty of reason itself demands it. Reason itself, as Kant shows in the Antinomies, cannot know or answer certain all-important questions; it even shows us that in the absence of trust or an acceptance of mystery, certain reasonable ways of existing are impossible. To acknowledge the truth of a mystery is not a wanton abandonment or a leap of faith; it is the recognition that there is a greatness to truth which exceeds the powers of our understanding, and although we must, perforce, abandon surety or certainty in such acknowledgment, there are other faculties of equal importance which allow us to recognize that it is possible to accept a mystery rationally, just as it is possible to accept a mystery irrationally. In the latter case, one accepts that which is inconsistent with the ways in which one exists; one embraces a doctrine that forfeits the other predicates of spirit, such as worship, suffering, and rapture; not to mention radiance and importance. However, this chapter is on the *meaning* of mystery, not on the technical canons by which one can distinguish a rational from an irrational acceptance of mystery. It is enough here simply to show that a rational acceptance or acknowledgment of mystery is not irrational in all cases.

The full significance of this list of the six ways of being reasonable is realized only with the final tandem. For it is with this sixth way of being reasonable or rational that the full effect of 'mystery' becomes revealed. We discover now that the primary function of reason is not to respond to the question: Is our knowledge about the world rational? (i.e., do I have sufficient reason or evidence to believe something is true?) but rather to respond to the question: Is our being in the world rational? That is, *being* reasonable or even being rational is not primarily a matter of epistemic clarity but of coherent and grounded *meaning*. In the very first pages of this inquiry I quoted Hamlet's famous question: If we were meant only to eat and feed, why has God given us *reason*? The answer cannot be *to know*. For Hamlet is not concerned with knowing, but with *being*. He realizes that *to be* like a beast is unworthy of his *being* a man, and the difference is his spirit. Hamlet uses the term 'reason', showing that he expects some coherence and rationality to his existence, not mere knowledge of facts. In a sense, the sixth way of being reasonable is a summation of the other five. This is what we are inquiring about. Is our *being* in the world—a part of which is to know it— grounded on reason, or is it, as it is with the animals, grounded on appetite? Hamlet's anguish is our concern. We seek to discover that being spiritual is more rational than being merely appetitive.

7

Rapture and Redemption

RAPTURE

At the risk of seeming highly unromantic and even caustic, I should like to protest that there is simply too much written and spoken today about love. In the sixties we were told to make love not war; the television evangelists assure us that God is love; social service messages tell us we can cure alcoholism with love. And of course, *everyone* is in favor of it, and everyone seems an expert on it. Like common sense, it is as universally proclaimed as it is almost universally lacking. Love is gentle, tender, sweet, good, kind, forgiving, healing, fun, exciting, and ubiquitous. (Can *anything* that plentiful be that good?) After all, murderers, rapists, liars, cheats, and sycophants are capable of love. There is scarcely a television program, a novel or a play, a message on a bumper sticker, or a sermon from a church lectern that does not convince us that love is the cure for all ills. Above all, love makes us feel good. It is the essence of God's law on earth, and all failures of human institutions are due to the single lack of this one passion or sentiment.

But this is romantic twaddle at its worst. There is no greater distinction between the great or worthy writer and the common hack than how they write about love. Those who are not afraid of the truth recognize that love is a dreadful disease: it causes the deepest possible torments of the soul; it makes men kill other men; it drives us to suicide, self-torment, and unbearable anxiety. Under the influence of this demi-god, we lose our reason and our dignity. We are driven to jealousy by it; we stoop to the lowest cunning and the most desperate conceit on its behalf. It

132

destroys far more than it saves. If God is love then we are all doomed.

Of course, there are various kinds of love. The erotic is the most dangerous, to be sure, but even that pearl of all love, parental affection, can be deadly and venomous. If you believe that love is sweet and gentle, attend one day's session at any child-custody court in the land. The love is genuine; but it is savage, cruel, violent, and desperate. The few successful loves are accomplished not by loving but by decency and respect. As early as Plato's *Phaedrus* love was called a kind of madness. There is no denying that under certain circumstances love brings us great delight, but that is the core of the problem. The delight is so overpowering, so alluring, our entire moral ediface comes crumbling down at the first appearance of this demonic passion.

And among the spiritual, those who are the object of this inquiry, the strangest claim in the entire storehouse of human utterances is the outrageous one that they love God. That is, *some* spiritual people claim they love God; the more cautious may feel it, subtly or overwhelmingly, but they shy away from overt acknowledgement, perhaps fearing its enormous significance when openly manifested. What can it possibly mean to love God? Or what can it mean to say that God loves us? Love today has become to mean one of only two possible things: the intense delight of sensually reciprocal sexuality, complete with all the self-indulgent psychological gratifications such as conquering, being taken, yielding, usurping, sharing, and mastery; or it means the kindly caring that makes us do nice things for others, to smile and share things, to hug our friends and help those in need. The first we can shorthand into the single term 'gratifying', the second with the word 'nice'. So love either gratifies, sometimes enormously, or it is nice, sometimes wonderfully. But how can I seek sensual gratification from God, or how can I be *nice* to God or God *nice* to me? The idea is rendered forfeit by the sheer silliness or smallness of the notion.

However, this is not an essay on love itself, but on rapture. I began by protesting that too much was said about love these days to emphasize how that curious term has been deflated, as all terms are deflated, when vulgarized to the common level. Rapture is often, though not always, a form of ecstatic loving, but neither of the 'gratificatory' or the 'nice' variety, which seems to constitute our ordinary meaning. As a predicate of spirit, however, it must be noted that rapture seems reserved for only a few among the spiritual or spirited people, so that one may possibly object that rapture is a mere occasional occurrence among the spiritual and not a true predicate. Before passing on this decision, however, it is essential to examine in detail just what rapture means.

Rapture, of course, is easily understood in terms of its etymology: one is *rapt* when one is seized by some overwhelming power. The term comes from the Latin, *rapere* which means to seize; and in early English uses it occasionally was used as a synonym for rape. In rapture, therefore, we are enveloped or abducted by a force or an idea to the exclusion of the immediate environment: it suggests removal, being taken away. It always carries with it the sense that the one enrapt is passive or even victimized by the rapture. The earliest English uses were primarily reserved for those who were seized by God and taken into heaven, and so it also became synonymous with Christian death. This is the original meaning. But the immediate metaphorical meaning has almost as long a history, and that is the phenomenon of being rapt by a passion or emotion, *as if* the passion had abducted our souls or at least our immediate concern away from the ordinary and everyday. In this acceptable and common sense, rapture inevitably becomes a characteristic of those overwhelmed by the passion of love. Romeo is enrapt by Juliet, Tristan and Isolde are both in a rapture so great that only death can either release them or fulfill the aching promise of the rapture itself.

In the previous chapter, the predicate of mystery provides us with a guide in understanding the epistemic paradox mentioned in chapter 2. It was noted that there seemed to be an unsolvable problem in considering spirit, that in order to understand one had to yield all understanding, or even: understanding spirit consists in not understanding. The harshness of this conflict is somewhat eased in our discussion of mystery. The present predicate, Rapture, is an easement of the second paradox, the metaphysical paradox, in which in order to be myself I must lose myself. The approach to the understanding of rapture is an attempt to defang the terrible inconsistency of the second paradox. For if we consider, merely as a model, the erotic rapture of lovers in which the private existence of one becomes absorbed into the overweening power of the Two, we can see that love-rapture does indeed forfeit the autonomy of the self in order to realize the fullness of the self in love. This we can grasp easily enough by even a modest degree of sympathy with great literature and music; and even if we have never experienced such things in their intensity as that found on the stage, we do understand Romeo's absorption in Juliet and Tristan's eclipse of his individuality in the *Liebesnacht* with Isolde.

It is surely prudent, then, to begin this inquiry into the meaning of rapture by concerning ourselves with the phenomenon of erotic rapture, especially as it is provided to us by the aesthetic media. The poets and the musicians, through their rare gifts of insight which are unsupported by argumentation but compel us to acknowledge them nonetheless, can tell us about such rapture; and from these insights we can examine the principles or the essential elements. On the surface, then, it seems that by erotic rapture we mean the joy taken in being overwhelmed by and absorbed in another's beauty. This provisional description relies heavily on the singularity of two key terms, 'joy' and 'beauty'. The singularity that is important here is that 'joy' is not the same as 'happiness', and 'beauty' (especially a beauty that enslaves) cannot be seen as 'good'.

What, then, is the difference between joy and happiness? Luckily we do not have to render a complete definition of either term, for that would require an encyclopedic analysis of the entire history of philosophy. We need focus only on their differences. And the most obvious difference is that happiness seems to be a quality which is within, whereas joy takes us out of or beyond ourselves. To be happy implies at least a sense of satisfaction or deep contentment with oneself or the way things are going; joy is almost the opposite, in that the entire experience elevates us beyond contentment and satisfaction. In other words, joy is *ecstatic*, in the literal, etymological sense of 'being outside of', *ex-statis*. In joy we are 'beside ourselves'; we feel ripped from the ordinary. Joy seems to be more immediate and more intense than happiness, yet at the same time it threatens to be dangerously short-lived. To an outside observer, someone enrapt in ecstatic joy may seem destined for deep regret after the glow of the moment is dissipated. Surely if one had to choose, it would be better to be happy than joyful; the former suggests permanence and sanity, the latter brevity and frenzy. This is especially true when the notion of 'joy' is conjoined with the adjective 'ecstatic', which it very often is. An ecstatic joy by definition cannot last long; its whole meaning depends upon the short-lived but intense depth of the experience. One does not live forever in ecstasy.

Unlike happiness, joy seems to be celebratory; as a kind of elation, it is often prompted by some kind of achievement (again emphasizing its intense but transitory character), as when an athlete suddenly discovers he has won the prize after many years of incredible hard work. There is a curious mixture of conflicting sentiments in this kind of joy: on the one hand the victor believes he has *earned* the trophy, on the other there is the irresistible sense that this delight is a bestowal, an unearned privilege, granted by some favoring deity. So that joy is both a celebration of what is deserved and a festival of what is bestowed and unexpected. A further insight may help us: the opposite of happiness is misery, but the opposite of joy is despair.

One of the more curious features of our species is our tendency to rank as most worthy those experiences which cost us a great deal of suffering. In a recent airplane hijacking, a middle-aged, middle-class, somewhat overweight man was beaming as he descended from the plane after the ordeal was over. The ubiquitous press immediately shoved microphones into his face, and as the brilliant glare of the television lights removed all shadow from him, he was bombarded with the expected question: "How do you *feel* now that _____ ?" "It is the greatest moment of my life" said the man. "I have never been so joyous in my life. The greatest experience ever." This is entirely believable, since he did not strike one as the type to whom great experiences came regularly. What made the obviously sincere outburst so very odd, however, was the fact that this man had just endured several weeks of terrifying captivity at the hands of ruthless thugs. One might expect him to be grateful, to be relieved at ending his ordeal, to be happy that he was free. But what he said was that it was the greatest moment of his life. Greatest? The suggestion is eerie. Can it be that, in order to achieve a great joy one must first endure great suffering?

Of course, the man was neither a poet nor a philosopher; he was not even especially articulate; yet we need not abuse him for his utterance. Apparently he knew how to use his own language. Why not take him at his word? This was the greatest joy, the most thrilling experience he had ever had. Now, surely no one would deny that such a sentiment is possible, if only because of the tremendous relief from the dreadful suffering that preceded it. Is this not merely a variation of the same old notion that the cessation of pain is not merely a negative thing but a positive one? Is joy relief? Or is it the case that this simple middle-aged, middle-class man is in fact no longer middle-class? That his suffering has purchased him a right, or an opportunity for privilege, that approaches greatness? Is it not more profound to realize that he was joyous not merely because he was relieved by the release, but that his prior suffering had rendered him a different person altogether, one entitled to a joy which nonsufferers cannot achieve? And if this analysis is correct, then perhaps joy is possible only to those who can suffer, or who have suffered. We are beings, after all, strung between suffering and joy, both of which are essential for self-understanding. But this simple man shows us something remarkable: his return to his home itself was not the cause of his joy, since he had been headed for home originally when the plane was hijacked. Had he returned home as planned, his arrival would have been a relief, perhaps, from the tiring plane trip, accompanied with grumbling about bad food and babies that cry during long journeys. What had changed him so that his return was now a joy? It was not merely that a terrible ordeal was over: he may have spent two weeks in the hospital at some time, fighting a serious disease, and when cured felt relief, not joy. Indeed it was not merely the fact of his suffering. It was rather the sense that this return was a form of salvation or redemption.

One might define a happy man as on who has avoided any considerable suffering; the same could never be said of a joyful man. But suffering alone does not explain joy; it is at best a necessary and not a sufficient condition.

Joy, as was mentioned above, differs from happiness in that it lifts us beyond ourselves, whereas happiness contents us with ourselves. What is the nature of this ecstasy, this being torn from ourselves and elevated to a new kind of awareness? We turn again to erotic rapture as a device. When Tristan and Isolde share their fated bliss, they recognize that in their rapture the self is eclipsed in order for the self to be. Why be a self unless it can be given, indeed totally submitted? Wagner has Tristan sing "ich Isolde, du Tristan," meaning they have assumed each others' identity, so that in losing their autonomy to the other, they achieve who they are. In raputre, then, to be is to be given; the worth of existing as an individual is completely eclipsed, but the realization is that being eclipsed in the beauty of the beloved is why one is an individual in the first place. One is reminded of the comic poet Aristophanes in Plato's *Symposium,* who praises eros simply because without it we are only half ourselves: to be is to be two.

A young lover takes his bride to bed. Her gentle caresses and her youthful nudity displayed for his sake gives him considerable pleasure. He is thus made happy: he benefits from the pleasure. But slowly he begins to caress her, to focus his attention on bringing her delight, and notes in this curious heightening of his own interest and elation. He is now no longer taking pleasure, he is giving pleasure. The thought pleases them both, and they sense that their lust is becoming love. This shared passion may soon reach frenzy in which all thought is excised by the hegemony of sheer pleasure, but even now the realization, though dimmed by the heat of passion, that they are making each other happy as well as themselves heightens the worth of the enterprise.

But as the intensity mounts, he may find himself pulling away from her simply to look at her, now flushed with a new kind of beauty, now authentically *his* in a way he had never known before. He looks on her, not with lascivious interest as earlier, but in a dawning joy that not only is she his, but he is *hers.* His own masculinity becomes meaningful only because of her femininity; he senses a startling new realization, that he will do anything for, submit anything to, endure all on behalf of what is before him. The moment is less frantic now than reverential; less carnal, more spiritual. It is almost as if he now fears to touch her, lest such touching return him to the earlier state of selfish gratification which has been replaced by a new realization that his worth lies in the thrall of her beauty.

This is a new realization every time it happens; for it's almost as if memory is too modest for such intensity. If he touches now at all it is with exquisite gentleness, a prayerful respect for such sacred belonging, no longer a willing slave of lust but now, quite simply, a captive slave of the beloved. He is no longer taken up in his individuality; his private pleasures and yearnings for delights, so recently afire, have transmogrified into this curious absorption of the self into another. He was happier before, when enjoying the immediate gratifications of his venereal hungers; now this radiant new passion is one of gentle slavery which makes his own pleasures a distraction. He feels he cannot endure the enormity of this longing, yet to yield to anything as a release would be sacrilegious. He is in rapture. Such rapture is, one might say, an enjambment with lust; the peak of desire is not on the same meter as the peak of joy. The syllogism of passion has run, then, from self, to other, to sharing, to an eclipse of self, to submission. But the final stage, submission, is not to any particular dynasty but to the total sovereignty of his beloved's beauty. In becoming this slave, he has achieved freedom.

But have we not completely reversed our original distinction between flesh and spirit? Has flesh become spirit in rapture? This is surely not an original idea: Hawthorne uses it in the *Scarlet Letter*, showing that the forbidden adultery was oddly redemptive; Wagner has it in *Tristan and Isolde;* Neitzsche screams in his "On the Despisers of the Body" in *Thus Spoke Zarathustra* that the body *is* the great spirit. Indeed, the latter part of the nineteenth century seems almost obsessed with this idea: intense erotic passion can be spiritual and even redemptive. The key is the notion of rapture; for in it one submits to an enslavement that liberates: it enslaves by making one a complete servant to the beauty of the beloved, but it liberates by removing the purely carnal gratifications as the essence of the union.

Just as there are many texts, particularly in the second half of the nineteenth century, which reveal in literature and music that erotic love can redeem, there are many texts which show that loss of individuality is something to be achieved, not dreaded. The most famous of these is the Apolonian-Dionysian distinction found in Nietzsche's *Birth of Tragedy*. Apollo is the god of light, and hence reason, and thus represents the *individual;* but Dionysos, the god of revelry, represents passions and hence the eclipse of the individual in the universalizing passion of the ritualist. The Dionysians sweep over the timid Apollonians and affirm existence itself. Ever since Nietzsche wrote those famous words at the tender age of twenty-four, hundreds of second-rate followers have reiterated his theme. The eclipse of self became a popular, even bourgeoisie belief, and the redemption of the self and the achievement of spirit through erotic rapture also became a middle-class, and hence vacuous, notion, though highly dangerous for all that.

But there are those who constantly remind us of the other side of erotic rapture: its total destructiveness. From *Therese Raquin* to the more sober analyses of Thomas Mann, the erotic demiurge does not produce spiritual redemption but desolate disaster. It should be remembered that the truly great authors and composers who celebrated the redemption through the erotic were deeply aware of the moral authority: neither Hawthorne nor Wagner ever denied that what Arthur and Hester did, or what Tristan and Isolde did, was morally wrong; they merely showed us that even the moral wrongness cannot completely overshadow the power of the erotic to provide salvation in a kind in rapture. Indeed, the likes of Tristan and Arthur Dimsdale are impossible without their own moral guilt being a part of their rapture. Only the imitators failed to recognize the dangers.

Rapture, then, at least as we understand it in its erotic form, is the joyful surrender of one's autonomy, in which the intensity of delight compels us beyond ourselves in ecstasy, to submit completely to the influence of beauty. We see the loss of a private individuality as a price paid for a higher reality that is possible only in union with the beloved. Joy is a positive term and thus the surrendering, even though it is forced upon us, is accepted and acknowledged. To the true believer in rapture, the union with the beloved is infinitely more worthwhile than the autonomy of the one: indeed, who one is can be fully realized only in such loss of self in order to achieve an even greater meaning, being absorbed in the other.

Even nonerotic instances of rapture, such as a listener's rapture in great music or an observer's rapture in great painting, has this ecstatic quality which fulfills the self by denying the self. The young concert-goer who is losing himself in the totality of a Beethoven symphony considers this Dionysian loss of individuation a boon and not a deprivation. So rapture, by taking us beyond ourselves, perforce, renders us up to higher ecstasy, by the power of the beautiful. What does it mean, then, to say that being spiritual includes the predicates of rapture?

Surely not all who are spiritual are constantly in a state of ecstasy. Indeed, if our first analyses of this predicate are correct, suffering must precede or even accompany such rapture. But if one is to be spiritual, one must acknowledge the will to rapture, even if dry and endless years of agony, doubt, mistrust, and even despair precede the moment of ecstasy. Indeed, the moment may never actually come; it is sufficient that the man of spirit believe in its worth and recognize that rapture is a possibility for which he is ever ready. But spiritual rapture cannot be the same as erotic rapture, even if the latter can, at times, become a propaedeutic for the former. Spiritual rapture is surrender to a beauty which is not seen or touched in bodily terms; yet, since beauty cannot be achieved through reason alone—Plato, Kant, Schopenhauer, Nietzsche all attest to this—this spiritual rapture must somehow be *felt* or sensed and not merely thought. And, of course, this is what makes the notion of spiritual rapture so difficult: How can we understand a rapture dominated by a purely spiritual reality?

We read of saints completely enrapt by prayer, visions, meditation, and even by rituals. These are not abstractions, they are not the result of a philosophical argument, like the ontological proof of God's existence. One cannot be led to rapture by inferences. Is there not here a great danger that the rapture is based upon a psychologically induced deception? Is it not possible that what the saints experience in their rapture is merely sublimated sexuality, or if that is too explicitly Freudian, at least an *illusory* sense of beauteous reality which is the product of fantasy?

Of course this is possible. It is likewise possible that the water I see on the desert floor is a mirage. The possibility of visual error does not make the notion of 'seeing' invalid. I am sure many young ascetics are enrapt by illusions; but that does not mean that all spiritual rapture is an illusion. We are not seeking to prove that any saint or spiritual person can epistemically verify the object of his worship or rapture: we are merely seeking to discover what rapture means and whether the possibility of rapture is an essential quality or predicate of being spiritual. So the question now is not whether the spiritual rapture might be illusory (obviously it often is, perhaps it usually is), but what it would mean if, just once, it were *not* illusory. What would it mean to be enrapt by something absolutely magnificent, something divine?

If it is impossible to experience rapture solely by means of thought alone, then once more we find the realism of spirit, as Plato suggests in the *Republic,* touching both the sensuous and the purely noetic. If authentic rapture with the divine is possible, then both the enrapt and the source of the enthrallment must be spiritual and not merely mental or rational. The divine cannot be sensed in the normal way, i.e., it cannot be the object of sensuous experience. Perhaps it can be gleaned by argumentation, as in a successful proof for God's existence. But only if it is grasped by spirit can there be rapture. Thus, all instances of spiritual rapture are either inauthentic inspirations of the imagination, i.e., self-induced delusions, or there is something actually graspable which is divine. To grasp the divine, not to reason or to experience the divine, would be the only possibility.

This, however, is in fact what the spiritual acknowledge. They do not accept the reductionist account of the psychologist, nor do they rely solely or even primarily upon rational proofs. To be spiritual is to be able to be overwhelmed by that which can be grasped. This shows the autonomy of spirit from either the senses or from reason. Thus, even though it is not a constant characteristic of the spiritual, it deserves to be called a true predicate of spirit; i.e., it is something we must try to comprehend if we are to grasp the meaning of spirit.

REDEMPTION

Redemption, in the narrow, theological sense, means that one's sinful state is purged by divine assistance, allowing the otherwise damned soul to enter into the eternal bliss of heaven.

There is no need for this term to be so demeaned by limiting it to this one, theological interpretation. Many sensitive thinkers and writers are aware of redemption without believing in a post-terrestial reward. Indeed, the precise theological account of redemption is actually a derived notion, stemming from a more fundamental notion, to the effect that the human species is by nature fallen in some original sense and that one cannot, by the powers we possess ourselves, elevate our status to what it ought to be or even what it was destined to be. Heidegger, in his a priori analysis of human meaning, identifies 'fallenness' as an essential category of existence. That is, when we turn our attention to the problem of what it means to exist, we *must* find that the species is understandable only in terms of reaching for something which because of its fallen nature it cannot attain without some transcendent assistance or illumination. Belief in redemption even in this vague and existential sense is essential for spirit.

Belief is some kind of redemption is ubiquitous. Marxists believe that mankind can be redeemed only by following the inevitable dialectic toward a Communist world-state. The National Socialists of Germany believed redemption was possible only by purging their race of the contamination of the Jews. Jews themselves believe in a future redeemer, the Messiah; Christians believe the Messiah has already come in the figure of Jesus Christ; nostalgists believe in the redemptive power of a return to a golden age; futurists believe in the redemption of the new order soon to replace the corruption of the old. All political reformers believe that their private schemes will produce some utopian salvation of humankind. Every one of these beliefs, from the noble religions to the despicable tyrannies of power and cruelty are alike in this: they look forward or backward toward a time in which humanity is no longer mired in the desperate meaninglessness and depravity in which it now finds itself.

For some, redemption requires a redeemer or savior, perhaps a noble hero who will show (or has shown) us the path to salvation. Honest men may admit that such beliefs are perhaps due to the simple cast of our nature, that the metal and the mold into which we were originally poured simply cries out for such a belief so that it becomes almost an a priori form of our existence. Kant even argues that *reason* itself *must* postulate some form of redemption in order to satisfy the cruel antinomy of moral reasoning which assures us that we are required by the principles of our mind to think that the just should be rewarded and the wicked punished, but since our experience tells us otherwise, we must rationally hope. It is difficult to find a culture which does not support some idea of redemption or salvation, so deeply imbedded is this notion in the human reality.

The primordial disgust with which we initiate this inquiry already supports the notion of redemption, though not necessarily a redeemer; why else turn *from* flesh *to* spirit unless there is a sense of redemption in being spiritual? Such a sense of disgust would be entirely impossible if there were not first some sense of unworthiness about the way we are. Of course, not all men feel this disgust, nor do all men have any real sense of redemption. And this is because not all men are spiritual. (They may be potentially spiritual, or truly spiritual but simply self-deceived, but they are not overtly and self-consciously spiritual and thus they scoff at any such notions.) However, to believe in some kind of redemption does not in and of itself assure one of spirituality: the Nazi vermin may have been convinced that redemption required a savage genocide, but they were not, *per se,* spiritual.

This must be stressed: a particular religious belief in a redeemer may or may not be justified, but its theological articulation is derived from the fundamental existential notion of fallenness which Heidegger talks about. We *first* are aware of our fallenness and then seek to find some way to redeem ourselves. The belief that such redemption cannot be accomplished *as we are* is the ground for all theological notions of redemption and salvation. That I can be something which requires being redeemed or saved at all may strike the purely secular mind as amusing, but it is a fundamental modality of our existence. And such redemption is simply impossible outside the realm of spirit. Thus, as we turn to examine a few examples from specific believers, it is not their particular faiths that we examine but the universal ground of realizing that *as we are* we are incomplete. The particular stories of actual human activities which manifest this profound commitment to redemption are multifarious and stirring. Some of the world's greatest events are grounded on this keystone of man's spiritual nature. Moses leading his fraught and troubled people in search of the promised land is an odyssey of courage and splendor. Christian saints, rapt in the realization of their redeemer, provide much illumination and admiration, even for unbelievers. Muslims making the arduous trek to Mecca and devout singers performing the *Messiah* attest to the belief in redemption and even at times a particular redeemer. But what does it mean to be redeemed? Why do we feel the lack in the first place? What is the nature of the lack? Why is the surge toward a redeemer so palpable and poignant? What is so terrible about the world as it is right now? And why is the conviction so deeply imbedded in us that, no matter how we articulate our redemption, it requires something beyond ourselves to accomplish, whether it be a godliness visiting our humanity or whether it be an inevitability to the course of history, like Marxism?

Nietzsche is rather brilliant in his insight in this regard. He tells us he is going to teach us the meaning of our existence, for the huge joke on mankind is that we do not know it. Then, to prepare us for this instruction, he reveals the coming of the superman (*Übermensch*). The superman is an existential redeemer. (At one point, Zarathustra describes the superman as "Caesar with the soul of Christ." Now, what is fascinating about this is that both Christ and Caesar were redeemers, the latter of the Roman State after the Republic grew too corrupt to rule; the former of all mankind by turning our attention to the love of God the Father.) So the 'redeemer', the superman, is about the meaning of our existence. There can be no doubt that Nietzsche treats the superman *as* a redeemer: he insists on establishing the *new* man, on changing our natures. In order to make his point perfectly clear, he contrasts the 'superman' with the 'last man', the man who has invented happiness, and blinks. The last man does not know the meaning of his existence, he is existentially asleep. The superman is alert and either knows or at least seeks after the meaning of his existence. This is redemption in its most fundamental guise: we seek to find out *who we are*.

But what does this atheistic, existential thinker have to say to someone who believes redemption is merely the ticket that allows him entrance into the heavenly paradise after death? (Or more tellingly, the ticket which keeps him from falling into an even worse situation than the one we are in: eternal damnation?) Although at first glance it might seem Nietzsche has nothing to tell the Christian concerned with saving his soul, in fact the analysis is entirely relevant. For in order to get this ticket to heaven, one must do certain things, or rather, one must profoundly change one's entire way of life. For the true Christian, of course, the path to salvation is not mere prudence. One enters heaven as a reward, or perhaps even as a bestowal. What must proceed such entrance is a discovery and a commitment as to who we really are. (This is why many Christians emphasize mere *belief*: once I recognize that I am the beloved of God, that we are true children to a loving Father, our salvation follows naturally from such *acknowledgment*. It is enough, say the Protestant critics, simply to *believe;* whereas the Catholic insists that good works must accompany such beliefs. This may be a semantic argument, since the conviction of both is that the true believer will in fact act decently and morally simply because he knows who he is. Both believe, however, that the entrance into paradise is not within *our* accomplishments: it is only because we are redeemed through the suffering of our Lord and Savior.)

Nietzsche's analysis fits into this theology because he too focuses upon the necessity of finding one's true self; but that must begin with the realization that we are *unaware* of that truth. Hence, we need to be taught. But I can be taught the meaning of existence only if I first am made aware that my existence as it is now has no meaning. In other words, to be redeemed from meaninglessness assumes that the disjunct between meaningful and meaningless is what redemption is all about. What then, is the *source* of our awareness of fallenness or of being like the last man, devoid of any sense of our own meaning? Nietzsche and Heidegger both assume it is a fundamental given, an a priori modality of existence which cannot be explained by more basic principles since it is itself primordial. And perhaps it is: perhaps the meaning of existence requires a distinction between one's being lost in the prattle of everydayness and one's being redeemed by a superman.

Yet not all thinkers share this view. Some place the origin of our awareness and the need for salvation directly in the structure of reason itself. Plato's entire dialectic presupposes the notion of excellence or ideality which, though necessary, can never be fully achieved by the human mind, at least on this earth. Kant, the supreme formalist, opens the most formidable book in all of literature, *The Critique of Pure Reason,* with the simple but direct claim that we *must* seek after questions which we *cannot* answer. Reason is therefore antinomic, and therefore discovers its finitude and the frustration of purely speculative thought. To offset these dire limitations to speculation and science, Kant insists that the mind of man recognize the *authority* of rational *hope.* (For Kant, hope is not a psychological state but a necessary function of antinomic reasoning; thus it becomes irrational not to hope.)

Neither Plato nor Kant are redemptionists in the sense that they provide, as Nietzsche obviously does, a redemptive model to show the path to salvation. Far less are they redemptivists: theological teachers who offer a single personal God or a heroic messenger from the divine. But both thinkers *do* insist that the *mind* and not the *emotions* discovers incompleteness in its function and range, and hence one must turn to some spiritual or moral understanding to redeem the antinomic drift toward misology.

But whether the awareness of one's incompleteness and the need to be redeemed at all lies in the a priori form of our existence or whether it is a purely rational thing, residing in the powers of the mind alone, there can be no doubt that this considerable array of respected and profound thinkers all agree that the human condition seems *fundamentally* so designed as to be conducive to the search for redemption, in some way or form. And since the concrete satisfies and attracts more than the abstract, it is small wonder that heros and saviors play stellar roles in our histories. Where would the Hebrews be without Abraham and Moses? Where would America be without George Washington and Abraham Lincoln? Where would Christianity be without the redeemer, Jesus Christ? Or the Marxist revolution without Lenin? Where would Elsa be without her Lohengrin?

Where would the spirit be without a God to worship, and to redeem? What, then, does redemption *mean?* Like rapture, redemption brings us out of our present unworthy state and changes, not our mere environment, but our entire existential structure. It changes who we are. The middle-class, middle-aged released hostage who walked down the steps on the hijacked plane glowing with joy simply is no longer the same man who originally walked up those steps on an innocent and unexciting vacation. To redeem means to fulfill, to bring to fruition the hidden greatness within the recumbent seed. And for most of us, however we think about redemption; it is usually in the future. Hence, redemption implies *hope*.

Redemption can be thought only if two conditions obtain: (1) I am now in an incomplete or inauthentic state; and (2) to achieve the fullness of my being an appeal must be made to some reality beyond my own individuality. The spiritual person not only is aware of this, he acknowledges it in a special way. It is not so much that he believes *he* is assured of achieving redemption; rather, he accepts the fallenness of his nature, and looks forward to, but is not necessarily assured of, achieving salvation. Among the greatest of the saints one finds the remarkable willingness to fail if one could achieve a greater devotion by doing so.

Given human weakness, even the notion of redemption can corrode into simple prudence. I act decently and pay my dues to whatever organized religion I choose in exactly the same way I brush my teeth in order to prevent cavities. It is this sense of redemption that arouses the deepest disgust from the secular critic of spirit. It does appear unseemly for an educated adult to perform little rituals of demeaning pettiness merely out of fear of some possible post-terrestial torment. But even the spiritual find such an attitude offensive. What we are discussing here is the fundamental existential awareness that we think about our existence in terms of fallenness and salvation, even if that sense is vague and unclear. We do this in part because the very nature of our reason is idealistic: i.e., when we think we do so in ideal terms. Every child knows that a 'perfect' circle is the only one worthy of guiding us in the rules of geometry; every lover knows instinctively how to idealize his beloved; the very growth of a child to adulthood manifests this developmental sense of reaching toward something which we do not now possess and which, in its absence, leaves us either flawed, unimportant, or incomplete. That some may abuse this notion by trivializing it is merely the fate that any worthy idea must endure if it is to be shared by the entire range of the species.

Up to this point the idea of redemption has been treated indifferently as to whether redemption was to be found in an actual redeemer or a movement or political achievement. It is now necessary, however, to reflect more seriously on the nature of the spiritual acknowledgment not merely of redemption but of a redeemer. It may be due to the peculiarity of our natures that we relate more intimately to concrete reality than to abstractions, but truely spiritual persons usually find their ideality directed toward a specific *person* whom they identify as their redeemer or savior. But I do not believe that mere concretization is sufficient to explain this: it seems there is entailed in the notion of redemption the idea of a bestowal, that the salvation is only partly earned and partly given as an act of grace. In order for there to be grace involved in the phenomenon of redemptive thinking, a personal redeemer is necessary and not a mere historical inevitability. Certainly among the more *piously* spiritual, redemption implies a redeemer. If this is so, the question we must now ask is this: How does one think about a redeemer? With fear and trembling? With awe and wonder? To be sure, these are a part of our thinking and even *feeling* about a redeemer; but such would be true of our worship, too. I would be in awe of a nonredemptive but creative divinity.

Surely if redemption is not inevitable, if it is at least in part a bestowal, then the primary characteristic of such thinking would have to be gratitude. And since surety is never guaranteed in such things, this gratitude is always hopeful. Earlier in this chapter I characterized the claim that one might be said to *love* God was outrageous. But it is not outrageous to love a redeemer; indeed if a grateful hope is essential for redemption, then love is entirely understandable. Hopeful gratitude is neither 'nice' nor 'gratificatory', but it can provide the basis for genuine loving. Since 'gratitude' will be discussed in a separate section further in the inquiry, it may suffice to reflect briefly on that curious phenomenon of the human spirit known as hope.

In Roman Catholic theology there is a remarkable doctrine concerning the nature of hope. (Many regard all Catholic doctrines remarkable, if not astonishing.) The Roman church teaches that there are two sins against hope: despair and presumption. The latter is conviction that one will indeed be saved; the former is that one is certainly damned. This doctrine provoked a high-school wag to summarize it this way: "If I really believe I'm going to heaven, I won't; if I really believe I'm not going to heaven, I won't; so I won't." It *does* seem a curious doctrine, for it seems to make assurance, one way or the other, *sinful.* Furthermore, the whole idea of being able to sin, not against God but against Hope sounds strange. It is easy to see why the Church would want to discourage people from despair, and to classify such deep despondency as sinful. But why make a sin out o presumption? And why not simply say that to despair is to sin against God? Why characterize either presumption or despair as sins against the virtue of hope? It would seem that of Paul's famous triad one can believe absolutely and love absolutely, but cannot hope absolutely.

Yet, as with all seemingly astonishing contortions of the theologies there is more in this curious doctrine than elicits waggish humor. For if I am indeed absolutely convinced that I am saved or redeemed, then I do not hope at all, I *know.* But hope is precisely a virtue because it celebrates our finitude and our ignorance. Since the notion of redemption entails the notion of at least partial grace or bestowal—i.e., redemption is never completely *earned*—one is required to trust in beings or forces beyond oneself to achieve the completion that our fallenness assures us we do not yet possess. Presumption—the absolute conviction that I am indeed saved—is a sin precisely because it is unnatural; it is to understand oneself as one is not, i.e., falsely. The point of this teaching is not to make us fearful, but simply respectful of our true natures.

The Pauline triad of faith, hope, and charity (love) may be entirely similar. Faith, like hope, is *not* knowledge; if it were, it would not be faith. And love, as we learn from the *Symposium* is possession and lack at the same time; like Juliet, we long but for the thing we have, making complete satisfaction and total possession inimical to true loving. But this does not mean that hope is an idle dream, a wish for the fantasical. As Kant shows in his argumentation, hope is a *rational* expectation, not a romantic or naive trust that things always turn out for the best. Optimism has nothing to do with spiritual hope; for hope is not the unqualified conviction that I shall be redeemed, but the simple trust that there is redemption. There can be gratitude for this redemption even if it is denied, although this takes an unusually highly developed sense of spirit to sustain.

The etymology of the term 'redeem' means simply to regain, or to get back what was surrendered or lost, as when we redeem what is pawned. This suggests that the original state of mankind was as it ought to be, then something happened which made us lose our natural position of innocence, and so now we must await some redemption to restore us to our former glory. There are, of course, countless anthropological accounts of myriad cultures which tell us of the various myths which reflect this basic attitude, including of course the Western traditional story of Adam and Eve. Two remarks should be made about this with regard to hope and redemption. First, the myths are responses to a more original existential awareness of 'fallenness'; and secondly, the account shows the structure of a *story*. Stories explain. They do not give causal explanations, but they make sense of things nonetheless. But a story, as we all know, has a beginning, a middle, and an end. We are born, we live for a while, and then we die. There is a past, a present, and a future. Redemptive hope is nothing else than the simple story-structure of explanation supported by one other principle: that our existence matters. Unless there is worth to existence, there can be no *story* which explains. The explanative power of a story presupposes the *worth* of existence. Why relate the past to the present and the present to the future unless this unfolding of time were not somehow significant? And the most fundamental story of all is of an original happiness lost through guilt and achievement of freedom, redeemed by something greater than the original worth that was lost. The very *intelligibility* of our temporal development demands that a future be pregnant with possible meaning, otherwise a *story* could not be told. But stories, even more than causal accounts, satisfy the mind's desire to *think*. Since our story is as yet unfinished, and since by definition the future is unknown, to doubt seriously the openness of the future is to doubt the historical character of self-understanding. Thus, to sin against hope, either by presumption or despair, is an offence against the very possibility of our existence being meaningful, since it makes a story impossible. To reflect on our own stories—

and to think of our own existence as structured like a story is itself revealing—is to remember (past), to be aware (present), and to look forward to (the future). If these three are without meaning, we have nihilism. Thus, even my projection into the open future must be meaningful: hence, hope is rational. Thus, 're-demption' is not the result of mere theological speculation; it resides as an essential way of thinking about our own meaning, which is the proper domain of spirit.

Nevertheless, it is important to reflect, even if briefly, on the claim that both despair and presumption are *sins* against hope. What is a sin? If we consider the entire range of possible ways to understand how one goes astray, the very list reveals considerable meaning. There are eight basic ways in which we, as human beings, understand our own deviation from what ought to be. The following list begins with the least objectionable and develops to the most objectionable forms of misbehavior. Each term is not only listed and explained but the presuppositions for each are also included. Thus, in the third column one sees what one must assume (or presuppose) if there is to be anything like that which is signified by the term being listed. By this list we can see that to err is not the same as to commit a moral wrong, and to do a crime is not the same as to commit a sin, and the highest kind of wrong is sacrilege. This list is hierarchical, and the presuppositions of the higher ranks assume the presuppositions of the lower ranks. Thus, it is impossible for there to be a sin if one cannot violate the moral law, for sin not only assumes the existence of a divinity, it also assumes the moral law and the consequent presupposition of freedom and the ability to be held responsible. (It is precisely because the presuppositions of the higher evils include those of the lower or lesser evils that some thinkers are convinced the higher ones should be *reduced* to the lower ones. Thus, to say that all sins, crimes, and moral wrongs are merely due to human ignorance or the taboos of a local community (numbers 1 and 3) is erroneous, for there are more presuppositions which must be made to account for the higher (or baser) violations. Such reductionism, though invalid and dangerous like all misrepresentations, has nevertheless a central truth: even number 8, sacrilege, must assume the same presuppositions as 1 and 2.

1. *Error*	A purely epistemic misjudgment. We say: I did not realize what was going on.	The sole presupposition here is the finitude of our knowledge.
2. *Mistake*	An error with practical, unwanted consequences.	We assume that our actions have consequences.
3. *Violation*	The breaking of a purely local and utilitarian maxim of prudence: don't pour steaming water in a cold glass.	We assume the virtue of prudence and the usefulness of guidelines.
4. *Moral Wrong*	An action which ought not to be done is done anyway, and censure necessarily follows.	We assume the reality of the moral law and our own responsibility.
5. *Crime*	An action which entails sanctions by the government.	We assume the existence of a society governed by laws.
6. *Sin*	An action which offends God or which violates the precepts of divinity.	One must assume that a God or gods exist.
7. *Profanation*	A violation of spiritual values.	One must assume the reality of the realm of spirit.
8. *Sacrilege*	A special kind of sin in which what is holy or sacred is defiled.	One must assume the autonomy of the sacred; that 'sacred' is not the same as either 'spirit' or 'good'.

Attention should be drawn to the rather subtle distinction between number 7, profanation, and number 8, sacrilege. The former is a violation, not a sin, and it is against the spiritual, not the sacred. This demands an explanation of the distinction between 'spiritual' and 'sacred'. This distinction deserves greater analysis than the present chapter permits, and it shall be duly considered in the section on The Essence of Spirit. But briefly: *we* are spirit; what we are in awe of is the sacred. Thus, offences against the former are far less serious than offences against the latter.

The point of this hierarchical list, however, is to reveal just what we mean by calling presumption and despair sins, and not merely vices or moral wrongs. They are morally wrong, since the higher-ranking violations include all presuppositions of the lower ranks, but they are much more. They offend the divine order. Partly because they usurp the divinity: i.e., these sins assume that man is god. But they are sins also because they are based on a misunderstanding of our spiritual relationship to the divinity or to God: we do not have *knowledge* or *certainty* about such things. Thus, hope is a virtue, and it is entailed in our special predicate of redemption.

For the saint, of course, rapture and redemption become fused: to be rapt is to be redeemed. This is not presumption, for in rapture one acknowledges the brilliance of the Now. As Auden says, in his poem describing carnal rapture: "we find our mortal world enough." Rapture, as a predicate of spirit, enthralls us as willing slaves to the beauty of our beloved; redemption is the realization that such beauty, in redeeming, is beyond us and must, therefore, in part, be bestowed as grace.

8

Adventure, Humor, and Nobility

ADVENTURE

To understand adventure as a predicate of spirit, a distinction must be made between the popular, everyday sense of adventure—that is, the pleasure one takes in new experiences and the delight in confronting danger—and the deeper existential sense of adventure, which means letting the world influence us as the ultimate ground of our meaning. The popular or everyday view is essentially one of *entertainment*, in which the excitement and danger of confronting new distractions are an escape or therapy against the jejune and boring. Having these experiences is fun; it is an activist existence rather than a reflective one. Events are there to please us.

But such a view is deeply distortive and even self-deceptive. Some adventures may indeed delight us, though usually this comes in the form of observing rather than doing. After all, being chased by thugs intent on mayhem, or escaping by a narrow margin the fangs of a crocodile in some jungle mishap may delight the viewer of a videoscreen, but for the participant it is usually terrifying. But even if one realizes that adventure in fiction is more delightful than adventure in life, the ordinary notion of adventure is dangerously deceptive. The youth entering into the world of adventure feels that experiences are his privilege, that they come like gifts, as gratuities from some youth-favoring fate, which are pocketed as extras, like tips for the good-looking waiter. Above all they are events that happen *for* him rather than *to* him; they are there to entertain, not to *alter* him or who he is. In this the youth is woefully deluded. Experiences have an au-

155

thority far greater than images on a videoscreen: they are about *us* and not merely about our perceptions of them. Unless we are willing to accept the influence and the power of experience—especially if it is a perilous or demanding experience, which is what adventure seems to mean—we shall be overcome, rather than entertained, by it.

Adventure is impossible without courage; otherwise it is not a true adventure but a form of entertainment or distraction. But what *is* adventure, especially as we are considering it an existential predicate of spirit? Fundamentally, it is simply this: that the world has more to offer and tell me than I have to tell or offer the world; the world is there to be studied and to learn from, not to use or take advantage of. It is a resource of things great and meaningful as long as I am open to them and always, always fascinating.

"The world has more to offer and tell me than I have to tell and offer the world." What are the implications of this? We can almost divide people into two groups: those who seek to impress upon the world their views of things and those who confront the world as a resource of possibilities not yet comprehended or confronted. It is when we contrast these two 'types' that we see the true import of this curious definition. For indeed, many are the nonadventurous sort: that is, they believe they already understand the world, at least its basic structure. There are delights to be taken, perhaps, and even misfortunes to endure, but the nonadventurer fundamentally expects no surprises, and the reason is not psychological dullness, but a sense that one knows what the world is all about. Such people may be quite content with what they know about the world, or they may try to influence the world to their own advantage. What they do *not* expect is that the world may offer them something magnificent or even horrific. After all, the stable, comfortable, identifiable world we are accustomed to is at least safe.

There are those who see the world as theirs—as a reservoir of opportunities to be taken, conquered, mastered, and influenced. These are the ones who run the organizations, who control and influence, using their skill and ruthless insight to manipulate events and people to their own advantage. To categorize these manipulators as 'adventurous' is to abuse the term.

They are antiadventure, for they expect nothing new, nothing altering or redemptive from the world. They may be powerful, they make evoke envy from the less successful, they may even be beneficial to society, but they are not adventurous. To be adventurous one must respect the future as unknowable and as a source of the unfamiliar, a willingness to be fundamentally, profoundly, and basically altered or changed by what is spectacular or enormous. The common—the nonadventurers—do not believe in the magnificent, and they are sure tomorrow will be very similar to yesterday, particularly as regards their own meaning. They are who they are and will never change.

But spiritual adventurers are spiritual in part because they are open to being profoundly changed. This is not optimism, for to be open is also to be vulnerable. The virtue of trust may be required, but spirit is not always trustful. But whether fearfully or eagerly, persons of spirit nevertheless see the future, and indeed the world, as offering more than they can offer it.

(A remark might be inserted here with regard to philosophy itself in this regard. One of the more distressing aspects of the profession is to see those for whom the world is a closed book, neatly categorized by some system or pattern of explanation. No truly great philosopher presents his 'system' as one which permits of no development or change. Indeed, the greatest of the thinkers, starting with Socrates, seem to possess this wonder, and openness for the multiprismed light of truth, seeking ever deeper and profounder truths because they acknowledge their own ignorance and hence the absolute need for 'openness'. In this sense, there can be no truth without adventure. Philosophy itself is an adventure in truth; it is not a storehouse of undiscovered facts, but a way of being that is ready for the world to reveal itself further and anew.)

It may be that only a few people are adventurous. But adventure is a prerequisite for spirit if for no other reason than it makes the world *matter*, and, as a part of this ever-new world, we ourselves matter.

Our earlier distinction between 'spirited' and 'spiritual' takes on special meaning here. There is little difficulty in seeing that the 'spirited' have adventure. After all, it was Plato's warriors who were representative of spirit in his account of the tripartite soul in the *Republic*, and few are as adventurous as warriors. But the 'spiritual' are even more adventurous, since they accept the richness of possibilities, including the darkest agonies of the soul, as ever a source of learning and instruction. For them the world is a source of meaning and always a resource of wonder. The world *changes* them because they seek the newness of meaning, even if this newness is nothing more than a deeper understanding of eternally true realities. But how is it possible for those of spirit to let the world alter them, or to learn ever new things from the world?

The answer is listening. The spiritual listen. Indeed, listening is a primary modality of all spirit. The more I involve myself with the business of daily noise and action, the less I can hear. For the modern, frantic busybody, the turmoil and noise of the everyday world simply eclipses the silence necessary for listening. Indeed, the nonspiritual cannot even listen to their own prattle: they are so ready to *speak* that 'listening' becomes nothing more than waiting for an opportunity to break in on the conversation and contribute more noise. There are too many speakers, not enough listeners.

But to whom, or what, do the spiritual listen? There are many voices which speak, sing, whisper, but rarely shout, to the spiritual. There is the voice of conscience, the voice of memory, the voice of duty, the voice of beauty; and in the stillest moment of all, there may be the voice of God. And what these voices reveal is the adventure of being authentic to one's spiritual nature. If we are without spirit, i.e., if we are nothing but highly complex mechanisms, then indeed all events happen *for* us, nothing can really alter who we are. We are machines. The perfect psychologist can remove any impairment to this machine so that it will run smoothly; indeed any alteration or change is seen as an aberration or distortion. But if I have spirit, or better, if I *am* spirit; then I can be fundamentally changed by experiences and events which happen *to* me and not merely *for* me.

This emphasis upon silence does not imply that contemplative spirituality is the only or even the best modality. But it does suggest that a willingness to let the world *be*, to listen, to receive, to be guided rather than to wander aimlessly about, is an essential part of spirit. The spiritual are rarely bored, for the reason

that they do not see the events of the world as essentially entertaining, but as genuine adventures, i.e., things that can and do
alter their existence. If the world's events are but entertainments,
then when the events seem irrelevant or idle, boredom becomes
inevitable. (Profound boredom can, of course, like profound disgust, awaken a sense that there *must* be something more to us
than membership in an audience.)

This rather ephemeral notion of existential adventure may
perhaps be clarified somewhat by contrasting two phenomenological pictures which reveal ways of being lacking in this openness or newness.

The Tourist

Why has this notion, this term 'tourist', been treated with
such contempt? Surely there is nothing unworthy about traveling
to new places and delighting in the art, architecture, and people
of another land. To see that magnificent temple, the Parthenon,
glowing on that lofty ridge above Athens deserves to be included
among the world's great experiences; or to stand before the
statue of David in the Uffizi Gallery in Florence is a privilege of
overwhelming beauty. If these are the things that tourists do,
why does the term imply deprecation? Yet there can be no doubt
that there is something belittling about being called a tourist.
"Oh, he's just a tourist" is the fundamental designation of unimportance, as if there were simply nothing worthy of consideration. In part, of course, the deprecation is due to the fact that
the tourist is merely outside, so to speak, looking in, not participating in what is the genuine worth of a land or place. But there
is more: surely there is something rather repulsive in the image
of a tour bus, carrying neck-stretching, weary observers about,
while they are informed in toneless amplification of the chrono-
logical trivia of the passing scene; or the image of a loud, impe-
rious midwesterner with camera and sunglasses gathering his
sunburnt family about him urging them to hurry up and get
their look at the Eiffel Tower. These are, to be sure, caricatures,
but they are helpful in isolating something very important. We
should perhaps distinguish a 'tourist' from a 'visitor', lest in in-

dicting the former we also tar the innocent. Not every tourist is a 'tourist'.

There can be no doubt that one feels genuine insult when one is observed like an animal in a zoo. 'If you look to your left, you will see a typical American, *homo americanus in sui loco*, performing his strange ritual of driving his huge automobile two blocks to the supermarket.' Safely behind the tinted panes of the bus windows, the eyes stare and the jaws gape as the tourist responds to the entertainment of seeing 'the real thing'. We are not specimens to be observed, we are people who matter, and this is why the tourist offends us. Unlike the genuine visitor who has come to our shores to share our life with us, the tourist has come merely to look at us and be entertained by this display.

Tourists often seem never to have left their homeland. The stereotype is of the American in Europe who eats at American restaurants, speaks only with his fellow American tourists, goes to the American bar for his drinks, and clicks his American camera (made in Japan) at everything he does not see. I once saw an American group of seven, apparently a family, all standing in front of St. Peter's Basilica, all of them taking pictures of the same building from the same spot. They did not even place one or two of their group in front of the building to identify their own presence. They went to a stall selling picture postcards and bought several cards of the same church, taken by a professional, to take home with them as mementos. They then left without entering the cathedral. One can image them later looking at seven badly focused pictures of this wonder, and saying, 'I was there'; but of course they were not *there* at all. They had never left America; it was surrounding them with the protection of a huge bubble of transparent plastic and piped in American air. What is offensive about this? It is not only that the tourist offends the locals by treating them as specimens, it is also the reverse, that tourists reveal themselves as merely observers, and hence they in turn are dealt with solely on an impersonal level. Such tourists will never be profoundly altered by their visitation; it will not, in any real sense, *matter*. But of course, a visit to Europe (or Japan or Africa) *ought* to matter. To see is not to be.

There is an academic version of the tourist: the cultural anthropologist who visits a primitive tribe merely to collect data.

Contrast this figure with the missionary. They both come from an advanced society and are strangers in an alien, primitive one. But the first has come to see, the second has come to change and be changed. The first is there because these people are different, the second is there because they are the same. The first sees the people he observes as specimens, the second as souls to be saved. But, one objects: surely the anthropologist is better than the missionary; the former respects the primitive's culture; he does not want to change it. The latter wants to destroy what is unique by converting them to a religion which is not theirs. Perhaps. But the missionary maintains that these aborigines have souls, and if they do have souls, and if that knowledge will help them achieve greater dignity, then the missionary is doing them a service. At least he accepts them as meaningful and not as specimens.

A few years ago the academy was astir in controversy over the television cameraman who had simply taped the self-immolation of a man as he poured kerosene over himself and lit it, going to gruesome death in a burst of flame. The argument was whether newsmen are there merely to record things, and so should not interfere, or should they concern themselves with basic duties to fellow human beings? The anthropologist and the missionary reveal the same duality; and on a more mundane level, the difference between the visitor and the tourist tells us about the same important distinction. In the existential sense, the tourist is a nonadventurer, the visitor is an adventurer. The one merely sees for the entertainment taken in observation; the other lives with what is new and strange and hence can be altered by it. There is much more to be learned in these contrasts, but it is sufficient here to leave it at this bald depiction of the difference.

The Ideologue

The Marxist who sees the entire history of our species as the struggle between the economically oppressed and the privileged few, some metaphysical feminists who read the rich tales of our ancestors as nothing but the oppression of one sex over the other, the National Socialist who reads the same history and sees the emergence of a new and superior racial hegemony are alike in that their ideological bias limits their appreciation of learning. There are many other things despicable about any and all ideologues, especially the moral deficiencies they manifest, but the present concern is simply with this analysis of the ideologue as one who is incapable of true adventure.

An ideologue may, of course, do many interesting things; he may even enjoy some of his activities and take pleasure in the anticipation of events. But fundamentally, as an ideologue, he is so limited in *being*, that the singlemindedness of his perception of the world resists any genuine learning. Karl Popper has pointed out that the political ideologue cannot accept the possibility of being falsified, and hence his view cannot be accepted. To be acceptable to our rational canons the principle of falsifiability must apply: what cannot in principle be falsified cannot really be true, either. This insight is sound, I think; but for the existential thinker it has a somewhat broader application: the ideologue cannot accept being *other* than he is. Nothing will change him, especially not the world. This is why, I believe, most ideologues are such grim and unsmiling types: they cannot accept grace or bestowals, they will not experience anything unexpected or novel, they do not allow the world to tell about itself, for they believe they already know.

There is no intent here to suggest a fetish for the unfamiliar. Constancy is a virtue, and a bold sense of one's self is essential for authentic existence. Indeed, one form of ideology is the worship of the new. Some of our contemporary aesthetics suffer greatly from this adulation of the untried. When artists are urged to 'create something new' at the expense of refining or achieving excellence, when school children are given high marks for being 'original' and not taught to spell correctly or to write grammatically, we know that serious trouble lurks ahead for the human race. Such misguided aesthetics and education is, indeed, a manifestation of antilearning. The worst of these ideologues do not want to *learn*, for that takes work; it requires a certain respect for what is already there. But to 'create freely' is easy, spontaneous, undisciplined, and fun. But of course learning is precisely the realization that the world has something to offer, that it is worthwhile to study the familiar and discover the richness of the real. Newness grounded in the world is *learning* and is

a predicate of spirit; but newness projected from one's own speculation, as in so-called 'artistic creativity' is mere self-indulgence,
and is not spirit but idleness. 'Creativity' in the narrow ideological sense closes off the world as a source of meaning and truth; it
ranks one's private perception above truth. Learning is far nobler than teaching, which is why genuine education is really
shared learning rather than instruction. To learn is to submit to
the authority of the world as it is and may provide genuine creativity as a response, but to play on the surface is to forfeit all
concern with excellence and truth, and hence is not to create at
all. Thus, ideologues, in adopting their speculative view of how
we ought to be, overlook entirely whatever truth there is to be
found in who we really are. All true ideologies are revolutionary;
they abandon the canons of evaluation and moral restraint
learned in the long course of our history, and replace them with
an ungrounded future. But in doing this they close off authentic
adventure.

   These two descriptions of the tourist and the ideologue reveal what is so fundamental about the possibility of spiritual adventure. To be spirit is to be open to the possibilities that change
us. To this extent, spiritual adventure entails a sense of *amor fati*,
and without some love of fate, spirit is impossible.

HUMOR

   It is curious that so few thinkers, even the most brilliant, are
anywhere near adequate when they attempt to write on humor.
Partly, I suppose, it is because the seriousness of philosophical
inquiry seems inconsistent with the light-heartedness requisite
for laughter. There are not many funny philosophers. Although
when they write about laughter, they are often so dreadful they
become funny in an unflattering way. Consider Descartes's definition of laughter found in *The Passions of the Soul*, Article
CXXIV:

> Laughter consists in the fact that the blood, which proceeds from
> the right orifice on the heart by the arterial vein, inflating the
> lungs suddenly and repeatedly, causes the air which they contain
> to be constrained to pass out from them with an impetus by the

windpipe, where it forms an inarticulate and explosive utterance; and the lungs in expanding equally with the air as it rushes out, set in motion all the muscles of the diaphragm from the chest to the neck, by which means they cause motion in the facial muscles, which have a certain connection with them. And it is just this action of the face with this articulate and explosive voice that we call laughter. (Haldare/Ross translation)

In reading this one is either moved to laughter or is fearful of never laughing again. Few examples show as eloquently as this the inadequacy of a purely mechanistic explanation for the things of spirit. Nowhere does Descartes even suggest there might be a special kind of awareness or surprise to the intellect that evokes such a curious response. This is definitely *not* the kind of thing we want to know when we ask about the nature of laughter or humor. It is comical in its absurdity.

But if a purely mechanistic account of laughter is inadequate to explain humor, then how can we approach this mysterious faculty that is so common, so intimate, so personal, that it seems to escape identification? There are several such "passions of the soul," as Descartes calls them, which seem forever shrouded in noncomprehension and remain only as manifestations of our ignorance. Sleep, for example, is as strange a phenomenon as there is, yet is a fairly common blessing shared by most everyone. Insomnia is a wretched curse so deeply hated that its opposite, sleep, seems a gift of rare grace. Yet do we understand sleep at all? How can a conscious being suspend his awareness in such an untroubled and mystifying way? Yet sleep, like humor, is as ubiquitous as the human species. So too is forgetting and recall mysterious: how can we forget a person's name, know we should remember, and then through some seemingly magical way, suddenly recall the correct name? What is going on? But surely one of the most remarkable human phenomenon is that of humor and the laughter that results from it. How are we to understand humor?

That humor and the response of laughter belongs to the world of spirit is as obvious as the above mechanistic description is false. Thus, if humor is a characteristic of spirit—for they say animals do not laugh—its explanation must be grounded in our understanding of spirit. So, we now can ask: what is the nature of our spirit which grounds our humor?

Not all laughter is grounded in humor; or rather, one's 'sense of humor' can be of several types, only a few of which are genuinely humorous in the spiritual sense. One can laugh *at* another's misery, for example, which seems a mere extension of cruelty. Or one can laugh wildly or madly, which seems a mere expression of instability. Or one can be overcome by an attack of the 'giggles', expressing one's lack of self-control. We sometimes laugh when we are ashamed, or frightened, or nervous, or tense. In these cases, laughter seems little more than a release from tension, and need not be thought of as a response to what is amusing or even funny. But there is also what might be called 'warm humor' or even *true* humor, in which the universality of human foolishness is fondly appreciated and acknowledged as one's own. It is this last type which deserves our attention as an essential predicate of spirit.

English-speaking nations seem to possess an especially wondrous sense of the humorous, and in part this is due to the titanic gift of William Shakespeare. This great dramatic poet has created the richest kind of humor possible in his masterful comedies. What happens when we laugh at Orlando marring the trees of the forest of Arden with silly love-poems to his beloved? ("Sweetest nut hath sourest rind; such a nut is Rosalind.") Or who can compare with the simple silliness of Bottom the Weaver, saying everything incorrectly but earnestly? ("The ear of man hath not seen, nor the eye of man heard . . .") Even the winsome cowardice of Falstaff as he spurns 'honor' seems warm and gentle. Somehow we seem to be laughing with rather than at; or perhaps we are laughing at our own foolishness, which is the best kind of laughter there is. There is also British wit, which seems the best in the world, which delights as it stings, and whose sparkle takes all resentment away by its sheer cleverness.

Shakespearean humor is profoundly Christian humor: it is the warm and yet startling realization of our own beloved foolishness. It makes us laugh because we acknowledge our finitude and feel good because of it. This is the humor of the spirit. It can be bawdy, touching, cathartic, gentle, and humbling: but it is always elevating. Somehow, through his genius, Shakespeare makes us glad we are fools. Fond fools, trusting in a generous forgiveness, delighting in our weaknesses and our foibles, always ready to approve of the antics of even greater fools whom we have grown to like or even love on the stage, but fools all the same. But why do we laugh at foolishness? Why do we favor so that which, by stern prudence, we should condemn? The question deserves more than the mechanistic account of Descartes. It deserves more than the transcendental account given by Kant in the *Critique of Judgment*. (Kant seems to account for laughter by the element of intellectual surprise at the unintelligible.) But it is a risky business to probe into this wonderful human mystery, since such great men have failed. Nevertheless, we are, perforce, required to give it serious attention.

Kant is surely correct in his essential insight: the nature of humor and its consequence, laughter, has to do with our being rational; and indeed, what makes us laugh is the unfamiliar violation of our expectations as to rational behavior. But not all violations of reason produce laughter, and humor itself is far richer than the mere outburst of uncontrolled expulsions of air. One can begin the inquiry into this familiar mystery by reflecting on what it is that makes us laugh. When properly conceived, we laugh at human foolishness, either our own or of those we love, in which case the laughter is redemptive; or we laugh at the foolishness of others, in which case we are contemptuous or derisive. So, what then is foolishness?

In the various attempts to isolate the 'essence' of man—an enterprise now frowned on by all post-Wittgensteinians as outdated and useless—we find such ingenuous attempts as man the thinking animal, man the laughing animal, man the willing animal, etc. But surely some attention should be given to the suggestion that man is the foolish animal. For only men are fools, the beasts may be ignorant, savage, dumb, and nonartistic, but they cannot be *foolish*, for to be a fool assumes that one can—and ought to be—wise, but is lacking in this virtue. Indeed, among the unfortunates of our own species we consider it unmannerly to laugh at true simpletons, just because there is no expectation of wise decorum. Thus, to be a fool is to fail at what is so fundamental about who we are: capable of reasoned and enlightened behavior. There is a tremendous difference, of course, in being foolish and being fooled, and still another difference between these and being made a fool of. But foolishness is not merely the violation of rationality: so too is error, immorality, and simple ignorance, but none of these are necessarily foolish. There seems to be a kind of aesthetic element to foolishness; i.e., the fool *appears* absurd, and our recognition of the incongruity of what we ought to be and the ribald manifestation of the opposite entertains us as onlookers. It is the *presentation* of our foolishness that evokes laughter.

We are, however, profoundly foolish, and never so much so as when we are intent on being proper and dignified. Foolishness is different from other violations of the reasonable in that it seems an entirely existential characteristic: I misjudge in error, I offend in wrongdoing, I miscalculate in assessing prudential odds, but I simply *am* foolish, and this brings foolishness directly before us as an indictment of who we *are*, not merely of what we have done. I may be contrite or at least guilty when I offend the moral law; I may be confused and bewildered when I miscalculate evidence and hence misjudge the facts, but I am sheepish and belittled when I reveal my foolishness.

Two sources of foolisheness must be contrasted. The first is history; the second is comedy. The former is nonspiritual, almost atheistic in its tone; the latter is divine. History, whether art or science, is a source of knowledge, usually knowledge of human frailty and outrageous incompetence. But comedy is the celebration of foolishness. In history, the distance provided by time allows us to reflect on the foolishness, especially of those in high places, and may evoke sadness or merriment. Foolishness by our contemporary leaders evokes chagrin and outrage, but when the history book cushions us from the disaster by placing the intervention of years between us and the failure, we simply shake our heads sadly at the foolishness of those who lived in the past. One of the reasons why many are inclined to accept some sort of determinism in history, whether it be dialectical (which is absurd) or simply the steady improvement of the human condition by a metaphysics of progress (which is outrageous) or the unfolding of the will of God (which is sacrilegious), rests on the very foolishness of the central actors. Surely the likes of *these* cannot account for our story. How can we grasp the total wretchedness of almost all great men, the supreme weakness of the fools who allow the mighty to abuse their power, or the hopeless self-deceit of those who have heretofore guided our destinies? Of course, from the vantage of hindsight, we *know* that the silly diplomatic moves in early 1914 were tragically foolish, that Napoleon ought not to have been sucked in by the Russians, that the French ought not to have let Hitler bluff his way into the Rhineland. And from this perspective of hindsight, the tragedy seems all the more grotesque, because just a little prudence would have avoided the cataclysmic eruption of so much senseless suffering. Thus, foolishness and not fate or inevitability is the true guide to history; were we elevated to sufficient height there would be no comedy quite as outrageous as the one we, the species mankind, have unfolded as our story.

But in comedy, the distance is not the past but the stage. And, because of the magic of this art, the same foolishness which makes history so sad makes the art of comedy the source of laughter. Of course, we laugh at many things besides formal comedies, but the comedy, especially in the hands of the true artists, seems peculiarly well designed as an objective entity to be studied as a source of our understanding the nature of humor. After all, the *object* of the comic artist is the human fool; as the antics of the fool on the stage evoke our laughter and hence reveal our humor, so the study of how the comedy does this should reveal at least a key to the mystery.

Shakespeare may be the greatest comedian of all time; certainly no other artist excels him in the genre. But there is a peculiarity about his comedies: they all seem to be romantic comedies; that is, they are all about lovers. This may be simply due to the fact that lovers are just more foolish than others, but there may be a more profound reason. It is at least a suggestion which is worthy of consideration: perhaps there is a link between humor and love.

One of the essential Socratic teachings about love, as found in Plato's two dialogues, the *Symposium* and *Phaedrus,* is the notion that love idealizes. That is, under the influence of the erotic demiurge, the soul is lifted to the level of universality (the Forms). Thus, when we see our beloved smile, we see it as the paradigm of all smiles; from that perfection we learn what smiling means. When our beloved sighs, we learn the perfect form (or universal meaning) of sighing. Indeed, through the eyes of eros the beloved becomes the paradigm which allows the soul to contemplate the universal form or meaning of things. In the *Phaedrus*, Socrates suggests that the soul, lit by the fire of eros, mounts up to the heights; the heat makes the soul sprout wings which allow it to soar to the level of universal or formal reality. Thus, human love becomes curiously epistemic: it *teaches* us to see things in their universal, or rational, form. In the *Symposium* the love of one body soon is replaced by the love of many bodies, and then this is replaced by the love of souls, until finally the soul in love reaches the height of passion in which beauty itself is grasped in its essence. We can take this remarkable instruction from Socratic eros and recognize its truth: in love, the soul begins with the particular, mounts through the intervening levels of meaning, and leaps toward the rational and the universal. This is what ideality means, to go from the concrete particular to the universal reality.

But if love is the mounting from the particular to the universal, how can we account for the opposite: the sudden departure from universal reason to the brute particularity of the individual? Is this not laughter, under the influence of the comedic muse? In humor, do we not suddenly drop from the reverential universal to the bumptious concrete and hence less rational? Humor is simply love turned upside down. In love the lover, through eros, goes from the particular (the sensuous) to the universal (the rational); in humor, the laughter goes from the universal and rational to the particular and sensuous. The fall from the heights takes our breath away, and this sudden loss of breath is laughter. But the form is still the ideality of eros.

It is a peculiarity that the greatest dramatist and the finest poet of any language should almost always place his love stories in comedies. As I noted above, the two love tragedies, *Romeo and Juliet* and *Antony and Cleopatra*, are not primarily about love as such but in the former case about fate and in the latter case about love versus duty. But in comedies love is the central theme and it is almost always wondrously funny. Indeed, in many of the plays, but particularly *Midsummer Night's Dream*, the point is not even who loves whom, for that is the tangle of merriment that makes the play so delightful, but simply that we should love at all. That there should be magic potions squeezed onto the eyes so that the anointed will fall in love with whatever they first see upon awaking is outrageous to one who takes loving a particular person seriously. Yet, love is not abused by these hijinks; rather it is enhanced. But why treat love always in comedic fashion? If the above paragraph is even close to the truth, the answer is obvious. Humor is inverted love; thus, love is best displayed as art when presented as a comedy. Further, both humor and young love are bright things, and they seem to belong together. When one leaves a performance of *As You Like It,* the title speaks the mood. This is how we like it. Love is warm, humorous, human, foolish, and wonderful. The laughter evoked by these absolutely precious plays is a laughter based on a sincere reverence for love, for love alone makes foolishness acceptable. (The etymology of 'comedy', after all, is from Greek 'song of the fool').

Humor is, then, the acceptance of foolishness or, if you will, particularity, under the influence of the Form of love. We laugh because our reason has been usurped by the foolish, but since it is on the ideality of loving, the rupture brings us delight, not chagrin. If 'adventure' is seen as the love of Fate, then humor is seen as the love of the foolish. But we can love foolishness only in the warmth allowed by ideality, which is erotic loving.

If there are saints, and if they do love their gods or God, then they must also have humor. Not the contemptuous humor which finds the foolish disdainful and laughs in derision, but the warm humor which finds the foolish, as the fall from the rational, beloved. To love our own foolishness is the essence of humor; all other forms of laughter, such as the derisive and the contemptuous, are deviant forms of the original laughter, which is the outburst of reason being evacuated by the fool down the ladder of love. In ideality the lover sees his beloved in universal terms, but in comedy, it is the opposite: Orlando loves Rosalind, but Rosalind is particular and scheming, indeed slightly devilish; Orlando, drunk by his erotic passion, plays the fool, and yet we love them both. Ordinarily foolishness must be condemned by the sober dictates of reason, but *this* kind of foolishness, love-foolishness, is the rebellious child of reason and so is not condemned at all but celebrated.

Humor, then, is love in its inversion. Because of this, in humor we find ourselves modest and outrageous, humble and haughty, dazzled and blind, wild and tame. Humor forgives all, it lifts the soul to heights just because it is an acceptance of our finitude. It is a link between our basic appetites on the one hand and our loftiest ideals on the other. And because it *is* a link, though an inverted one, between reason and flesh, between mind and body, between the high and the low, it is spirit.

To test this, albeit indirectly, consider the various clowns in Shakespeare's comedies, such as Bottom and his crew, or the Dogberry constabulary, or Trinculo and Stefano. Their antics would be but vulgar farce if they were removed from the love story that gives them their profundity. As Bottom's crew performs the comical tragedy of Pyramus and Thisby, our laughter is not the mere hilarity of the outrageous, it is the warm and deep humor which is eternal. We know they are honest, good, warm-hearted fools; and the lovers, watching, represent us, the audience: this gives the wild, erratic silliness a wonderful glow; it teaches us to laugh heartily and lovingly; indeed, it teaches us the essence of laughter itself: beloved foolishness, the child of rational ideality, upsetting the order of things. How could we not laugh at this? How could we not celebrate this foolishness, since it tells us so much about who we are? Humor is thus an essential predicate of spirit: it shows us how to celebrate our own foolishness. Without this, we would be in the thrall of despair; for if we cannot laugh at our foolishness because we are lovers, then we can only weep bitterly at our irrationality. We have already seen that joy is necessarily a spiritual and not a physical passion. True humor cannot be otherwise.

NOBILITY

The final predicate of spirit is in a way the culmination of the other nine. Early in the current of this extended description, with the second predicate, importance, it was noted that the spiritual seek to achieve meaning: i.e., they are important. Both the ground and the consequence of that importance is the predicate of nobility. The noble are radiant, important, worshipful, self-sacrificing, respectful of mystery, enrapt by beauty, ready for redemption, adventurous, and humorous. The truly noble stand out as paradigms of human existence, manifesting genuine dignity and recognizing the worth of others. The modern world has almost forgotten how to use this term: whom do we today identify as noble? Yet, it is a term we all recognize and usually reserve its usage for the rare and magnificent among us.

To be noble usually means being outstanding in character, radiating the moral loftiness and dignity that is inherent in humanity but manifest only in the few. The etymologists tell us that the term comes from 'know' (or 'gno-' in the Greek derivatives); hence it is equated with all that is special and significant about the knowing species, humanity. It also suggests that the truly noble are those who have knowledge, but of a special sort. They know what and how to be; they know who they are. The derivation from 'knowledge' in no way suggests that the term refers to the encyclopedic or the academic; indeed the noble are often contrasted with the merely erudite.

Nietzsche, in his curious masterwork *The Genealogy of Morals,* argues that the noble-ignoble distinction is actually prior to and is the source of the later terms, good, bad, and evil. One is first noble, and then *because* one is noble, one does what is good. Whether or not Nietzsche is correct in his analysis there can be no doubt that 'nobility' has this existential priority to moral goodness. In some usages the term 'noble' seems almost to be equated with 'spiritual', for both terms suggest a superiority to and indifference toward the base, the common, and the earthly. Both terms also suggest loftiness of rank, regardless of how that rank is established. We look up to the noble, not because we fear them, but because they demand respect and because they illuminate their existential worth. Nobility seems to be a quality of character, so that it is not achieved by dint of many good works; one does not *do* the noble, one *is* noble. Superiority of demeanor, self-worth, and existential status seem the qualities best describing the noble; but in addition is the awareness of one's superiority and the grace not to abuse such honor. There is, in the noble, a pride about one's being who one is, but there is no arrogance.

But herein lies the final snag, for nothing is without struggle or torment in this inquiry. The spiritual are noble and the noble are proud; and so it would seem the spiritual are proud.

But is not pride, at least in the Christian ethic, the supreme source of evil? Did not Satan fall because of pride? Or, if one is suspect of remaining too close to our own tradition, do not the Greek tragedians build their magnificent dramas around the polarities of *hubris* (pride) and *sophrosone* (accepting one's place; temperance)? Thus, if one takes the moral interpretation of tragedy, once again the greatest ill is *hubris*, that disease of greatness which all magnificent heros seem to possess within them like a festering wound or cancer. "Such a man I do not want under my roof, such a one I do not want near my hearth," Chorus says in one of the most famous lines in all tragedy, from *Antigone*. The great ones seem to attract hubris the way honey does flies. And hubris is what brings a man down. Hence it is a vice, not a virtue. And surely the Christian saints were said to be *humble,* not proud. So how can they be noble, if nobility entails a conscious awareness of one's superiority?

This is a profound paradox of judgment. On the one hand, nothing offends us so much as the braggart, the arrogant, haughty overachiever who, even when accomplishing amazing feats, is so prolific in self-praise there seems to be no need or inclination for others to add to it. On the other hand, few things offend us as the mousey, meek, frightened nay-sayers whose cowardly self-deprecation and fawning sycophancy inspires in us a belief in the very baseness they affirm about themselves. Without pride, one is nothing; with it, one is too much.

This dilemma cannot be resolved by Aristotle's appeal to the golden mean. We cannot defuse the sparkle by saying one should have some pride but not too much. I simply cannot have too much pride when my own dignity is threatened and the dignity of those who belong to me. How much pride should a warrior have? A leader of men or nations? A champion of justice? Who would provide a measuring stick for nobility or courage? But is not pride the very foundation of both? To be sure, one can and must distinguish between pride and arrogance; but arrogance is simply bad manners, whereas pride is a fundamental quality of character.

A few years ago I was offering a course in philosophy at the state maximum-security penitentiary, for the in-house educational program for prisoners. Somewhat uneasy on my first visit,

I walked down the long, grim corridors and I noted the demeanor of the men about me. Some appeared sullen, of course, some angry, a few seething with outrage, some seemed terrified. Most, however, seemed simply stupeified into a zombielike automation. The guard who was accompanying me saw my interest and made this remark: "There are two kinds of men in here: those who meekly submit to the system and merely wait, and those who are proud. I don't like the proud ones; they give us all the trouble." But as we observed the vast numbers of shuffling, downcast men, one could not but wonder if the trouble was not worth it in the end. To live with some dignity in a prison requires leonine pride. There, to survive at all as a man, one needed as much pride as was possible to develop or achieve. Sometimes the demands on a convict's pride were so enormous as to be literally awesome. In the prisons gangs thrive and racial tensions mushroom, and even the seemingly petty identities of place of birth, accent, and type of crime establish bases for identity, for belonging to something that matters, for pride in being someone. Of course the guard was, perforce, wary of these men. But when one saw the proud prisoners and then the submissive ones, who were by far the larger number, the choice was clear. Racism and gang-identification are genuine evils, but they are sources of meaning, and in a place where the meaningless looms as vast, enclosing walls, pride in who one is matters as much as survival itself. But one cannot kill the anger without wounding the pride, and when pride is scarred, so is self-respect. Do we really consider humility or meekness to be virtues when the greatest threat of all is the eclipse of our own meaning?

One is tempted to resolve this by semantics. The pride that 'goeth before the fall' is simply not the same thing as the pride one must have in oneself and one's nation in order to live decently and with respect. They are just two different things, and perhaps there ought to be two different words, good pride and bad pride. But the Greek tragedians and the Christian moralists and the existential philosophers all support the opposite view: pride is pride, and distinctions created to resolve a problem on a purely semantic level provide only semantic solutions. The fierce, angry pride of a caged youth may be more threatening and violent than the dignified pride of a noble leader, but the inner quality is the same: I matter, and being true to who I am is a supreme duty. I know it is possible for me to become base and defiled—look about me and see the horde—but I shall not yield that integrity which is mine, for I am *proud*.

There can be no greatness without pride; but without pride there is no hubris, and no fall. To acknowledge this and bear it as a fundamental quality of who one is, is nobility. Thus, nobility is pride in being proud, and to that extent it is controlled. There simply is no resolve: the same force that drives us up to the level of dignity can drive us beyond our limits. No verbal distinctions can resolve this truth. Oddly, the awareness that one's own importance can bring one down is itself a part of pride, though it is often called humility. (Humility is one of the most tantalizing and frustrating of all virtues, for it seems to suggest one ought to debase or degrade oneself, and that is surely counterintuitive. We do not accept the obsequious self-deprecation of Uriah Heep: that cannot be a *virtue*. Perhaps genuine humility is simply a modesty in being proud. Or, it may be a recognition that ephemeral trappings of public adulation are distracting from inner worth. But humility cannot seriously mean that one tries to be *less* than one's true worth.)

The recognition that pride, as hubris, is tragic, that to elevate oneself is to prepare for the possibility of failure, is not lost on the truly noble man. Nobility is pride in existence; and with this pride comes the awareness, terrifying to all who contemplate it, that one can fail at existing. It is possible to *be* badly. But this makes *being* dangerous. To exist at all is a hazard. Not because I may one day cease to exist, but because my own existence may go astray; I may not live up to what it means to be. However, if the very meaning of existence itself is dangerous, then one who excels in being, the noble, must have courage. This special courage, the courage to be who one is and the pride one takes in excelling at being who one is, manifests itself as praiseworthy and even beautiful. The Greek term *kalos,* ordinarily translated 'beautiful', is also the term used for noble. The courage found in the recognition of one's own excellence radiates an aesthetic as well as ethical worth: we not only admire but delight in what we see.

Courage surely is essential for true nobility. But courage itself is possible only when one's own personal interests, pleasures, comforts, and desires are sacrificed for some higher worth. To put myself in danger makes sense only if there is a loftier reason for doing so than avoiding danger, otherwise it is mere foolishness. So, the courage imbedded in the noble consists in the resolute ranking of things in terms of their worth. This willingness to sacrifice the base desires for the loftier good reveals that, for the noble, not even one's own life is as important as honor. But honor here does not mean the idle praise bestowed from without; it means being true to one's own word, one's own role and calling, in short, being true to oneself.

This phrase, 'being true to oneself' is a dangerous notion because it is so easily misunderstood. To be true to oneself does *not* mean that the individual becomes the sole and determining ground of all value and truth. Nor does it in any way imply that my own particular interests, much less desires, have an authority beyond any constraint. It does not even mean that since I am *different* from everyone else, I must find out my own private rules or guidelines to govern my conduct. Quite to the contrary, 'being true to oneself' is the acceptance of universal and objective principles. I can be true to myself only if my word matters, for example, or if my obligations are acknowledged as an essential part of who I am. In Herman Melville's classic novella *Billy Budd*, Captain Vere and the members of the court-martial were all deeply revolted and disgusted by the onus that their merciless duty had put upon them. But in deciding to judge the innocent sailor as guilty of killing the master-at-arms, Claggart, they were 'being true to themselves'. It is perhaps unfortunate that this phrase, so noble in its original meaning, has become so relativistic and so excusatory in our present age. But this inquiry cannot be dissuaded from using the proper terminology merely because it has been abused by the thoughtless and the popular. Honor, itself a nonmodern term, must be seen as truth.

And so the argument finally rests on that philosophical jewel, truth. Not truth conceived as epistemic certainty but existential truth—that is *being* true to one's existence, to who one is. This is the fundamental sense of nobility: a courageous acknowledgment of the truth of one's own worth, the consequences of that worth, especially if it is superior, and the unwavering, sterling commitment to that truth which cannot be swayed by any appeal that ranks beneath it in dignity.

It is perhaps the greatest indictment of our age that 'nobility' is no longer an active, meaningful notion in our daily assessments. We can still call our heroes courageous and valiant, brave and dynamic, clever and charismatic; but whom would we ever call *noble* today? Is nobility even *possible* in an age of egalitarian justice and economic judgment? Or is it, sadly, that our only use of the term 'noble' occurs in quotations from earlier times:

> Is this the noble Moor whom our full senate
> Call all-in-all sufficient? Is this the nature
> Whom passion could not shake? whose solid virtue
> The shot of accident nor dart of chance
> Could neither graze nor pierce?
>
> (Othello, 4.1)

All the elements are there in this magnificent passage: poetry telling us exactly how we think of nobility. It is 'all-in-all suffient': passions do not shake it; the barbs of accident and chance are disarmed before it. In short, nobility is *above* these petty, base, and transient things. But 'being above', being lofty, is dangerous. All heights imply the fearful drop, the fall, the plummeting to earth, broken. But if the height here means being true, then the fall must mean: being false. So, the ignoble are those who are false to themselves, not only in self-deception but in *being* false; i.e., existing untruly, not in accord with the authentic and genuine reality that one is. It is this deep commitment to truth in the existential sense of being true that makes the noble synonymous with beauty. So once again, beauty is truth is nobility. We now can add: beauty is truth is nobility . . . is spirit.

With these ten predicates we now have a sufficient understanding of the subject to render a description. But, the analyses of these ten predicates were not carried out merely to provide a list: a table of contents would suffice for that. In the analyses each predicate was examined in terms of its existential meaning, and in the course of the description, various important characteristics develop which illuminate the question of how we think about being spirit.

The various predicates seem to present at times counterimpressions: worship and rapture, for example, seem to indicate a passive role, whereas suffering and nobility indicate a strong sense of one's own worth. But there is one thing that seems to run through all these analyses: in all cases the predicates are shown to presuppose the *autonomy* of the existential judgments which one must make in order to think coherently about spirit. The image of a sacrificial, listening sufferer acutely aware of his fallenness and urge for redemption is quite in contrast to the radiant and rapturous youth endowed with importance and nobility. Yet both pictures are a part of spirit. This of course is what is needed in a *description;* we are not reductivists, at least not at the beginning of an inquiry. In spotting these ten predicates, it is not inherent that each person of spirit possess each predicate, though most of the predicates seem to entail some awareness of the others, as worship suggests both sacrifice and redemption. But rapture, for example, even if it belongs as an essential quality in the understanding of spirit, is surely the least ubiquitous of the list. But of course, the entire purpose of making such a list, of describing in this way, is to prepare the investigation for the deeper penetrations which must now follow.

It is not enough to recognize that by spirit we mean being characterized by radiance, importance, worship, sacrificial suffering, mystery, rapture, redemption, adventure, humor, and nobility. It is necessary to begin with such a description, however, as a preparatory survey. But in this description were uncovered some rather interesting principles which will assist the attempt to isolate the essence of spirit. The inquiry itself began with a serious consideration of three rather dreadful and terrifying paradoxes: the epistemic, the metaphysical, and the ethical problems which seem to make any success a highly unsanguine hope. But the predicates themselves do much to ease the misology of the paradoxes, though the tension must remain. What does it mean to be spirit? The predicates *locate* this question, and that is crucial; but they do not satisfy. To achieve that we must now dig more deeply. And so we ask: granted that these ten predicates are an accurate description of spirit, what is it that makes them possible? How can I make rational judgments about them? What are the ultimate presuppositions? To these more challenging but no less interesting questions, we now must turn.

PART III

The Essence of Spirit

9

The Metaphysical and Ontological Presuppositions

THE METAPHYSICAL PRESUPPOSITION

Confronted with the formidable threat of misology found in the three paradoxes, and convinced of the soundness of Immanuel Kant's reasoning in *The Critique of Pure Reason* that pure speculative metaphysics simply cannot be done, one might be forgiven for trying to introduce metaphysical speculation indirectly. Now that we have accomplished a description of spirit, it may be tempting to ask: If this is what spirit is, then what must we presuppose, metaphysically, in order to ground this description in what is real? The argument would go something like this: If we can show that it is more rational to be spiritual, then we can assume that the metaphysical entities necessary for this account, such as God and soul, really do exist. But if we can show it is more rational not to be spiritual, then we can assume that soul and God are not really necessary and probably do not exist. Such thinking, though understandably attractive in our present frustration, is not only invalid, it is also beguiled. For such argumentation presupposes that what *really* matters is speculative metaphysics and the consequential priority given to the existence or nonexistence of entities. Whether an entity exists can be judged solely by our experience, and even then we are restricted to understanding such an entity as we experience it and not as it is supported by invisible powers or metaphysical substances which can only be thought, if even that. Thus we cannot sneak in the back way any metaphysical apparatus and assume that, be-

181

cause we have accomplished an ontological analysis of meaning we can thereby argue for the existence of anything whatsoever.

Nevertheless, the existential account given of the description of spirit is not without presuppositions which can indeed be isolated. These presuppositions, however, cannot determine whether any entity, be it soul, body, God, or spirit, exists. If we carry out the inquiry successfully, there should be no need to do so.

Metaphysics is the study of appearance and reality. That is, the primary concern of the metaphysician is to isolate those principles which reveal the meaning and nature of reality. He also contrasts these principles with those which illuminate the nature of how the world appears. Thus we distinguish appearance and reality; and if our analysis is even approximately correct, it is obvious that by 'reality' we cannot mean 'that which exists'. In itself, there is nothing prohibitive about making the distinction between appearance and reality; but too many thinkers, both modern and ancient, have utilized the obviously valid distinction between appearance and reality and employed the distinction as a justification for reductionism. But to distinguish appearance from reality is not to reduce appearance to reality or reality to appearance. The term 'appearance' does *not* mean the same as 'illusion'. Appearance means exactly what is says: how things appear to us: i.e., the world as the object of experience. Reality means that which grounds whatever is true. Thus our understanding of the *true* meaning of justice, for example, shows us that justice is real when we make specific judgments about individual and specific acts. Reality is also seen as 'the ground of the true' even in our ordinary experiences: we say the sentence 'This dog is brown' is true if *in reality* the dog is brown. But reality need not, indeed cannot, be restricted to entities like brown dogs which support claims about dogs being brown. Reality grounds the true in any and every use or meaning in which the term 'true' can be coherently applied. Appearance, on the other hand, means the experience of things as they happen in the world; but experience by itself obviously cannot provide us with the real, since in order for the experience to be true it must be grounded in the real.

Kant, for example, distinguishes appearance from reality in his account of the difference between what we interpret through the categories (what he calls 'phenomena') and that which grounds our understanding of the ideas (what he calls 'noumena'). This is a legitimate use of the distinction. In no way does Kant 'reduce' his phenomena to noumena, nor does he claim that the world or experience (appearance) is ever real. (Though many unsympathetic critics of Kant like to interpret his writings as saying precisely that, which then renders him vulnerable to self-contradiction. But Kant carefully avoids such silly reductionism.)

The distinction between appearance and reality must, therefore, be assiduously separated from any and all reductionism. But reductionism is precisely what many thinkers, especially mechanists, materialists, and hedonists, have in mind when they appeal to the honored and valid distinction between appearance and reality. Their argument goes something like this: all that people believe about spirit, soul, and God is merely appearance, i.e., illusion, which *in fact is really* nothing but subjective psychological reactions of fear, wonder, ignorance, and imagination. What *really* exists is nothing but matter, and by matter is meant the smallest imaginable particle functioning according to discernible laws. This view not only distinguishes appearance (belief in soul) from reality (our understanding of nuclear physics), it also *reduces* all nonphysical things to physical things or explains the nonphysical away as mere illusion, hence nothing.

There is something enormously seductive and alluring about this kind of reductionism; and we must recognize its authority on our minds. Mechanism, particularly if it is atomistic, is the fundamental, instinctive metaphysical system. Hedonism is the fundamental, instinctive ethical system. Both materialistic mechanism and selfish hedonism are extremely powerful and seductive doctrines, so overwhelming in their reductive simplicity and powerful in their allure that many thinkers seem to believe that merely by defeating them one must uncover the truth. A great deal of respect, however, must be given to both mechanism and hedonism, for they are, philosophically anyway, very often far superior in their coherence and soundness to most of their opponents in the intellectual arena. Spirit, of course, is impossible in either of them, but these powerful and almost 'natural' systems of thinking are by no means so impoverished as to be incapable of accounting for all that we have discovered up to now about the meaning of spirit. Materialistic mechanism and subjective hedonism are deeply false; but they are not easily dismissed, nor should they be.

Unfortunately, what many thinkers imagine themselves to be doing when they speak of the spiritual, is nothing else than 'invisible' mechanism or 'post-terrestial hedonism'. That is, to maintain that there exists a soul, independent of a body, but that it exists somehow 'within' a body and functions as an efficient causal agent in the operations and responses of the body, is to concede to the authority of materialism and the explanative power of mechanism. The soul is, according to this pseudo-spiritual account, really just another element of the physical, natural world, except that it is *invisible*. Such a view is hardly more sophisticated than a child's willingness to believe in invisible ghosts, tooth-fairies, and fifth-dimensional aliens because of the fun it allows the imagination. But the naivité of such a view is no barrier to its popularity. We speak of the soul being 'in' the body, without realizing that this gives the soul a very physical characteristic indeed, namely that of having a place, which is nearly the same as taking up space, which is reductionism. What *really* exists then, in their account, is what takes up space on the smallest level: the ideal 'atom' or in current terms the smallest subatomic particle. Now, just as in this room there are radio-waves that I cannot see but which nevertheless can activate the aerial and be amplified into audible sounds were I to turn on the radio, so there is a soul in the person, which, though not seen, is merely a rarefied or colorless physical entity, made up, just like our bodies, of billions of ultimate particles.

If one arranges or alters the balance or proportion of these busy and ubiquitous dots of energy, one can account for the 'soul's' guilt-feelings, love, sacrificial reverence for the divine, and even respect or disrespect for the moral law. Morality itself is merely the result of certain atomistic arrangements of primary elements, so that in the end, only matter exists, and the only explanation of events is through the mechanistic account of efficient causality. This is 'invisible mechanism' and it is as false and silly as any reductionist account, but unfortunately it also has the status of being a seemingly natural way to think.

The same can be said for hedonism, which in my view is the most powerful ethical system in the entire repertoire of human speculation. Consider a man calculating what he must do to achieve his lustful satisfaction with a reluctant woman. If he is powerful enough, and the situation sufficiently dark and isolated, he may simply rape her. If he is clever, he may seduce her. If he is rich, he may engage her in the oldest profession. But eventually he will take his pleasure one way or the other and afterwards completely forget her. We think of this as hedonistic, and it is. But consider another man. He too wants delight and pleasure. But, either because he is more calculative or because he is dismally meek, he estimates that his highest pleasure will be the reward awaiting him after living what is commonly called a decent life. What motivates his actions? Are the motivations not the same as the first man's, except that the first is perhaps a bit more honest about his character? Merely because the second man has *delayed* his pleasure until a later existence and is 'good' because he fears punishment does not disqualify him as a hedonist. He is either much smarter or much dumber than the first man, depending upon which metaphysical system happens to be true, but the *reasons* for doing anything at all are the same as those of the first man. So, post-terrestial hedonism is no less a form of selfish gratification than the more charming, physical kind of hedonism. And 'invisible mechanists' are no more spiritual than the gratification of hunger by eating.

In this inquiry into the meaning of spirit, it is essential that the reductionist allurement of both mechanism and hedonism be overcome. The point is, both mechanism and hedonism do indeed explain things and much more successfully than most other explanations; however, *what* these systems explain is not always *what* we are asking. This is why, throughout the inquiry, the form of the questions have been carefully structured: we ask, not what is *a* spirit (that gives it the status of an entity), but what does it mean to be spirit? Speculative metaphysics, as Kant shows in the *Critique of Pure Reason*, simply cannot compete with naturalistic and mechanistic explanations if one insists upon using only mechanistic principles or of restricting thought to the determination of a thing's existence. For many thinkers, the inability of nonmechanistic thinking to account for efficient causal explanations is tantamount to their invalidity, but such a protest is simply begging the question. Thus what is so attractive about both mechanism and hedonism as systems is their *reductive* and economic simplicity: I do not need to assume very much to render intelligible the entire universe if I 'reduce' all entities to their atoms and all human action to the impetus of pleasure. Matter and pleasure are obvious and recognizable; they are the fundamental 'givers' of our experience, and since all explanation is essentially analysis, one need only 'break down' the complexity of a notion (i.e., 'reduce it') to these obvious and untroubled notions, matter and pleasure, and all will be clear.

But are matter and pleasure really that clear? Or, as Auden says, perhaps "Love, like matter, is odder than we thought." In fact, matter remains one of the most mysterious notions we have, and to listen to a reductionist shrug and say that the seemingly nonmaterial is 'really' only matter, one wonders what the term 'only' means, to say nothing of what 'really' means. The principle which seems so effective in normal, everyday materialistic accounts, efficient causality, itself is thwarted in our account of fundamental matter. What, after all, causes the subatomic particle to act the way it does? To say that gravity is *explained* by the attraction that a huge mass has on a smaller item leaves out most of what we want to know: *why* does the larger attract the smaller? *How* does it attract? What makes it the way it is rather than otherwise? To assume we know what matter is because we are familiar with it opens the door to the countersuggestion that we 'really' are more familiar with spiritual notions like prayer and worship than we are with tactical properties like weight and color. Before judging, let us wait for the materialistic reductionist to finish the job—which promises to be a very long time indeed—and in the meantime we shall continue to wonder.

Far less obvious is pleasure. Do we truly understand pleasure, especially if it is conceived as the ultimate reduction of all motives? To say of the self-sacrificer that he is 'really' doing that which benefits him, and benefit in the last analysis is always hedonistic, is not so much a false claim as it is a meaningless claim. For in this 'reduced' state, pleasure is so far removed from our everyday, uncomplicated understanding of it that it fails to provide any illumination. We certainly do not say that an ascetic is receiving the same delight as the sensualist, yet the sensualist's kind of delight is what we normally mean by pleasure, so to reduce the former to the latter means we must rethink the meaning of pleasure. But to do that spoils the immediacy and appeal of the account. If I must rethink pleasure in order to account for sacrifice, then what good does it do to appeal to my ordinary sense of pleasure, which is quite other than how I ordinarily think of sacrifice?

But even 'ordinary' pleasure is mysterious. Is there ever truly pure pleasure? Even the simple delight of a cool drink when I am thirsty, a warm fire when I am cold, or the sensuous delight of a lover's touch, seem to be somehow *more* than *mere* pleasure. Does not the satyr take as much delight in reflecting on his own image as he does in the carnal reaction of his nerve-endings? Can we escape some sense of gratitude or at least fortuity when the cool breeze brushes the heat from our brow? Since it seems impossible for there to be pleasure without consciousness, then how can it be rendered explicable by materialistic metaphysics? To explain pleasure as the easing or the satisfaction of our wants and needs does no good at all, for we want to know why we want and need what we do, and also why the satisfaction of them is judged worthwhile. Pleasure, like matter, is odder than we thought. But if, by the 'body' we mean simply that which explains through efficient cause and which itself is explained through reductionism to the smallest thing, then it is not only the case that the body cannot explain the spirit, it is even true that the body cannot explain the body. For the body surely makes sense to us in terms of pleasure and pain, but pleasure and pain cannot be explained without consciousness, so that which makes body *intelligible*—pleasure and pain—cannot be understood by the principles which explain the body as an object.

The speculative theory known as mechanistic materialism is seductive because of its appeal to reductionism. I can reduce all phenomena to atomistic activity. This is analysis. By analysis we mean breaking down into primary elements, understanding by division into primary simples, or at least, less complicated complexes of further simples. But synthesis is the opposite: we understand the parts by seeing how they fit into the whole. Kant argues that synthesis must precede analysis: I must somehow think of a complete thing before I can think of its constituents, for the raw grasp of constituents by themselves affords no unity. For Kant, the very act of judging is the unifying—hence synthesis—of two concepts. Thus the ontological ground for our final rejection of mechanistic materialism is that it violates the priority of synthesis over analysis. Analysis, after all, is merely of what we already know; we gain a *kind* of knowledge by dividing the thing into ever smaller parts but we cannot learn the fundamental principles through this method.

Our search for the ontological presuppositions of the ten predicates of spirit therefore must avoid any analytical speculation. We must avoid the natural temptations to drift into either mechanism or hedonism in our attempt to isolate whatever principles might explain the nature and meaning of spirit. But these reflections on materialistic mechanism and hedonism reveal something further. In our attempt to discover the true principles of spirit, we must resist using the metaphysical nostrum of any reductionism based on the distinction between appearance and reality.

When the hedonist argues that seemingly altruistic acts are 'really' just oblique forms of selfish gratification, it is not only the reductionism that is suspect but the enthymatic premise that 'reality' and 'appearance' are basic presuppositions which support the explanation. When the mechanist argues that the spiritual elation one has in prayer is 'really' nothing but a psychological, and hence ultimately biological, response which in turn can be explicated by the busy speed of atomistic energy, he too is engaged in an enthymeme. What does the term 'really' mean? The distinction between appearance and reality lies at the foundation of all speculative metaphysics.

But is it always justified? By means of microscopic lenses one can produce a rough, cratered, and uneven landscape on the screen. The technician assures us that this is not what it seems. By changing the focus, the rough and unsightly surface becomes a smooth, velvety face of a child. "What seems to us to be a smooth as silk is in reality a rough and cratered surface," the epidermist might say. But the camera technician might say: "What seems in this picture to be rough and cratered is in reality the smooth cheek of a lovely child." Both use the distinction between appearance and reality. In this case, of course, by 'reality' one simply means from a certain perspective. But which is the real picture? They both are real, depending on one's point of view. This deflates the importance of the metaphysical distinction.

However, the distinction is not always so innocent. The passions *really* are nothing but reactions to stimuli. We can also turn this around: these meter readings of the body's reaction are *really* the experience of fear. Merely because fearing, loving, and guilt can perhaps activate different readings on meters attached to our skull and wrists does not mean that the passions *are* the readings. We simply think about them differently. It would be surprising that one who is experiencing fear should not have different testable physiological reactions from one experiencing love, but this does not lead us to the absurd conclusion that what activates meter readings is what we *mean* by fear and love. Yet such reductionistic judgments are made all the time by appealing to the metaphysical distinction between appearance and reality. There may be a legitimate distinction, in fact surely the distinction *is* important, but it cannot be used as the basis for *establishing* the correctness of any reductionist account.

But if the time-honored distinction between 'appearance' and 'reality' cannot isolate spirit from flesh; and if, as we have seen, the apparent 'simples' of matter and pleasure are far more mysterious and rich than one might first expect, so that even if some kind of reduction could be carried out it would not change anything since we would not be any further along in out understanding, what then, is left? To what resource can we turn? It was noted that in refusing to accept the meter readings as the true account of love and guilt, we objected that meter readings are not what these passions *mean*. And this is the clue. Whatever principles can throw light upon the isolation of spirit and the distinctions necessary to carry out an ontological support of the ten predicates, they must, perforce, be principles which reveal and determine the *meanings* of whatever primary notions are assumed in making sense of spirit. We shift, in other words, from *kinds of entities* to *meanings*. Whether we label such inquiry as phenomenological, existential, or heuristic is unimportant—indeed on behalf of truth and this inquiry, it would perhaps be more felicitous if we avoid such labels altogether and remain on the fundamental level which explains without becoming technical or jargonistic. The question now is: if we must abandon the traditional distinctions of appearance and reality, and further abandon any reference to the existence of any kind of entity—thereby suspending, perhaps forever, the satisfaction of such questions as whether the soul or God or freedom *exists*—then how can we proceed?

THE ONTOLOGICAL PRESUPPOSITIONS

A fundamental way of understanding our existence is in terms of what certain pronouns mean when they are isolated from their normal function of referring to an entity or person. In these special cases we are not the *referent* of the pronoun, rather we exist in the way in which the pronoun has fundamental, existential meaning. The term 'I', for example, in philosophical discourse, has a fundamental, existential meaning prior to any specific or concrete reference. Immanuel Kant argues in the "Paralogisms" in his *Critique of Pure Reason* that the 'I' presupposed in all acts of cognition is a formal and necessary precondition of all knowing. Hence, for Kant, this transcendental 'I' does not refer, rather it functions as a necessary but formal condition for knowledge. Of course, anything and everything can be the referent of a pronoun, but in this special philosophical sense of a priori meaning, only conscious beings are aware that, as conscious, to be at all is to be in the modality expressed by certain pronouns. For us, to be is to be a pronoun. This does not mean that my metaphysical status has suddenly been changed and that I am now merely a part of speech. Rather, it means that my existence is grounded on fundamental ways of being which can be designated by pronouns. In the unreflective, everyday experience this pronoun is the first person singular, 'I'. Sometimes philosophers use this pronoun when they inquire, depending on their methodology. For example, Descartes begins his *Meditations* with an awareness of his own existence, "I think, therefore I am." To begin thinking in this way *presupposes* the meaning of the pronoun. He does not say: Descartes thinks, therefore, Descartes exists, precisely because this proper name has a history and empirical basis; it is not pure like the pronoun 'I'. Grammarians define a pronoun as a substitute or surrogate for a noun; and its etymology suggests the same thing: a pronoun is a term which takes the place of a noun. This seems to make the noun primary and the pronoun derivative. But in philosophy this ranking is reversed: it is not René Descartes who thinks, but simply 'I'. Now, it may be assumed that Descartes would want us to universalize this 'I', and perhaps it is possible to do so. But much of what is peculiar and indeed disturbing about Descartes's philosophy is his initiating his inquiry with the pronoun. Since for him the 'I' is set up over and against the world as something other than itself, the true pronominal relationship for Descartes is *I-It*. The tandem pronoun 'I-It' simply means that one sees the world in terms of the personal subject observing or objectifying external reality, the world.

However, many other thinkers are hesitant to establish such high ontological status for the individual conscious of himself in a world which is his object. Kant, for example, prefers to think in purely formal terms and speaks instead of knowing self or 'I', of 'consciousness in general', which is not even the sum total of all such 'I's' but the formal condition of such 'I's' being able to think at all. The subject of knowing, for Kant, is thus not the 'I', but the 'All', and insofar as the All has universal principles which it uses to govern the individual experiences, we can describe his total pronominal relationship as All-It.

But tandem pronouns, in all such cases, are fundamental presuppositions. That is, their meaning is prior to the concrete instantiations which give them identifiable names or tags. Kant, for example, explores the principles and rules which govern the make up of 'consciousness in general' (the All) and applies these to the external world (the 'It'), and unless these notions are presupposed to have some meaning, the entire endeavor collapses, for unless All and It are meaningful it makes no sense to say that we All have ways of knowing It. Thus, the meaning of these pronouns must be presupposed.

Martin Buber has written a book entitled *I and Thou* in which he contrasts the 'I-Thou' with the opposing 'I-It'. One is immediately aware of the difference. I deal with a person, whether another human or God, differently than I deal with a thing. If Buber is correct, the difference is existentially profound. But he too assumes, perhaps more self-consciously and alertly than the others, that there are a priori meanings to unattached pronouns. (By unattached pronouns I simply mean the pronoun which is not immediately referring to a particular thing or person, i.e., something which is designated grammatically by a noun.)

If we assume that all possible tandem pronouns which serve as fundamental starting points for any philosophical system must contain at least one pronoun capable of conveying consciousness, we recognize that there are only three pronouns which can represent our own immediate awareness essential for an epistemological starting point: the 'I', which is particular and existing actually; the 'we', which is more than a plurality of single 'I's' but which represents a way of being conscious as opposed to others; and the 'All', which represents any consciousness at all, whether actual or possible. If we assume these three pronouns as essential and recognize the six pronouns established by the rules of grammar—the first, second, and the third persons in both singular and plural forms—we have: I, Thou, He, We, Ye, and They. However, these are all personal pronouns, and so we must add an impersonal, objective pronoun, 'It.' Modern English does not discriminate between the singular and the plural of 'You', so I have used the more ancient forms of 'Thou' for the singular and 'Ye' for the plural. English also has no gender-neutral third person, so I have used 'He' in the generic, not in the gender sense. (I find the locution 'He/She' unacceptable or at least inelegant.) Thus we have, with the three pronouns which alone can be ascribed as conscious, I, We, All, in possible combination with seven others, so that altogether the complete list is as follows:

I-It	We-It	All-It
I-Thou	We-Thou	All-Thou
I-Them	We-They	All-They
I-Him	We-Him	All-Him
I-Me	We-Me	All-Me
I-Us	We-Us	All-Us
I-Ye	We-Ye	All-Ye

We must disregard all tandem pronouns in which there is not a first person (or an 'All'), such as They-It, for there is no immediate consciousness internally available for the inquirer. I do not deny that other tandem pronouns may proven beneficial in other inquiries, but this is a specific investigation, testing whether pronouns have any a priori, independent meaning and for that we need at least one of the two pronouns to be self-conscious.

These tandem pronouns are fundamental ways of existing, and they also serve as irreducible and nonderivative *principles* which explain or illuminate our existence. Because they are both fundamental and a priori they provide the thinker with an exhaustive and complete list of existential building blocks. Each tandem has its unique and fundamental meaning, and although it is not necessary to discuss each at any great length, it is essential to render a fairly thorough account of the tandems which are important for this inquiry.

I-It: This, as we have seen, is the ultimate presupposition used by Descartes and any thinker who begins his analysis with a self-reflective simple. The tandem indicates that there is an individual, knowing consciousness which is aware of a separate other entity, whether the entire world or a single object. Under the influence of this principle, one sees the world as the object of his or her thinking or experience, and the subjective awareness is individual, i.e., a single unit. Now such a modality is possible for all minds, and indeed it is a genuine way in which we can and often do exist; it is also a way in which we think about ourselves and the world. But it is *not* the *only* way, and thus to appeal to this modality or tandem as the fundamental metaphysical system simply overlooks the fact that there are at least twenty-three other modalities, each of which is equally primordial. To rank one of these tandems above the others gives a definite cast or quality to one's metaphysical outlook; but to exclude the other tandems as fundamental is not merely to characterize one's metaphysics, it is an ontological mistake. The extent to which Descartes makes this mistake is fully explicated in Kant's criticism of it in the section called the 'Paralogisms' in The *Critique of Pure Reason*. It should be emphasized, however, that the I-It tandem is a legitimate modality of existential awareness and must be included in any adequate account of the ways in which we exist in the world.

All-It: This is Kant's substitute for the flawed use of the prior tandem as the only one available for the epistemologist. Kant's point is that the self-reflective 'ego' presupposed by all consciousness is not a specific substance as the prior tandem suggests but is merely the system of principles or categories which must be assumed in order to account for human knowledge. This tandem, as an existential modality, is as legitimate as the first; it is superior as an epistemological starting point for the reasons Kant gives; however, it does not forfeit the possibility of an I-It. One can still think of oneself as an entity which perceives the external world as something totally outside oneself, but such a way of thinking cannot establish the substantial reality of a knowing subject, nor can it deny that the world may be more than an external entity. Kant does not make the mistake Descartes made; he does not argue that the All-It (not his terms, obviously) is the *only* modality. When you and I think about the world as made up of entities, such a way of thinking is certainly justified. If we instantiate our own existence on the basis of this thinking, it is a misuse of the I-It; if we recognize that the self presupposed in such thinking is purely formal, we are using the modality of All-It. We think as metaphysicians or as scientists when we adopt this modality, and as long as we do not exclude the other modalities, such a way of thinking is legitimate. We give this modality a *priority* when we adopt such a way of thinking. Such ranking is not in itself philosophically unjustified, as long as one recognizes that this ranking is done solely as a device for keeping straight what field of inquiry is being used. A physician, operating on a friend, must adopt such a modality if he is to be successful as a surgeon; but he immediately abandons this priority or way of thinking when he concerns himself with the friend as friend. Thus, we shift our modalities and the priorities we give them constantly in our daily affairs. As we will soon see, it is also possible to rank one modality above others for a fairly consistent or even permanent duration of thought; but whether such ranking is always or even ever justified is moot.

I-Thou. In ordinary human existence this modality is that which establishes the possibility of love and hate. Unlike the I-It, in which the object of our subjective awareness is first and foremost a thing or entity, the I-Thou establishes a personal meaning which cannot be understood merely as a special kind of entity with personlike qualities added on. The I-Thou is fundamentally different than the I-It. There is no one single attribute, such as 'having a free will' which can distinguish a person from a thing, for that approach merely adds on the attributes to a thing. The very principles of intelligibility which reveal the meaning of a thing are different from those which reveal the meaning of a person. For this reason the fundamental distinction is recognized on this primordial level of tandem modalities which cannot be derived from each other. In the I-It or even All-It modalities, the primary principles are those which account for a subject becoming aware of an object, to the extent that the object is always conceived as other or external. But in the I-Thou modality, concern for and caring about replaces the notion of recognizing and dealing with an object. In the modality of I-It, the primary principle is use; in the I-Thou it is love or hate.

When the I-Thou modality is raised to the level of the supreme ontological principle, there is a personal relationship with whatever forces or powers govern the universe: this is usually (though not always) seen in terms of a personal God who cares for and is in turned loved, and not merely revered or obeyed, by his created offspring or children. However, the true picture of the I-Thou is that of a saint in rapturous contemplation with the divine creator, and as a consequence, a willingness to see all things and events within the world as an extension of this loving (or hating) rapture. The diabolical is just as spiritual as the holy, though not equally as good, and both are manifestations of the I-Thou. This single modality by itself deserves a book-length analysis; fortunately for our purposes it is enough merely to point out the differences, for our chief concern in this section is merely to develop a sense of how this fundamental ontology of pronominal tandems allows us to establish such primary and crucial differences in our thinking.

I-We. This modality is the source of our understanding of ourselves as social beings. It is important here because one should not tend to derive the I-We from the prior modality of I-Thou. In other words, the I-We is *not* a mere plurality of I-Thou's; indeed, the I-We is quite distinct. Through the I-We one recognizes duties, obligations, and privileges that develop in a society; there is not rapturous loss of self as in love, nor is there the reverential awe and wonder of the aching majesty felt in adoration. The I-We is a more practical, a more everyday modality. It is, however, no less important for that, for under this principle we come to realize such important notions as justice, patriotism, and social conduct. As with the other modalities, the I-We cannot be derived from other principles or other modalities: it is a priori. (Thus, attempts to ground and explain the social systems by reference to a 'contract' or by an appeal to 'natural rights' founded on our most basic wants and needs are misguided and ultimately doomed to failure. I can explain the state only because one of the fundamental ways to be is to be I-We.)

I-They. If the I-We modality is the ground of all social interaction, the I-They is exactly the opposite: it is the ground of all alienation from society. By the tandem I-They is meant that principle by which we set ourselves off from others, either in good or bad will. Thus the I-They can be used to understand both the criminal and the recluse. In this list of tandem pronouns, the term 'They' always represents others as opposite to what is our own, whereas the term 'We' or 'Us' represents what belongs to us or to which we belong. Thus, the I-They contrasts with the I-We; the latter is the basis for community, the former is the basis for isolation and loneliness. At times, of course, the I-They may be necessary for educational or even moral reasons, as when the matyr is sacrificed by the community for that which he alone realizes as true. Again, however, the point that is so important is that these various modalities, manifested in the list of tandem-pronouns, are a priori and nonderived. I cannot explain the I-They by appealing to a mere flaw in the I-We. Nor should this modality always be seen as negative: after all, each of us *does* retain an individuality which cannot and should not be sacrificed for the commonwealth. Insofar as I have a unique characteristic and a private and important personality, yet at the same time I desire to fit into society with my own uniqueness, I am participating in both I-We and I-They.

We-They. This tandem is one of the most important for the social thinker, for it is the ontological ground of war. In war, men do not fight for justice or what is right, they fight for meaning. Wars are not the result of economic conditions—though they may contribute to the cause—but rather because it is necessary for one to think in terms of who *we* are as opposed (or threatened) by who *they* are. To lose this basis of our meaning, the 'We,' is absolutely unacceptable for those who seek an authentic existence, and so inevitably we divide the world into those who belong, the 'We', and those whose very otherness threatens, the 'They'. I do not mean to suggest that this distinction is always bad, indeed some realization of belonging to a 'We' is essential for coherent meaning; nor am I suggesting that to resort to arms in defence of what is one's 'We' is always wrong. On the contrary, at times it is immoral not to defend who we are. The point that is important in recognizing this modality, however, is that the tandem pronouns We-They are here recognized as a priori modes of existence and hence *not* a relationship between any two entities. This of course is true of all of these modalities expressed in the tandem pronouns: the I-It, I-Thou, All-It, We-They, etc., are not to be conceived as relations between entities, as if the entities exist *first* and then they establish a relationship of the sort implied by I-Thou or We-They. On the contrary, the modality expressed by the tandem pronouns are *prior* to being an entity. To be an entity is to be in the tandem modality of All-Me; that is, the self is no longer an 'I' but a 'Me', and is thought of in terms of being the object of another's experience (the All as any possible mind, including my own).

Thus, if we are to understand the phenomenon of war, we must focus our attention on the a priori modality of We-They, recognize its authority, and understand the hierarchy it plays in self-understanding. All other accounts of war presuppose the We-They distinction; and those which pay it little heed are simply giving ad hoc explanations for an enormous problem. Most attempts to explain war focus solely on the immediate political events which precede the outbreak of hostilities; but such accounts, especially the economic ones, are grossly dissatisfying, for why should one group identify itself as a 'We' over and against another, recognized as 'They'? Nevertheless, such identification is *always* a prerequisite for war happening as well as for understanding the event of war. Thus, the We-They modality is an important source of understanding who we are.

We-Ye. If We-They is war, then We-Ye is peace. That is, the We-Ye modality is the acceptance of there being more than one unit by which people identify themselves and the celebration of it. We as Americans or English are glad there are Italians and Germans, not only because of what they have contributed to world culture, but because the existence of other nations adds meaning to our own. How is it that the 'Ye' becomes a 'They'? To answer this we must study history—not merely political history, but cultural and religious history as well. Indeed, these modalities should warn us against misreading history without taking into account such fundamental ways of existing. To be sure, peace (We-Ye) is preferable to war (We-They), but a simple appeal to peace without respect for the legitimacy of the We-They modality of our existence is simply self-deception. One cannot argue for peace and at the same time disregard the agonies of those who have lost their own identity or nation. The fundamental need for recognizing that one belongs to a 'We' is too sacred to be disregarded. It would be nice if our diplomats could figure out a way to rank the We-Ye as paramount without destroying the notion of We and Ye, but of course that is what mindless pacifists who see only the horrors of war and not the equally nihilistic horrors of statelessness do when they simply protest that war is the greatest of all evils. Being without meaning is a greater evil. The 'We' of the We-They modality, of course, need not always be a nation. It can be a religion, a sect, a class, or even a race. But once these unifying agencies arm themselves, they take on the characteristics of a state almost inevitably.

We-All. The term 'We' in these various tandems always has a specific existential meaning, such as "We, the American people" or even as vague as "We, the society"; but the term 'All' refers not to the sum total of every 'We', or even the sum total of all minds, but the universal principles, laws, and categories found in all minds and conceived as 'consciousness in general'. Thus it is possible for there to be a tandem between the 'All' and the 'We', and this modality is the moral law. That is, we understand that *We* (those of us in a society, even if that society is the largest possible, the human society) must yield to the authority of that which is universally shared by every consciousness and that can only be the moral law. There is no doubt that in particular instances, when the dreadful onus of making a moral decision falls upon one person, the modality may seem to be I-All, for I am then concerned about how I particularly and individually fit into the scheme of things. But the necessity for universality, so admirably expressed in Kant's moral writings, shows that the proper tandem to express the moral law is the We-All. It might be argued that guilt, which is *not* universal but always particular, best expresses the modality of I-All.

All-Thou. This is immanent theism. If the religion is racial, the modality would be *We-Thou,* as I suppose Judaism must be characterized. The 'Thou' here refers to a divine person, and the use of the intimate form is important, because theisms of the immanent sort stress the intimacy between the divine person and the human person. The closeness with which a particular culture is identified with a particular religion may manifest this religious modality into We-Thou rather than All-Thou; but when thinkers reflect on the nature of their religion, it seems obvious that the daily practice of a culturally identified religion (We-Thou) should be explicated rather in terms of All-Thou. But immanent theism must be contrasted with:

All-Him, which is transcendent theism. The 'Thou' shifts to 'He' in transcendent theism, because of the necessary separation between God and the world presupposed by such theism. Immanent theism is the belief that God dwells intimately among his own, or even among all of us; transcendent theism emphasizes rather the 'otherness' of God. If God is infinite and we are finite, it seems that only a transcendent theism is possible; if, however, the distinction between the infinite and the finite is modal rather than substantive, an immanent theism is possible. But the immanent theism of All-Thou and the transcendent theism of All-Him must be contrasted with deism: He-It. Precisely because deism has no self-conscious pronoun (I, We, All) it is suspect as a sound articulation of the ways we can be said to exist. It should be noted, though it is hopefully obvious, that when I say that All-Him *is* transcendent theism, I do not intend to identify the terms. Any actual religion, as the various forms of theism, for example, is characterized by much which comes from tradition, history, culture, art, theological disputation, and ethnic variation. The principle All-Him contains none of these riches: it is merely the principle which must be presupposed if such theism is possible. That is, only if it is possible for me to exist in such a way as to participate in the modality of All-Him is it then possible for me to articulate a specific, theistic religion.

A few other modalities may here be briefly mentioned to show the significance of this approach. The *I-Ye* represents the possibility of leadership or governance; the *I-Me* is the inauthentic modality in which I view my own existence as a substantial entity or as object rather than subject. Such a modality is not inauthentic when, for example, I consider myself *as* an object for a provisional but important reason, i.e., when I test myself medically or reflect upon my ills to help a diagnosis. But if my dominant modality is I-Me, I am guilty of the error of translating a modality into a substance. *I-I* is therefore the authentic modality of self-awareness. *All-They* is the realization that a special group (they) can constitute a threat to the very meaning of universal humankind, as the Islamic fundamentalists judge all non-Islamic sects, or as the Allies judge the Nazis in World War II. This modality takes on especially sinister meaning in certain religions in which Satan or Satanic cults are viewed as inimical to all humanity.

There is no suggestion or even hint that these descriptions are in any way complete. Nor do I deny that variations with a certain modality may exist and may well enrich our general understanding of how we exist within the world. The purpose of the above sketch—and it is little more than that—is simply to show that the complete list of tandem pronouns do provide us with a fundamental list of existential modalities, i.e., ways of being, and that it is possible for various reasons to rank some of these modalities above others, either for a brief period in order to accomplish a specific endeavor (as when we adopt the modality of We-They during the time of war, but revert to We-Ye in a following peace); or it is also possible to rank one modality permanently as a sustaining and metaphysically dominant source of self-understanding, as a materialist would insist upon All-It and I-Me as modalities which outrank all others in illuminative power, whereas a theist would rank We-Him or All-Him as the dominant and consistent modality. The arguments that sustain these disagreements may never be resolved; it is important to stress, however, that whatever modality is ranked as dominant by a thinker, it is *always* a profound ontological error to eliminate or disregard the entire range of such modalities, and it is an even greater mistake to *reduce* a fundamental modality, which all of these are, to another. Of course, as we have seen, what makes many metaphysical systems *interesting* is their reductionism of many modalities to one, as is usually done by most mechanists and hedonists. But the present analysis of the various modalities grounded on the grammatical presentation of the tandem pronouns should at least warn the would-be metaphysician that how we think about our own existence is fundamental, but it is also diverse. There is no way one can 'reduce' a 'we' to an 'it'; and so all of these tandem pronouns which represent fundamental modalities are a priori and nonreducible.

But this analysis was not done solely or even primarily as an exercise in existential ontology. The purpose is to isolate those modalities which account for spirit. In the very first chapter Plato's *Republic* was cited as a possible source for understanding spirit, and it was there noted that spirit comes into being when the interests of the 'I' are replaced by the concern for the 'we'. If this is correct, then surely the modality of 'I-We' is a possible source of spirit. So too is the rich suggestion of the I-Thou; and if one wishes to include religious spirituality, then the two forms of theism, All-Thou and All-Him would also be included. There may, indeed, be more, but these four are sufficient to provide a starting point in our refinement toward an essence of spirit.

But these observations provide an excellent starting point. The earlier distinction between 'spirited' and 'spiritual' can now be explicated in terms of the warrior's I-We and the saint's I-Thou. The theologians can argue about the All-Thou and All-Him; but since the former is more personal and less formal, we can now suggest that being spiritual is to be in the modality of I-Thou and being spirited is to be in the modality of I-We; to formalize our understanding of our spirituality is to be in the modality of either All-Thou or All-Him, with a slight existential preference for All-Thou. These are the only presuppositions needed.

10

The Essences

With the ten predicates we have established a guiding description of spirit; now however we must plunge more deeply into this term and establish a *definition*. In order to do this, we must consider the *essence* of spirit. There are, upon serious reflection, three possible candidates for the essence of spirit: (1) nearness, (2) transcendence, and (3) gratitude. Each of these suggestions will be considered separately.

NEARNESS

There are those whose fundamental way of existing seems to be distance. They are distant from others, distant from themselves, and distant from anything sacred or divine. These are not necessarily lonely or even antisocial beings, for there are many forms of social existence which are profoundly distant, for example, politeness can be extremely distant. The reward for such distance is sometimes understood as a kind of total freedom; indeed many seem to seek out this 'total freedom' precisely by distancing themselves from any and every commitment, obligation, promise, bonding, and intimacy. They may be sexually active, since one of their commandments is to achieve a fairly wanton diversity of pleasure at the cost of a readily dispensed nearness of true affection. This freedom has remarkable allure; by severing all nearness one accomplishes gratifying autonomy. Such freedom may be highly selfish, but it is liberating, and it seems to have become the dominant life-style of the West in the twentieth century. We distance ourselves from our tradition, our culture, our religion, and our history and thereby become autonomous individuals whose dominant concern is self-fulfillment and self-realization. We become bachelors; even those who marry remain bachelors. For distance is the guarantee of this freedom; and we would rather be free and alone than close with chains. Friendships, which bind, are replaced by acquaintances which please. Relationships are dropped when they become onerous, for there is no independent worth to a 'relationship' as there is to a friendship. Love becomes a mere opportunity for passion, which makes us feel important. Our fellow independents solemnly assure us that this new and supreme virtue, self-realization, must yield to no other claim on us. We divorce any mate which threatens our autonomy, abort any unwanted fetus even though we produced it, for it is not *ours;* we send our living children to day-care centers and summer camp lest one of us must remain at home and lose the income. We isolate ourselves like a precious and lovely flower in a pot, where no other plant, not weed nor flower, is allowed to grow: an unnatural soil, artfully watered and sunned, stilled in all germination. But we treasure this ceramic enclosure that keeps out alien roots, for in it we are unencumbered, without bondage to any person, thing, belief, or system. We are unique unto ourselves. We are free, and modern, and distant.

We are even—or perhaps especially—distant from ourselves, for we have ceased reflecting in solitude; we do not think. The primary goal of our everyday lives seems *distraction*—though we often call it 'entertainment', or perhaps 'having a good time'. Nothing distances us from ourselves more than noise, and hence our leisure times are always full of loud and cheerful fellows whose constant din keeps all nearness away. Even our music has become loud noise, with a primeval and pleasant beat. Even our *thinking* has become distant; for literature and art and music and poetry are now conceptualized, meaning that they no longer elevate or move the spirit but merely delight the intellect. For centuries we have been working on this isolation—we call it by various names: the ultimate right of the individual, the freedom of our own conscience, the right to self-achievement. Our history shows us a steady emergence of the supremacy of the individual, even above family and friends, above nation and religion, above anything that would bring us near. And there is much, much good in this:

we no longer own slaves, we insist that our governments care about the poor, we pass laws prohibiting any decision based upon a group or class or people. We hate discrimination and argue all should be equal, and this is surely just and right. But in focusing so vehemently on the individual, we have forfeit all possibility of authentic nearness: we are then, even in our highest success and our most admirable achievements of justice, distant. We are *good* in our distance. We are distant in our goodness.

But we are beckoned. Beckoned or called to draw near. We know this nearness threatens the cheerful, noisy, autonomy we think of as liberty; but it beckons all the same. Nearness and farness: how are we to think of these terms? What does it mean to approach, to come near, to *be* near? This at least we understand fundamentally: we are near that which is our own. It is possible, of course, to disavow anything *as* our own, and then we are truly distant. But if we seek to achieve nearness, or to be near, then we must surrender at least the trappings of complete autonomy, for that is part of how we understand nearness: that there is something that is our own, and being our own, *matters*. Abstractionism, as it is manifest in conceptual art, literature, and even philosophy, prohibits this dreadful claim upon us. As totally free we do not want *anything* to matter. Could it be that perhaps total freedom is therefore inauthentic?

For spirit, nearness is all. We seek to draw near, and in this nearing we feel the enclosure, the ligatures that bind, as one would bind up a wound. The I becomes We; the I-It becomes the I-Thou. To grow near is to approach the presence of; it is to embrace reality rather than to confront that which exists.

And so we must ask this question: Who are we that allows us to be near? That is: what is the nature of our existence such that we can draw near to something or be distant from something? Perhaps indeed we should leave off the substantialist language and rephrase the question: What does it mean to be able to grow near or to be distant? Surely we are not speaking of mere physical proximity, as we would say that Paris is nearer to London than it is to Moscow. I am not near when I am in the same room, or even the same bed; yet I can be near to one on the other side of the planet. It cannot simply be how we feel, either; although feeling is perhaps far nearer to what we seek than geography. Nearness is a way of being. But it is a way of being which can be lost, or at least overlooked. Nearness, however, in its most fundamental sense, is spirit. And if we retain our first comprehension, if nearness is spirit, then distance or farness is flesh.

To be near is not accomplished by *doing* anything; at least it cannot be accomplished merely by doing something. Actions that do bring us near are meaningful beyond the range of their being actions. Nearness is the acknowledgment of belonging; in this sense it is not accomplished at all but rather discovered. For I cannot, indeed, achieve nearness; rather I must find it. Nearness is not the product of my creation; it is rather the discovery of my own being. Granted we speak of 'growing near' or 'approaching', and these terms make us think of nearness as an accomplishment, but this must be guarded against; for approaching in the true sense is self-discovery, the way a teenage boy suddenly 'discovers' girls; a devastating self-discovery that forever changes the boy, destroys the boy, and makes way for the man. All nearness is of this sort: it is not something one can decide one day to do, as one might decide to grow a beard or buy a new suit. And yet, nearness is not a natural thing either, assured and guaranteed as is puberty. For farness is equally possible; and since farness is equally possible, then to draw near must to some extent be chosen. But it is a choice in the sense that whether one allows oneself to be deceived can be a choice: it is a way of letting a certain way of being establish itself as a part of us.

It is important to realize that nearness is not something one can achieve merely by making an effort or choosing to be near; it is equally important to realize that nearness is not inevitable, nor is it a natural gift, like having blue eyes. But if I can neither 'choose' nearness nor inherit it as a right of the species, then how can it occur? There is freedom involved, and there is also inevitability involved, but neither by itself accounts for nearness. Perhaps it is possible to suggest that one freely *succumbs* to nearness, as one succumbs to persuasion. This may be a dubious suggestion, for it seems to make nearness an accident of fate to which I must submit. Yet I should like to argue that one does succumb to nearness; I suppose in the same way one might say that we succumb to falling in love, or succumb to a mood. It is not totally without choice; we can resist it. But then neither is it totally ours to achieve merely by deciding to do so. For do we claim that one can simply choose one fine day to be spiritual?

To say that nearness is the essence of spirit is to say that to be spiritual is to be near, or at least to be able to be near. Being near does not refer to a static state, perhaps it would be better to use the locution 'nearing', for being spiritual manifests itself as an approach to that which brings full realization to who we are. To be spiritual, then, is to draw near or to approach, and in this nearness we succumb to the persuasion of that which is sacred. In spirit we near the sacred.

By drawing near the sacred we must yield, to a certain extent, the persistent ideology that individuality is the supreme good and that complete liberty and the absence of any restraint is the only way to achieve the fullness of existence. Perhaps it is not even the way to guarantee one's happiness, although that is a judgment based on experience and prudential wisdom. But surely spiritual nearness is impossible without submission, and indeed a positive yielding to the presence of another. This presence is often called God, but it is more precise to understand this presence existentially, and thus we identify it as the sacred.

The Sacred

But if nearness is that modality of existence which constitutes the essence of spirit, and that which one approaches is the sacred, it is impossible to continue the inquiry without considering now what has been lurking in the background for quite some time. What do we mean by the sacred? At first glance it might seem that the sacred is precisely that which *cannot* be neared. By the sacred we seem to mean that which must not be touched; one does not enter the sacred precinct without first purifying oneself through ritual. Only the few, the virgins, the priests, the selected ones, can touch the sacred objects, look upon the sacred icon, enter into the sacred rooms. There is a legitimate sense to this: by the sacred we mean the untouchable, and hence that which cannot or at least should not be approached or neared. The Old Testament tells us of the man who was struck instantly dead because he merely *touched* the Arc of the Covenant. This resistance to being touched, especially by common or unwashed hands, is an especially important notion which helps illuminate the flesh-spirit distinction. The flesh is touched, the sacred is not. To be in the mode of the tactile is to be far, but to be in the mode of that which is sacred is to be near. Does this not sound backwards? Surely if the essence of spirit is *nearness* then one would expect *touching* to be its supreme resolution. Why approach something unless touching it is the seduction which prompts the approach?

But the sacred does not mean that which is untouchable absolutely; rather it means that the ordinary senses of touching, which are either to use, or to caress and give pleasure to, or to take pleasure from, are forbidden. The nearness must be achieved in another way. Perhaps it is near because it is essential for understanding who we are.

Anthropologically, the sacred represents that which unifies or even establishes a people or clan; it is the center of the ancient stories, the fetishes and symbols which sustain a people as a people. Mecca is a sacred place to Islam in part because of its history, a history which is relived daily by devout Muslims who pray facing toward Mecca; Jerusalem is not merely another city for the Jews, nor even for the Christians: it is the city of David and the city of Jesus, and thus it becomes a special place of worship. In this anthropological sense, which is a genuine though incomplete characterization of the sacred, there can be no such thing as a personal or private sacredness. To be sacred is to represent the community. It reflects who *we* are, not who *I* am. Thus, the notion of sacred is tied up with that of our history, especially the history of our origins. Its reverence consists of the communal recognition that without this place or event, the unit as such would not even exist. (This suggests an overlap with the third candidate for the essence of spirit: gratitude. If Bethlehem and Jerusalem make up what used to be called 'the Holy Land' it is because there Christ was born and died, theologically accomplishing the redemption of the Christian peoples. In revering these places as special, holy, or sacred, Christians manifest their *gratitude* for the privilege of their religion.) Most, if not all, cultures have stories which account for the origin of their tradition, and these stories usually take place in a particular spot or by means of a particular kind of thing which is then the object of special veneration. Thus the sacred cannot be separated from the history or the story of a people.

This anthropological approach is helpful, but only up to a point. It may be true that special places or objects are revered as sacred because of the role they play in the origin either of our species or of a particular religion, but this in no way helps us distinguish the special type of reverence given to the sacred. I may revere someone simply because I respect or love them; I may hold a special remembrance in my heart for a specific little spot where something precious happened to me, but these are not the veneration restricted to that which is truly 'sacred'. (I admit we often make a metaphoric use of this term, and say: "this is sacred to me"; but if this analysis is correct, such uses are nothing more than metaphoric, so that they mean: this is to me as the sacred is to a community.) Surely to venerate something or someone as sacred is far more than to isolate that one as having special importance. The *kind* of specialness is critical in understanding the sacred. The anthropological analysis suggests that what makes the sacred unique is the necessary relationship it has with our origins, either as a specific people or even as the human species. This is surely correct. But at the same time, the notion of the sacred seems to isolate our own private existence as being peculiarly important or even precious. To enter into the sacred temple or to visit the sacred place seems to make the individual visitor favored or blessed. Thus the sacred is at once that which is revered because of its historical significance as the origin of who we are as a community (or religion), but it is also that which singles us out as favored by the powers that represent such origination.

Because the sacred represents the veneration given to that which accounts for our origin, it demands a particular kind of awe. This is the special awe that comes from reflecting on the fact that we exist at all. It is the recognition that, as contingent and finite, we are nevertheless existing, and the power, the entity, or even the place where this existing is brought forth fills us with the wonder that we should have been selected or chosen to be. This awe is also reverential in the sense that demands a certain quietness or hush, a sense of supreme delicacy and gentility, and a sense of being removed from daily or trivial concerns. We do not laugh coarsely in a temple or church, we do not yell obscenities in a holy shrine. Our actions in such places are moderated, cautious, dignified, slow and muted.

In the presence of the sacred we recognize not merely that which is precious or of value, but rather that which *grounds the possibility* of the precious or the valuable. In this sense, the sacred is a bestowal, like a gift, which promises elevation and importance, but an importance which is singularly otherworldly, as if the everyday is profoundly without meaning. We are hushed at the presence of the holy because this meaning, we fear, can be denied us if we do not hear it. In order to grasp more profoundly the meaning of this notion, it may be helpful to consider the holy or the sacred from the opposing notions of its violations, profanation and sacrilege.

The profane is that which violates the sacred from without, as the infidel profanes what is sacred in part through ignorance or simply by not sharing in the mystery. The etymology reveals that *pro* + *fane* means "outside of, or not within, the temple." Profane does not mean wicked, it means "not spiritual," coming from another (i.e., unspiritual) world. Profanation is the intrusion by that which is alien. But sacrilege is the violation against the holy by the initiates, the believers, by those who already are within the realm of the sacred precinct. Hence sacrilege is worse than profanation because there is, in addition to the violation of the holy, a further outrage in the treachery or ingratitude of one who knows of the importance but turns against it. When we speak of "the sacred and the profane" we mean the two worlds, that of light *and* that of darkness; but when we speak of the sacred and the sacrilegious we mean the treacherous violation of what is holy by one who has fallen from light *into* darkness. In a subsequent chapter we shall consider evil as a spiritual reality, but the present reflections on sacrilege and profanation are here employed as devices for understanding.

So, we now ask: granting that we accept a nonreductive account of such things as sacrilege and profanation, what does this tell us about how we understand the sacred? Certainly it shows us that the sacred has a high preciousness about it, because when we learn of a sacred thing, person, or place being violated either by profanation or sacrilege we understand it as a gross violation of the very *source* of our worth. It can be compared to the way that medieval kings established treason as the highest of all crimes because in violating the regency one violated the very possibility of crime and justice. Crimes are manageable within a system of punitive justice, but the state itself must be presupposed. So, to commit treason is to threaten the very *being* of a state, and hence from the point of view of government, there can be no worse crime than treason. Even today, when the personage of the ruler is not regal, and hence the government is not equated with the individual president or prime minister, the crime of treason has a special status. For treason threatens the state itself, without which there would be no crime nor redress; there would be sheer anarchy, not only of political activity but of cultural and religious activity. So, too, a violation against a sacred institution is not merely another sin, but a threat to the entire *intelligibility* of what is holy.

These reflections support the insight that what we mean by 'sacred' is the very ground or support of all meaning that is not accounted for by the simple, brute animality of our spatio-sentient existence. If we count as anything beyond our flesh, there must be some fundamental ground or ultimate reality which makes any grasp of this meaning possibly true. That is why it is so precious to us; for if we should lose it, then the very possibility of any preciousness whatsoever is forfeit. But the sacred is more than the mere reality which grounds the truth of all our possible claims of meaning: it is also an external Other whose radiance and magnificence beckons us to approach it. We cannot find the sacred merely as a category from within, nor as a feeling or psychological need; we simply do not *think* about the sacred in these ways. For, in order to be sacred, it must be neared or approached.

If nearness is, then, the essence of spirit, we must consider how this nearness manifests itself. There is nearness to the sacred in such manifestations as prayer, sacrifice, worship, ritual, sacraments, and formal ceremonies. In all of these, the spiritual self looks beyond its own existence to some ultimate Other which beckons or calls and which, because of its supreme magnificence, demands devotion. But even more than that, by isolating nearness as the essence of spirit, we focus on the reality that the approach to the sacred *alters* us, indeed transforms us. As we approach the sacred, we are no longer who we were. Nearness, which in human relations is best understood in terms of love, is quite distinct from mere relation, because the point of departure is not two distinct entities which somehow add on a third quality which then relates the two; rather, nearness profoundly changes the one approaching. Indeed, the change wrought by this approach is so intimate that many spiritual believers accept the view that their reverence for what is holy comes solely from within. They assert this because the change wrought by the nearing is so intense and intimate that many feel it is inadequate to express in any terms other than language of private and mystical insight. But for all the enormous light thrown on this modality by such thinkers, it seems to me that the very point of nearness cannot be explained *solely* by the change that is wrought within; it must also take into account that which is neared: the sacred. The point is, we as human beings are not sacred; rather in being spiritual we are near the sacred. The English language may allow us here a very subtle distinction: perhaps we should allow one to identify a person as 'holy' but not 'sacred'; the former term meaning that one is in the state of nearness, whereas the latter term denotes that which is neared.

This quality of Otherness which seems essential for the sacred gives some support to the transcendent theist. If the essence of spirit is nearness, and that which is neared or approached is sacred and other, then it is a fairly easy step to imagine that spirituality is simply nearness to God. One cannot use this as an argument on behalf of a theistic religion, of course; but it can be seen as a reason why so many devout people think about God in the way they do. The sinner is one who offends God, not necessarily one who is distant from God, for as we have already seen, to admit the existence of sin as opposed to mere immorality is to recognize the realm of spirit. According to this view, atheists are profane, but believers can commit sacrilege; and the saint is one whose nearness to God explicates the ten predicates which describe spirit. The mystic, within this account, is one whose nearness to God is privileged, secret, and gratifying; but the sacrificer is one whose commitment is not dependent upon such personal and immediate satisfaction. But even some mystics admit of "the dark night of the soul" in which the nearness to God takes on the character of a great abyss. These analyses need not be simplistic; the concept of nearness is rich and varied, and surely cannot be reduced to pietistic self-satisfaction.

We must reiterate that the present inquiry is not an attempt to prove the existence of anything. Many who may feel themselves very 'near' God may of course be deeply deceived by the mere psychological feeling of well-being that comes from adopting views which fuel their self-importance. There is an enormous difference between the pious, who are virtuous, and the pietistic, who are arrogant and opinionated. But there can be no doubt that transcendent theism provides us with an admirable theological system which accounts for spirit as nearness. On the other hand, if *nearness* is emphasized by itself, without the sacred as Other, then an immanent theism rather than a transcendent theism would be supported. However, there simply cannot be, in this analysis, any decision regarding specific theological views. In order to throw light upon a notion, it is not prohibited to appeal to theological insights, but this inquiry must resist any reduction of the philosophical to the theological.

TRANSCENDENCE

No one seemed to understand her. She was a pleasant, cheerful 'ordinary' child, without any seeming outstanding qualities, except perhaps for a remarkable sense of devotion; but that is fairly common among young girls who are still in the stages of attractive idealism. When the doctor told her she was suffering from a minor deficiency in her diet and should eat more red meat, she smiled sweetly, accepting the truth of his diagnosis, but secretly knew, and hence smiled the more, that she, as a Carmelite, would never eat red meat. She had eaten it before her entrance; she did not think there was anything wrong with eating meat, but as a daughter of Carmel she would not. Her understanding of her severe order was simple: here, she said, one serves him—and she never used his name or title, but always simply referred to him by the use of the pronoun—through suffering. Not through good works, not through mystical rapture, not even through love: there were other orders for that; she would serve him through suffering. And she did. And because she did so absolutely and so awesomely, she was unintelligible to those around her who knew her, cared about her, and loved her. Not even her father could grasp what she was doing. She asked no compensation, nor reward. Like Francis DeSales, she sought to love and serve without any hope of reward. In her youthful, almost girlish simplicity, she offered him her willingness to go to hell—in which she had a total and complete belief—so that there would be one soul there who would love and suffer forever for him. She endured small, annoying, petty, afflictions with a curious, silent joy. There was no great torture, no hideous agony of the more violent sort that is visited upon the great martyrs or the heroes of a battle. She simply accepted suffering as her offering to 'him'; almost as if she recognized in her smallness and unimportance this was all she could offer. She was not a genius who could solve the knottier problems of theology and hence illuminate our grievous ignorance; she was not a stirring speaker who could move immense congregations to splendid works; she was not an artist in any field whatsoever, whereby she could inspire others to glory. In fact, all she had was her capacity to suffer, and so she made that a magnificent offering. But she denied herself even the solace of such sacrifice, for she asked not to be comforted; indeed she sought out the loneliest, darkest kinds of wretched agonies, the miseries of self-doubt, despair, abandonment, loneliness, and the chilling doom of total failure; for only by enduring these things could she suffer enough to warrant his attention and offer his deserved worship. Her name was Therese Martin and her small, hand-written notebooks have survived to tell us of her mighty suffering and her absolute desolation, done cheerfully for "him," for the one who never granted her a single blessing or radiant glimpse of her worth. From her notebooks we learn that "he" granted her what she asked: that she suffer without any support. And that formidable institution of venal popes and a thousand glories raised this unimportant, silent, smiling sufferer to the lofty level of sainthood. But still no one understood her. She would have wanted it that way: she was not someone to be understood; she was merely someone to be noted and then to wonder at.

I had known him for several years. Ours was but a casual friendship, not an intimate one, but when we did get together, usually at his house for dinner, we knew our friendship was solid and good, and would weather the frequent intervals of noncommunication. This Egyptian friend had a teenage son whom he loved with unusual ardor and beaming pride. He would pretend to worry about his son's "Americanization," for he was a devout Muslim, though not a fundamentalist. I had not seen him for several months, when I saw him one day in the elevator in our office building. We were glad of the fortuity of our meeting, and we asked each other the obvious questions of concern. I asked about his son. There was a sudden, grey shiver of absolute grief that dulled his eyes briefly; but he smiled, shrugged his shoulders, and said: "Allah's will be done. We lost him. May Allah be praised." He said no more; the terrible, swift grief had been replaced by the incredible solace of this divine fatalism, which left the critical and doubting instinct of my philosophical nature stunned. I felt dumbly tragic, incapable even of offering solace for fear I upset this obsequence to the will of his God. This, I shuddered, is not the stuff of this world. I knew he loved his son deeply; I knew he *must* grieve over his loss. Yet here was the serene acceptance of a Will beyond his own so important to him that he must submit even if it meant restraining the natural demands of grief for the loss of what was supremely precious to him. Yet he was not a particularly 'spiritual' man in his daily affairs. Few who knew him would have called him spiritual. But his awesome fatalism, his curious religion which admits of no truck with the calculations of this world, removed him from our common understanding.

These two, the first spectacular in its mighty mystery, the second far less wonderful but still stunning, more so for being rather ordinary, reveal to us that one of the most important ways we think about the 'spiritual' is that it is not of this world. We even have a term, 'otherworldly', which seems to characterize what we mean by this mode of being. Spirit is that which transcends the world; spirit is transcendence. It is, to be sure, dangerous to use a term like 'transcendence' in this account, since it is a philosophical term, much in use by great thinkers and hence much interpreted or misinterpreted, depending on one's perspective. Indeed, in two of its formulations, 'transcendent' and 'transcendental' it means totally different, even opposing things. The 'transcendental method' of Immanuel Kant has nothing to do with the transcendent theists who argue that God is totally 'Other', and can be approached intellectually only by analogy. But the original meaning of 'transcend' is simply to excel or to go beyond, and it is this primary meaning that I utilize when I submit as the second candidate for the essence of spirit the quality of transcendence. I mean: "not of this world"; going beyond that which is intelligible; being of another and higher realm or plane. And when so understood it seems obvious that transcendence should be designated the 'essence' of spirit: for what else do we mean by spirit than that which goes beyond or transcends this world?

But there *is* only *one* world. Granted, we use the term 'world' very often as a synonym for 'realm', as when we speak of the world of football or the world of ballet. We might talk about the difference between the worlds of East and West; and when we use the term in these ways we mean that the realms of ballet and football are unique, that they have their own nomenclature and rules and advocates. When we speak, however, of the 'worlds' of East and West, we mean more than that they are different realms, we also mean that they are contrasting realms. But, in the strictest sense, there is still only one world. It is the same, single world that we of the West share with those of the East. And if we understand world as the universe, there surely can only be one. What else does *uni*verse mean? It is the one ultimate place where all other places take their reference. Indeed, 'world' is not really a place at all, since in order to 'have a place' one must already be in the world. To be sure, Leibniz talks of 'possible worlds', and he recognizes that the mind can entertain not only a logic of possibilities with this world, but also other possible worlds. Leibniz does not deny, however, that in the final analysis there is only one real, actual world.

It is important to see why philosophy makes this demand on our proper usage. If we were to admit two worlds, we would have to invent some broader notion or term to include the two worlds.

Whatever that term would be is the role played by the term 'world' used in its proper philosophical sense.

Indeed, our popular uses of the term in its plurality, speaking of the various worlds of art, sport, science, and commerce, is in fact a dangerous technique. "Oh, you live in a different world," unfortunately dismisses what is most important: that the great differences of the diverse sections or parts of the single world must somehow accommodate each other, or at least grant others their place. To dismiss the appeal of a strange and singular agency on the basis that it is simply of another world is to close off the enormous and powerful influence of values and perspectives other than our own. The saint and the sinner, the cruel sadist and the sensitive child, the wealthy plutocrat and the devastated indigent are all part of our same world. That is what the term 'world' really means, the repository of all the variant and deviant modes and things which are unfamiliar and strange. But they are still in the world. To use 'worlds' as designating simply different beliefs or values is to introduce a dangerous relativism under the guise of tolerance. And so, we cannot speak of spirit as belonging to another world. Spirit is of this world; though to admit this is to expand the realm of what we mean by 'world'.

Spirit is transcendence. By this we mean that the values and concerns of our daily lives can find no existential place for the extraordinary realm of spirit. But we do not mean that there is literally another 'world' of spirit, for if spirit is truly of another world then it has nothing to do with us at all. For if we are in 'this' world and spirit in 'that' world, then there is no sense in talking about it. For if spirit is not in our world it may as well not even *be* at all. So, when we assert that spirit is transcendence what do we mean? We do not mean that there is a metaphysical difference between our world and that of spirit, for again that puts us entirely out of reach, and thereby renders spirit not only unapproachable but unimportant. Nor do we mean a realm governed by ontologically different rules, as if there were a sixth and seventh dimension which our sensitivities simply cannot grasp. Nor do we mean that the object of spiritual veneration or worship is a transcendent God. The term 'transcendence' applies to those who are spiritual, not to the object revered by the spiritual. Hence, to say that spirit is transcendence is *not* to say that one's godhead is a transcendent entity. *Being* spiritual is to be transcendence.

But if transcendence does not mean dwelling in a different world (since there can be only one world, strictly speaking), and if it does not mean dwelling under totally different ontological or even metaphysical rules, then what can transcendence mean?

Let us look more closely at what is entailed in our judgments. Suppose we admit that the life of Therese Martin transcends our normal understanding. We mean that she is, in the last analysis, simply not comprehensible by the ordinary values and estimates of what is important. We do not doubt that she is a real person, and that her interests are originally similar to our own. But somehow she has surpassed the limits of our expectations and desires. We shudder at the idea of actually embracing suffering as a permanent way of devotion. It disturbs us to think of what kind of God there must be who would take delight in watching his favorites go through such agony. We also feel almost estranged, perhaps even slightly repugnant at the notion of service through suffering. It is an unclean, or at least unhealthy thought. Yes, we can admire her courage and her devotion; we can especially admire the strength of her character, but we do not seem to want to *approve* of it. We think: she should have found a better way to serve her God. Enduring petty and ignobling torments in a joy of bestowal is dangerously near the perverse. Why not serve 'him' with laughter, ecstasy, rapture, delight, pleasure, gratitude for the good things of this world? Therese makes the spiritual frightening and ugly. If 'transcendence' means "going beyond," then surely Therese has done precisely that: she has gone beyond the limits of acceptable behavior.

But has her endurance of courageous suffering truly gone beyond 'acceptability'? We must repeat that there is only one world, and Therese is a part of that one world. We are not merely repulsed by a life of subservient but noble suffering, we are also inspired by it. And so the task of explaining transcendence has become precise by these reflections: we must account for transcendence without an appeal to some 'other world', and at the same time we must render our understanding of transcendence as being genuinely 'beyond' the perspectives of the ordinary. But this would mean that the one world we dwell in is both spiritual and crass, noble and ignoble. And of course, this is precisely what we must recognize if we are to grasp the true meaning of transcendence. The spiritual transcends *within* this world, not from this world to another. It is precisely because Therese Martin is of this world that her extraordinary devotion and sacrificial love so astonishes us and amazes us. But if she must be of this world, and if she is spirit, then spirit must be that which reveals hitherto unrealized dimensions *of this world.* (Indeed, if there is a God, then he too must belong to the world, even if he is the creator of the world: he is 'in' the world 'as' its creator.) The terrible danger that ensues from admitting several 'worlds' in the cosmic, metaphysical sense is that we open up the possibility of totally unintelligible reservoirs into which we can toss anything we do not readily comprehend and somehow believe we have said something intelligible. One instance of this danger is the overly-ready ease with which we submit pestiferous problems in human behavior to the 'other world' of the insane or the mentally ill. To call a deviant mentally ill is to place him outside the 'world', and hence we no longer can, and hence no longer should, *think* about him. But by dismissing the mentally ill from our world, we abandon all necessity for moral behavior, respect, and even the rights to life and dignity. To be sure, the mentally ill are *different,* and they may be required to forego certain liberties if they are dangerous to themselves and others, but they are still a part of our world, and hence we must think about them. The same must be said of the spiritual: it is part of our world. We could not even talk about it if it were not.

So, when we say that spirit transcends, we cannot mean that it leaves the world. One cannot restrain ordinary conversational language, of course, and it is quite proper for one to use the metaphoric distinction between the 'world' of spirit and the 'world' of everyday concerns, as long as we realize that we are *not* establishing two differing metaphysical cosmic systems. After all, the English language allows the use of the word 'world' as a synonym for "realm within this world," and that is what is truly meant when we say the spiritual are 'beyond' our world. But in the important sense, this terminology threatens the abuse of language and logic mentioned above, and so we must be alert to it. Therese's transcendence is not only 'other' than our own, it is also 'above' our own; that is, as a mode of existence her devotion *excels* the modes we have adopted for our own existence. It is the very repugnance and fear of such a severe life that makes us both resist it and admire it; but she endures it for a lofty reason, for a *spiritual* reason. We seem to equate the transcendence of spirit with a kind of loftiness. This appeal to the lofty not only anchors several of the existential predicates (like 'importance' and 'rapture') but also grounds the initiation of this inquiry in our disgust with flesh. The loftiness of spirit is a refuge, whether we actually go there or not, that beckons us away from the meaninglessness of our common existence and toward higher modes of existence, in which even suffering can be offered up as a kind of worship or praise.

Thus, that *to which* the transcendence of spirit beckons us is the loftier modalities of existence, those which matter, those which allow us to glorify that which we revere. It does not beckon us to a totally *other* world, but to that which, by its loftiness of meaning, allows *this* world to be celebrated, even or especially in those modalities which, like suffering, seem so repugnant to the non-spiritual mind. We call it lofty because it appeals to excellence in itself: in the same way that a lover or frequent listener to music will suddenly discover an absolute masterpiece, and recognize that, although he still likes the music of his prior experience, he must acknowledge the perfection of what music can attain. We are often moved to express of truly great works of art precisely that they constitute what the genre is for. We express this colloquially in such phrases as; "Now I know what music is all about," or "This is what painting really means. This justifies my being able to *see*." The great works of art thus inspire us to recognize the ultimate or the finest example or paradigm, and in this way they can be said to *transcend*. Exactly the same thing can be said of spirit: it transcends our existence by showing us what the supreme or ultimate modality of existence can be.

Yet, there can be no doubt that built into the very notion of transcendence is the rejection or denial of the ordinary and common modalities of existence. When Saint Benedict first opened his monastic retreats, they were recognized immediately as places of extraordinary meaning, simply because in the severity of the life offered they *rejected* the fleeting distractions of 'this world' and did so by elevating the consciousness to a higher modality.

However, these examples are not meant to equate religious with spiritual existence. To be sure, many religious modalities are also spiritual, but not all spiritual existence is necessarily religious. Therese, saint though she be, is more spiritual than religious. Indeed some religious qualities are not spiritual at all, since they depend upon a specific theology. Both religious and spiritual modes have a common rejection of the temptations of a purely hedonistic existence, but religion far more than spirituality tends to be *equated* with this rejection. Nietzsche's indictment of the purely ascetic consciousness is more antireligious than it is antispiritual; indeed it is probably not antispiritual at all. And this, of course, is what so elevates us in the contemplation of Therese, and this is why she should be called spiritual rather than religious. Granted her life is extremely ascetic, but her joy in rendering this suffering and severity into a bestowal is grounded in her spirit, not her religiosity.

In order to concretize this modality, consider the following rumination. Suppose I am about to endure an enormous amount of pain and I recognize that I have an option of sorts. I can simply confront the misery with howls of outrage and whimperings of pitied lamentation, which strike me as unseemly or unmanly. I could, rather, endure the pain and suffering stoically, refusing to become debased by it. Why should I? Well, one might say that a certain amount of self-respect and dignity will not allow me to be reduced to a crawling worm. We all recognize that the latter approach is superior to the former, if only because we recognize the reality of the virtue of courage. However, suppose I want to confront the grim experience positively. Suppose I would like to make the suffering not just endured but worthwhile. If I could confront the misery joyfully, what must I assume or presuppose? If I were to endure considerable agony for the sake of someone I love and offer the pain as a kind of sacrifice, then obviously I would render what had been something to be endured into something to be celebrated. This is possible within the ordinary range of human love: we can undergo some discomfort, even pain, for the sake of one we love and thereby render it a positive rather than a negative encounter. But suppose I wished to go even further and actually celebrate the suffering itself as a supreme sacrifice in which the bestowal of what I endured is a triumph. In order to do this I would have to assume the meaningfulness of spirit. Most would rank this as higher even than the stoic endurance of pain, for the simple reason that it *transcends* the limits of those virtues which improve the character and provide us with a sense of self-worth.

Since all of us must endure some suffering, and eventually all of us must endure the final measure in death, our options are not to avoid such things but to confront them more or less successfully. To cower before these inevitabilities is surely less noble than to endure them courageously; but to endow them with a special meaning by rendering them bestowals of devotion is even loftier than the endurance of them stoically. And so we ask what must be presupposed in order for this to be possible.

The most important presupposition is the one discovered in the prior chapter, that we must rank the modality of I-Thou and He-Us above that of I-It or All-Me. If Therese Martin is merely a subject which knows and attends on the world, her sacrificial greatness is rendered meaningless. Or, if she is merely an entity within the world, which is then later accoutered with the trappings of personhood and holiness, she is also rendered unintelligible. For that kind of sacrifice demands that she exists as I-Thou in her personal way of being in the world, and that the world as such is dominated by the He-Us modality. Only if the modalities which allow for such singularly personal notions as offering, giving, enduring for the sake of, and bestowal, as well as gratitude and mattering, are esteemed as higher and more fundamental than the more common ways of being and thinking about who we are, then such sacrifice is not only repulsive and alien, it is ultimately *Unintelligible*. However, to rank I-Thou and He-Us as the highest modality of *our* existence is nothing less than fundamental *transcendence:* i.e., to put it in the vernacular, I can transcend 'this world' and dwell in the higher, spiritual world only if it is possible for there even *to be* the possibilities of existing as I-Thou and He-Us, and if we in fact do indeed exist in such a way so as to rank them as the primary modalities of existence.

Because transcendence seems to make the modalities of I-Thou and He-Us primary, and because transcendence seems to ground our ordinary way of speaking of 'spirit' as belonging to another world entirely, we consider the arguments to designate transcendence as the essence of spirit to be well-founded. For surely there is one indisputable reality about spirit: when we see it in others or try to achieve it in ourselves, instinctively we begin to distinguish the value or the worth of two different ways of existing, although we usually identify these differences in terms of different 'worlds.' As long as this usage is not seriously ultimate, there is no fault in using these terms; but in philosophy one must be more precise, and so we have provided a superior though not as familiar nomenclature. The essential point remains the same however: to be spiritual is to belong to another world, understood philosophically as being in loftier modalities which make spirit meaningful. Even in our daily, tedious, and unspectacular life we seem to be aware of more important and loftier realms which are not entirely out of reach but are kept from us by indolence, distraction or venality. Furthermore, as in the case of nearness, the candidate of transcendence has this advantage, that transcendence seems to ground all the predicates which make up our description of spirit. Perhaps then transcendence is the essence of spirit. At least by considering it as a possibility, we have learned a great deal about the nature of spirit, and that, of course, is our ultimate goal. One of the ways in which we 'transcend' our lower virtues and reach the loftier ones of spirit is through prayer. It may seem at first glance that prayer is a purely religious and not a spiritual function; but this claim is not obvious upon reflection, and even if prayer is fundamentally religious, it is a spiritual religiosity that is manifest in the performance, so it behooves us to consider as an ancillary to our discussion of transcendence the meaning of prayer.

Prayer

There is a verbal, though silent, outpouring of entreaty that seems a universal characteristic of language which is ubiquitous throughout the species. All who speak must articulate this internal appeal; it makes no difference whether the speaker 'believes' in anything, so long as he is a speaker at all he will be able to announce to himself this modality of entreaty. Some may even feel slightly embarrassed at these internal utterances of supplication, gratitude, worship, or outrage which make up this silent call, for it does seem that if one is to 'pray', there must be something or someone to whom one is praying. But whether or not such beliefs are sound, there can be no doubt that, as speakers, the internal articulation of entreaty toward some higher modality is not only possible but inevitable. We may dismiss them as psychological tricks or inherited superstitions, but all men, even avowed atheists, pray in this fundamental sense. Often the impulse to articulate this silent entreaty is provoked by dire need or impending catastrophe, or on occasions of enormous relief or gratitude. When a disbeliever utters "Thank God!" or, when confronting a possible outrage, "Dear God, No!" we do not infer that the speaker necessarily believes in a deity. But, upon analysis, we *do* recognize that such powers of silent speech (or even overt articulation based upon the same impulse) seem always to appeal to some higher plane or even reality. Perhaps we are simply "talking to ourselves" when we do this, but if so, we are speaking to ourselves in the modality of that which transcends the voice which utters the appeal. Once again we find the existential inversion: men do not first pray only after they have a fixed belief in God; rather they believe in a God in part because they first pray.

When the articulating consciousness, even when silent, lifts itself to an appeal or entreaty concerning the powers of fate, greatness, or graciousness, it is fundamentally prayer. We can, after all, 'pray' to another in a quite ordinary sense of entreaty, as when one says: "Pray, lend me a hand," or when we urge someone to yield, "Do not do this, I pray you." In these uses, the term 'prayer' simply means to entreat. But few would deny that we also entreat the fates, the stars, the powers that be, or even God. It is because such entreaty is always of some cosmic power or superior reality that the theological definition of prayer is 'the lifting of the heart and mind to God,' in which the key word is 'lifting' and not 'God'.

Thus, all men, even atheists, at some time or other, pray. In doing so, they exercise transcendence; that is, they go *beyond* themselves as speakers and entreaters to that which might possibly hear or grant. We do not need to establish any discrete, metaphysical referent, then, to analyze what 'prayer' means, and why it is an essential part of spirit, particularly when spirit is conceived as being essentially transcendence. Nor is there any intent here to discuss the 'efficacy' of prayer; i.e., whether there is any reason to believe that our prayers are answered. Prayer can still be meaningful even if none of them are answered. For the religiously spiritual, it is enough simply that they be *heard*, not granted; for the nonreligiously spiritual, it is enough that they be uttered at all. For the purpose of the inquiry is to reveal what it means to be spiritual, not what other kinds of things might exist in the universe that would gratify or answer our spiritual entreaties. What does it *mean* to make such entreaties? This can be asked no matter whether the entreaties are ever answered, or even if they are ever heard.

What being able to pray—i.e., to make entreaties about our meanings, whether these meanings be illumined by fate, the will of God, or just our own stories—means is that *to entreat* is *to be* spiritual. One cannot be spiritual without this capacity to entreat beyond ourselves, and this means that being spiritual depends on our being speakers. Language thus plays a fundamental role in our understanding of spirit: I cannot be spiritual without language. (This does not mean 'talking'; indeed 'listening' is probably far more spiritual than talking.)

We must guard against trivial descriptions of language. Language is by no means just for 'communication'. Communication of what? Ideas? But ideas themselves are not possible without language. Nor should we think of language as a specific cultural form of expression, such as the claim that English is one language and German another. Language here rather means the ability to articulate or to manifest meanings; it also means to hear or to listen to the articulation of meanings. When language is lifted to the level of ultimate entreaty, it is prayer.

But entreaties presuppose two modalities: first, that I lack or want; and second, that I do not deserve what is asked. If I deserve, I do not entreat, I demand. Thus, in prayer, I manifest both my lacking and my existential worth; for why should God grant that which is not deserved, unless I first assume that there is something about me which evokes a willingness to bestow. This must be stressed: when I pray I am asking, not because I deserve the boon, for that would permit of a demand; rather, I ask on behalf of my being who I am. (Is this not the true existential reason for religions speaking of human beings as 'children' of God: not because they were created by God, for in this theology so is everything else created; but rather because children are precisely those to whom we bestow gifts simply because they are ours.) In prayer, this sense of 'belonging to' the entreated is existentially compelling. For in the very petition I acknowledge the gratuitous and gracious. This raises a fascinating question: is it, then, impossible to pray for justice? For I *deserve* justice; it is incoherent to say I deserve mercy or pardon, since the very notion of such gratuities is that they are not deserved. So if prayer is essentially the entreaty based upon our existential rather than our moral worth, it would seem one cannot properly 'pray' for justice. And though this seems counterintuitive and even sacrilegious to many, there are good reasons for saying this. One may believe in a post-terrestial justice, as Kant points out; but one cannot *pray* to be treated justly, since *terrestial* justice is our affair, not God's. I might entreat a threatening man to treat me justly, but if I do I am deceiving both myself and my would-be tormentor; for I ought to demand justice, not entreat for it. (Now it may be *prudent* to entreat rather than demand, but that is an entirely different matter.) For, by entreating for justice rather than demanding it, I am assuming that justice is nothing else than the willing bestowal of my threatener, and that is to do violence to the notion of justice itself.

But surely people pray for justice all the time. The fact that they do does not mean they should or that their actions are consistent with the proper meanings of the terms. To *pray* that God himself treat us with justice is, of course, outrageous, since it suggests God would treat us unjustly without the entreaty. To pray to God that he arrange the circumstances of our existence so that others treat us justly is to ask, not for justice, but for good fortune; for unless others be denied their freedom it must always be possible that they unjustly offend us. If we ask to have things arranged so that we simply do not confront unjust men, that is an undeserved boon which we could ask for but *not* demand; for I have no moral right that I never confront unjust men. So it seems one cannot truly pray for justice.

Can I, then, pray for any virtue? One of the most frequent prayers is that for courage; and here it seems one can indeed pray for this virtue. For courage is not a right as justice is; it is a quality of character. To pray for courage then recognizes our own weakness and frailty but entreats to be bestowed with a strength that is not ours by right but by grace. Of course, if one already has the moral strength known as courage, there is no need to pray for it. Yet, surely, the most courageous are those who, in the confrontation of the dreadful, entreat God to bestow strength. This is explained by pointing out that the fear, which is necessary for courage, is not of a misfortune that will occur to us, but that we will prove lacking in terms of our existential worth. What we pray for in the entreaty for courage is not success in the venture, but dignity and nobility in the acceptance of either victory or defeat. Not knowing if we have sufficient strength we ask, as a bestowal and not a right, to achieve that sufficiency.

Reflection on the peculiar gracious or existential meaning to prayer thus reveals why discussion about 'efficacy' of prayer is philosophically irrelevant. Since, *if* there is such a thing as an 'answer' to prayer, it would always be bestowed as a gift and never as the right, the determination of *whether* it will be granted or whether the bestowal depends on the sincerity or urgency of the prayer is entirely beyond the grasp of our knowledge. It is to confuse granting with deserving. The Christian quotation: "Ask, and it shall be granted unto you" does not mean, therefore, that *whenever* you ask it will always be given. (We *know* that is not true. Too many good Christians have entreated desperately for very worthy gifts and been denied.) Rather, the quotation can be taken to mean that if our prayer is granted, it will be provided as a *gift* and not as a *right* (that is: it will be *bestowed*, not *paid*).

It might be objected that our analysis overemphasizes the etymological meaning to prayer, that what many people mean by prayer is not entreaty but simply correspondence of some sort. To pray, they would say, is to visit verbally with God; perhaps to listen to the quiet whisperings of profound depth and beauty which happens only in the inner soul. There is no logical reason why one should deny the possibility of such a thing, but if it is truly in the nature of a kind of divine chat, it should not be called prayer. But if it is more than that (and I assume this is what is usually meant), if, for instance, it is the spiritual, almost mystical listening, to a divine presence, then it is surely prayer in the noblest sense, for once again such events, if they do occur, are privileges and not rights. The praying one may not specifically have entreated for this particular boon—i.e., the boon of having God speak inwardly to a person—but it is understood exactly in the same way we understand an entreaty: it is a bestowal granted because of who one is, it is a privilege and not a right, and it cannot be demanded, as justice can. To receive such a boon is to be in the state of entreaty or prayer. For those who have received such boons, if there are any, the honor of having received such grace cannot be due to any right or even any ritual. That is, there exists no formal set of ritualistic conditions which, if followed, will guarantee this bestowal. The rites may indeed be sacred and revered, but that is because they constitute, or at least are meant to constitute, the *asking*, not the *receiving*. No technology of procedure can ever be designed to guarantee efficacy in entreaty, either to the divine, in prayer, or to the human, in beseeching. For if the procedures or rites were guaranteed, the intrinsic and essential notion of bestowal or granting would be lost.

To characterize prayers as the articulation of our consciousness of bestowal in an entreaty to that which is beyond our normal comprehension, may seem as if we have merely taken the theological definition of prayer and removed the term 'God' simply to satisfy the agnostic or atheistic reader. Certainly to one who devoutly prays the notion of prayer is meaningless without the notion of God. And, the term 'God' here means a being who can at least listen and who can, though need not, bestow. In no way is our analysis intended as a mere softening of theological understanding to accommodate a wider audience. Rather, the aim is to put the notion of prayer in its proper, existential perspective: to pray is to entreat, and to entreat is to be in the modality of a lacking, which we wish to be fulfilled, not by right but by bestowal. The acknowledgment of the bestowal is an affirmation of the autonomy of our existential worth: for one is bestowed solely on the basis of who one is, not on the basis of what one does. By this analysis, then, no attempt is made to excise theistic belief and hence reduce prayer to a mere psychological phenomenon. It *is* to deemphasize concern for efficacy, for the essence of prayer lies not in the assurance of one's request being granted but in the entreaty itself. Many among the saints pray devoutly without asking for anything; indeed among the boldest of the saints are those who eschew efficacy precisely because such concern distracts from the primary meaning. It may well be the case that those who pray most profoundly are those who have a solid belief in a divine hearer; but if this is true it merely reiterates the principle: people do not first believe and then pray; they first pray, and *because* they realize they pray, they then believe. This existential inversion in no way lessens the authority of prayer as a modality of belief. Indeed it has already been shown that transcendence, of which prayer is but an essential part, is possible only because of the I-Thou and He-Us modality of our existence.

The notion already noted that 'lack' is essential for prayer must now be clarified. In a very real sense, as long as I am a human being, I cannot 'lack' my moral worth. That is, as long as I qualify as a person, I have certain rights. These rights, of course, may be denied me by misfortune or the wickedness of others, but if so, we say I have been wronged, and there remains an eternal appeal that, so wronged, I deserve to be compensated or avenged. But it is exactly the opposite in the case of spiritual transcendence: for here I do not have rights but privileges. To entreat is to reveal myself as *lacking precisely in that modality which can only be fulfilled by bestowal.* In entreaty, then, I supplicate with the recognition that the sole basis for my language of prayer is the acknowledgment of the possibility of grace. In this way, no matter how supplicant or humble the one who prays may be, nor how obsequious his behavior may seem, the act of prayer acknowledges one's existential worth. In the same way that a beloved child may entreat his parent for an undeserved gift and thereby reveal his lofty status as a beloved and not a mere wage-earner, so one who prays ennobles himself, or lifts himself to the level of being assessed solely in terms of his autonomous worth *as* one to whom something can be bestowed. In this way prayer elevates; not merely by drawing the attention of the mind to a higher reality, but by raising the ontological *status* of the one who prays.

The notion that such supplication is an entreaty to grace suggests that the essence of spirit consists in the transcendence of bestowal over justice. But 'grace' is a term which deserves richer analysis. To fulfill this it is now fitting to turn to the final candidate for the essence of spirit.

GRATITUDE

Earlier, in the discussion on sacrifice, appeal was made to the characters of Goneril and Regan in Shakespeare's tragic play, *King Lear*. It was there noted that the lack of gratitude indicts these 'pelican daughters' as particularly ignoble, since the violation is not merely against propriety and the moral law but is an insult against the generosity of their father's bestowal. At that time it was suggested that the notion of gratitude plays an important role in our understanding of spirit. Here, however, the suggestion is even stronger: that gratitude is the *essence* of spirit. In order to initiate this suggestion, reference is made to yet another literary masterpiece.

Dante's "Inferno," the favorite part of his massive epic *The Divine Comedy*, tells us of the various levels of hell. By depicting the kinds of suffering meted out to the differing kinds of crimes, one grasps how we think about the ranking of our wrongs. The lower the level, the worse the offense. It is perhaps surprising that the ranking of depravity should so fascinate us, but by noting the *degrees* of wickedness one learns a great deal about how we think not only of the failures, but also of the virtues which have been violated. We note, for example, that murder, terrible as it is, does not deserve the deepest indictment; and part of the reason for that is that sins against dignity and grace, though they may cause less suffering to the victim, are simply more detestable and repugnant than violence. Furthermore, murder is a violation against the body and may be prompted by huge passions, whereas cruelty or sins against grace seem to suggest a meaner spirit. Neither poet nor reader usually takes these assignments as theologically beyond dispute: the point is to reveal, through poetry, how we react negatively to certain crimes, which then in turn reveals to us our priorities concerning our virtues and the good life. And so it is a capital inquiry to ask: who are those in the very lowest place in Dante's hell?

In the very bottom of hell, according to Dante, hunches the torso of a three-headed Satan, locked in the icy grip of a vast and frozen lake. Each of the three faces of Satan is gnawing on the embodied soul of an infamous traitor: Judas Iscariot, Brutus, and Cassius. These three, it is explained by Virgil to Dante, are suffering the worst torment of all because their peculiar sin was not merely treachery, but betrayal of one who had loved them. From this we learn that the moral outrage of treason is accompanied by the spiritual outrage of the betrayal of one who loved and honored the offenders by granting them bestowals far beyond their station. Judas, Brutus, and Cassius were not only traitors, they were offenders against generosity and love. For this they are placed forever in the frozen pit of the deepest hell. Two remarks can be made to initiate this division of our inquiry: the punishment is peculiarly fitting, for in the frozen lake they have no warmth at all, and warmth is a metaphor for closeness and even affection. The punishment for abusing affection is the total removal of all memories and hopes of affection: bitter cold. Secondly, the depravity of these crimes is simply without peer: there can be no sin as sacrilegious as the betrayal of graciousness, for the offense is not a mere violation against the *moral* law, but against the generous bestowal of affection.

Brutus, Judas and Cassius are, of course, not the only betrayers of affection. There are many other souls whose punishment is to be locked in this frozen lake where no warmth and no movement can occur. Dante says of them:

> So, to where modest shame appears, thus low
> Blue pinch'd and shrined in ice the spirits stood,
> His face each downward held; their mouth the cold,
> Their eyes expressed the dolour of their heart.
> (Cary translation, XXXII, 34–38).

The passage positively shivers with suffering and regret. And so we must ask: why do both Dante and Shakespeare, master poets and profound observers of the human heart, seem to agree that there simply is no more heinous violation against our spiritual sensitivities than that of ungrateful betrayal? For it must be restressed: it is not that these souls in Dante's hell and the unsavory daughters of Lear were merely treacherous, but that they were singularly ungrateful in their betrayal. Of course, all betrayal is a violation of gratitude, but these five, Goneril, Regan, Iscariot, Cassius, and Brutus, have been pointed out by our master poets as paradigms of ingratitude. Their acts of betrayal are rooted in their ingratitude, and for this they are are poetically damned to frozen misery. Why? How are we to understand this artistic indictment of the worst sort? Do we, in fact, agree with it?

Our agreement is certainly not a request for a poll. I submit it here merely as a private consideration for the reader. It surely seems as though we should feel a special sense of revulsion at these crimes. For the offense is not against the moral order, from which both excuses and pardons can redeem us, but against the very source of all pardon: the gracious. There may, in fact, be some crimes that are morally worse than treachery, but there can be no spiritual offense to equal it, since the object of the offense is the loving bestowal, granted without deserving or merit, and the betrayal thus offends spirit itself. To be ungrateful, therefore, is to offend the very meaning of spirit, and if this is so it may suggest that gratitude is thus the true essence of spirit.

"Thank you." These two words reveal a curious modality of our existence. On the one hand, they express that an appreciation is acknowledged for a benefit received that was not one's due; but they also elevate, because the very acknowledgment of being given what is not one's due is to assert there is a higher or more lofty modality which transcends mere moral obligation and rests, rather, on the capacity to be favored, befriended, or loved. To thank is not merely to acknowledge the gift; it is also to express appreciation of a new status achieved by having received the gift, that of the favored. We have already seen how, in the ranking of kinds of giving discussed in the passage on sacrifice, the meaning of bestowal demands an ontological difference between the modalities which receive rights and those which receive gifts. Gratitude is the acknowledgement both of the generosity of the giver and the elevation of one's own status as being favored solely in terms of who one is rather than what one does.

Consider the following frustration. Suppose I have enjoyed a series of remarkable boons which are not deserved but which endow me with considerable joy and delight. It is possible, of course, simply to feel lucky and to render some acknowledgment of the sheer fortuity of our world. I can, in other words, take these undeserved benefits, declare myself fortunate, and simply delight in the possession of them. But if these boons touch me in a way that provokes a need to thank, whom can I designate as the bestower of my good fortune? If I am religiously spiritual, I may of course give thanks to God; if I am a spiritual agnostic or simply confused about the nature of a supreme reality, I may recognize some Providence to thank, without quite knowing what that means. But if I feel thankful and acknowledge no spiritual basis for this gratitude, I must simply understand my being grateful as an illusion, or a trick of psychological deceit. But in that case, my being grateful is without ground, and hence foolish. The gratitude that I acknowledge for these boons must then be denied; I accept them either as rights deserved by the fortunate or as sheer fortuities that provoke no gratitude at all. Thus, when I am confronted by any such bestowal of undeserved good fortune, the urge to be grateful evokes at the very least a sense of my worth as one who can be favored or befriended, as well as an indebtedness of thanksgiving to whatever bestows such joy. There is nothing more frustrating for a person with sensibilities than to have no spirit to acknowledge within oneself as the reason for the bestowal, and no possibility of thanking. As a result I can only assume myself not to be favored but lucky and hence must remain unable to acknowledge the bestowal of fortune. This is difficult to sustain as an existential modality, so the only likely replacement is the inauthentic one of deserving. Denied the opportunity to be grateful, and frustrated by the sheer acceptance of mere accident, I become convinced that in some way I *deserve* these benefits. But this is to become arrogant and boorish as the result of good fortune, which is surely a depressing thought. The occurrence of unexpected benefit inevitably turns the mind to either gratitude or self-gratulation. Why is being grateful to sheer fortune any more rational than gratitude toward Providence, or in the case of religious spirituality, God? To say that to be grateful to God requires an unacceptable reification of a metaphysical entity may be a protest, but is the reification of Luck any less arbitrary or ungrounded? The simple point here is that to be the recipient of such undeserved boons evokes a powerful, existential modality of gratitude which can be replaced only by inauthentic modalities such as belief in Luck or simple indifference to one's good fortunes.

Oddly, the reversal of this does not seem to follow. If I am confronted by considerable misery, also undeserved, the mind does not seem unduly persuaded to blame some powerful evil force. For some reason, the endurance of suffering can appear intrinsically virtuous, as a Stoic might argue; whereas the experience of unexpected delights evokes an existential need to thank. This acknowledgment of the need to be grateful is an essential characteristic of spirit. We would surely identify the indifferent as lacking in spirituality, and those who opt to account for their good fortune as deserved we would indict as arrogant.

Suppose I try to account for my gratitude at receiving undeserved benefits by an appeal to such amorphous notions as fate or luck. We often hear such accounts, as when one asserts that "it is my fate to have been born wealthy," or "we were fated to love," or even "I thank my lucky stars that I am clever." How are we to understand such notions as 'fate', 'luck', or even 'destiny'? Kant calls these "unsurpatory concepts," which means that we use them as if they were genuine explanative concepts but which, upon analysis, turn out to have no explanative force at all. Thus, to say "I was fated to be wealthy" turns out to be the same as "I am wealthy"; i.e., the addition of the term 'fate', since I do not know what fate is, simply adds nothing to the sentence. If I have a metaphysical notion of some determining power, like a mythological notion of fate, of course, the sentence "I am fated to do x" *does* mean something other than "I do x"; but such metaphysical beliefs are far less acceptable to the canons of reason than gratitude to a divine being. If I say, "The reason I am so charming is that I am lucky," it is obvious that upon analysis I have misused the term 'reason'; 'luck' is not a determiner in the sense of an agent. Thus, to say I am lucky to do x means merely that I do x. This is why Kant calls such terms 'usurpatory'; they *seem* to explain but really do not. Their inclusion in a sentence does not *add* anything to a sentence. And so, since fate, luck, and destiny do not *add* anything, to appeal to them as *explanations* of my good fortune is absurd and to render gratitude toward such empty notions is just silly.

This, of course, leaves the notion of 'chance'. We say, "It was mere chance that I happened to pick the right lottery ticket." But chance means nothing else but ignorance of the elements or laws involved. If I flip a coin and let 'chance' decide, the ensuing result, that the coin comes up heads, is obviously due to very precise and real laws governing the determination of physical activity. If I knew the exact amount of pressure my thumb would exert on the coin, if I knew the wind currents in the room and the principles which determine revolving coins, I would *know in advance* the coin would turn up heads. Thus, when we appeal to chance, we appeal to our own ignorance. This is at least honest. I am saying: I do not know what accounts for my good fortune. But such ignorance, when left as an *explanation,* merely repeats the sentence: to say the coins come up heads by chance is to say the coins come up heads. Chance, then, tells us nothing at all about the one favored. But of course, that is precisely why gratitude is so important, and why I cannot be grateful to chance. Chance does not respect persons, it is merely the ignorance of physical laws which, had I known them would render the event predictable. But gratitude reveals something about the grateful one: that there is something about him which promotes the bestower of benefits to favor him. In other words, not to thank is to deny the significance of my being able to be favored.

In ordinary human intercourse, we confront the thankless everyday. We consider it a breach of politeness or manners precisely because it offends the very graciousness of the bestowal. We feel sorry for the thankless because such a person is lacking a certain understanding of himself as being favored simply because of who he is. Most of us recognize that authentic gratitude establishes an acknowledgement between the receiver and donor, such that the receiver recognizes that the donor has favored him. Merely to be polite and say the terms 'thank you' does not establish gratitude; nor does obsequious behavior designed to provoke more benefits. True gratitude demands that the recipient of favors acknowledge that he is favored beyond what is his by right, and thus that he realizes something about himself which is more fundamental than rights and that he acknowledge the favoring agent. To thank is to celebrate this existential modality.

But suppose we speak, not of thanking a person for a specific boon, but of the modality of thankfulness for existing at all. Is a gratitudinous existence a meaningful modality? Can I, in other words, reflect upon the fact that I exist, realize that such existence is fortuitous, and then acknowledge gratitude for my existence? Unless I simply refuse to think about the meaning of existence at all, it would seem I have three alternatives: (1) I regret my existence and hence am not grateful but angry that I am; (2) I am indifferent to my existence and could not possibly care one way or the other; or (3) I am grateful for my existence. But to whom? I cannot be grateful to fate, chance, or the laws of nature, since it has shown above that in order to be grateful I must acknowledge in myself that quality which provides for my being favored, and neither chance, fate, nor the biological laws of nature can favor. Thus, if I am grateful for my existence, I must be grateful to something which can bestow, and more importantly, I must acknowledge myself as being able to be favored. But this is exactly what spirit means. To be spiritual is to acknowledge the autonomous worth of being favored; i.e., to be spirit is to *matter* to someone or something, however vague, rather than to be explicated solely by principles which do not provide a sense of mattering or caring.

The point can now be made more simply. It is logically possible to account for my existence, or even for the enjoyment of undeserved boons, solely by an appeal to the laws of nature. But in such an account there is no provision for making sense of mattering or caring; i.e., there is no provision for being favored and hence no way to account for gratitude. In such an account, the phenomenon of gratitude would be restricted solely to gifts bestowed by living human beings who favor me because of who I am; there would be no possibility of my being grateful for my existence. Thus, a grateful or gratitudinous existence is the supreme mark of spirit, for in the absence of some quality about *me* that allows me to be favored by some power which *bestows existence* (and that quality is 'being spiritual'), I can only accept the fact of my existence as a mere event, which, if it is a purely natural event, cannot be appreciated gratefully.

One might want to argue that this provides one with an existential reason for belief in a bestowing Providence or God; and perhaps that can be defended. However, it is not the purpose of this inquiry. The present analysis is not concerned with who or what bestows, but with what it means to be favored. From the ordinary human interchanges of gifts, we can understand the meaning of gratitude, and recognize, as Shakespeare and Dante do, that the thankless are the most despicable. But when we lift the notion of gratitude to the acknowledgment of existence itself as bestowal, an entirely different modality is demanded of us. The existential change is profound. For now, my very existence is characterized *essentially* by meaning, mattering, caring, and being favored. The argument here is simply that this is what we mean by being spiritual. For if the ten predicates of spirit used to describe the term are correct, they seem to support the notion that a gratitudinous existence is the fundamental ground of spirit. We think of ourselves no longer as entities having certain qualities, but as modalities, of which the gracious is the paramount. Surely this explains such predicates as rapture, mystery, adventure, etc., as well as the other two candidates, Nearness and Transcendence. The argument is thus laid down to support the third candidate: gratitude is the essence of spirit.

"*The End.*" These two words evoke, even in the simplest child, the termination of a story. They are found at the final moments of older films, on the last pages of premodern novels, and even today of children's stories. But these two words may also designate the termination of our life: this is the end. We are going to die. Certainly any account of spirit which omits the importance of death in our understanding of spirit would be deficient. Many cynics believe that the *only* reason for belief in spiritual things is the purely psychological one of fearing death. But does this seeming isomorphism between the final words of a story and the impending collapse into nothingness of a human reality have any basis other than a mere accidental use of similar terms? Or is it the case that the term 'the end' is profoundly storied, such that our own ends can be made intelligible only as the finality of a story? In other words, does this similarity of the two uses of the term 'the end' suggest that the proper way to understand the meaning of our existence is as a story? Are we stories? And if so, what does this reveal about spirit and the possibility that the essence of spirit is gratitude?

It is remarkable that, in spite of the fact that we make sense of so much through the telling of stories, philosophers rarely spend much time or energy in analyzing how a story works, how it is that by arranging a sequence of events in a proper order, sense is made not only of the individual moments but of the entire collection of moments that go to make up a story. There is a test given by psychologists in the examination of intellectual capacity of the subject in which the subject is given a set of cartoon pictures at random. The point of the test is to see how quickly, if at all, the subject can arrange the squares into a coherent story pattern. I am not qualified to judge whether this is a good procedure for testing intelligence; but I do know that most people eventually can arrange the cartoon squares into a proper storied sequence and that if they cannot do so, there are grounds for believing the subject is seriously lacking in intellectual skills. This suggests that the structure of a story is almost innate: we seem to know almost a priori that a certain sequence will reveal a meaningful tale, whereas a mere random arrangement of these moments will yield nothing coherent. And yet, we are presented in our daily lives with disconnected moments, not as a story, but simply as a series of events. What is it that allows us to select, arrange, and present these moments in a pattern that makes them intelligible? Surely it is something essential about the way we think of our own existence as unfolding through time.

Kant has pointed out that time is the form of the inner sense; that is, that time is not an object of perception but a form or way of perceiving. We do not see time, we see through time. But this temporal structure allows us to arrange events in terms of conditions and their effects (first we light the fire, then we feel the heat). There is nothing storylike about the mere sequence of causes. Rather, a story makes of the sequence of moments through time a meaningful appreciation of the significance of the actions. Stories have a beginning, a middle, and an end. But stories also have character, plot, and theme. The six elements: beginning, middle, end, character, plot, and theme do not make up the story; rather it is the story that provides meaning for the six elements. If the story provides the meaning to the elements, it must be formally prior to them. Hence, I cannot explain the story by means of these six elements, since the explanation is from the story to the element. Stories are thus a priori forms of meaningful existence: i.e., in the absence of a story, the various moments of existence remain incoherent or at least isolated and disconnected.

Without stories, whether factual (history) or fanciful (novels), we could make no sense of our existence. Yet a story is totally unlike the categories of cause and effect, or the understanding of one moment as a condition prior to the subsequent moment. We do not think the various moments, chapters, or episodes of a story are in any way lawlike, the way categories are. They are, however, nonetheless necessary ways which must preexist the moments if we are to make sense of the unfolding of time. Since they are not lawlike, as the categories are, they are bestowals to our understanding. That is, the capacity to understand our unfolding in time through the structure of a story is more like a gift than a law. If anything, it is our aesthetic consciousness rather than our scientific consciousness that provides the story structure. To be able to understand ourselves as the unfolding of a story is a bestowal, and this bestowal may be essential for an authentic, i.e., meaningful existence. Certainly one who reflects on one's various moments, developments, and alterations merely as a disconnected series of random events is lacking in the fundamental grasp of one's meaningful existence. If I cannot tell my story, I cannot present my own existence as having meaning.

The three formal elements, the beginning, middle, and end, can be determined easily enough simply by the calender. The three structural elements, character, plot, and theme, can be provided first by ourselves: we are our own character; secondly by our adventures: we live through the events which alter us; but from whence comes the theme? This is provided by the gracious bestowal of one who would hear (or perhaps even tell) our story. When Hamlet lies dying in the arms of his friend Horatio, he begs: "If thou dids't ever hold me in thy heart,/Absent thee from felicity awhile . . . to tell my story." It is not egregious that such a duty is to be carried out by a friend and by a friend willing to absent himself from felicity.

Those who argue that spirituality, especially religious forms of spirituality, are grounded in the sheer fear of death, have, I think, misprized the human reality. For do we truly fear death so much? Do we fear it at all? We may fear the pain of dying, or the grief we shall cause our beloved ones when we are gone; but how can sheer emptiness frighten? Surely what we fear in dying is not death itself—for as long as we are, we cannot meet death, as Epicurus points out—but the dread lest we are taken away before our story is finished. Thus it is life uncompleted we fear rather than death itself. And life uncompleted is simply a story cut short, a story not finished. It is, if you will, a nonstory, since a story should have an end commensurate with the beginning and the middle. Belief in an afterlife merely prolongs the story.

Yet stories need not end in death. When the child hears the familiar end, "and they lived happily ever after," the listener is not being asked to believe in eternality; rather he is being informed that the story is finished, not the life. Though the united prince and princess may be happy, their lives are, for the story-listener, no longer interesting. Thus, it is the story that provides the interest, not the mere happiness: that may be reserved for the period *after* the story is completed. We thus have a series of events or disconnected moments which are unified by the power or authority of the structure known as a story, and this structure provides interest or meaning. Our lives can, of course, be seen merely as a series of events or moments, possibly pleasant moments, possibly wretched, but most likely a mixture. But a special grace is added if these events congeal together in some way to make a story.

But if our lives do make a story, then we have spirit. The final element of a story is the end; if our life is a story it can be so only if we have an end: our death. Being spiritual thus embraces death because it completes our story, not because there must be a post-terrestial continuation. Yet, for there to be a story, there must be a teller and a hearer. To think of one's existence *as* a story is to assume it can be told. But there is no logical necessity to this; there is only an existential necessity, which is to be grateful, because the moments that, when added up, make up our lives, need not tell a story; but if these moments *do* make up a story, that is a bestowal.

It seems an essential characteristic, then, of spiritual beings, that they think of their own existence in a storied way. So, one seeks for spirit, not out of a fear of death, but out of a fear of a meaningless life, which is what an untimely death means. Our very lives can provide a story but only if we assume spirit. To be at an end is to be the end. We are stories. And the telling of our stories is possible only through the gratitudinous bestowal of spirit. We do not merely die if we are spirit, we come to the end. And that is a powerful difference. That is the spiritual difference.

I have presented the three candidates for the essence of spirit without any determination of preference. It seems one can argue the essence of spirits is nearness; or that it is transcendence; or that it is gratitude. Each of these candidates is so different from the other two that the approach reveals a great deal about how we think of spirit. It is perhaps not necessary for us to decide which is *the* essence; but it is important to consider the arguments, given in their respective presentations, for the attempt of this work remains that of inquiring into the meaning of spirit. It is important to argue that gratitude is the essence, and not transcendence or nearness; or to maintain that nearness and not gratitude is the essence. For in these arguments we find ourselves seeking ever deeper penetration of the elusive prey in the murky depths of our ignorance. Perhaps in some way a single notion can be found which somehow integrates nearness, gratitude, and transcendence. But if so, the reason for accepting such a unificatory notion is because of the argumentation provided in the above sections.

It is insufficient merely to say that spirit includes the notions of nearness, gratitude, and transcendence. For these are not characteristics or qualities that are somehow 'added on' to the notion of spirit. They are candidates for its essence, and that means that in thinking of spirit *as* transcendence, gratitude, or nearness, we are isolating the fundamental way to think about the notion. The ten predicates which *describe* spirit are, with these three suggestions, unified in a *definition*. That the inquiry presents three possibilities rather than one actuality in no way alters the classical authority of this distinction between description and definition. We might remind ourselves that one of the predicates of spirit is mystery, and if there is still some uncertainty as to which candidate best deserves the title of essence of spirit, it may be due to the importance of mystery even in the inquiry into what the term means. Before we turn to the final reflections, one more chapter is necessary to complete the task of description and definition. And this need rests upon the very richness of the term: spirit is not always good.

11

Spiritual Evil

Once we have established the autonomy of spirit—that is, once we have recognized that we matter as *belonging*, in addition to what we do—it then becomes obvious that this new realm of spirit contains not only the benefits of independent worth but also the failures. In doing this we have passed from the moral realm of what is bad and wicked to the spiritual realm of what is evil. There are those, of course, who would reduce the latter to the former and insist that by 'evil' we mean merely extremely severe cases of moral wickedness, so that there is no special or autonomous meaning to evil. The following is not an argument to convince the would-be critic that there *is* a realm of evil which is autonomous of bad or wicked, rather it is an inquiry into what evil means if it is to be thought as nonreductive to the moral deviations of bad and wicked. (I take 'bad' to refer to the immorality of actions, and 'wicked' to refer to the corruption or delinquency of character.)

What must I assume if there is to be a special realm of what is improper as spirit, i.e., spiritual evil? If it is separate from what is bad or wicked what constitutes its wrongness? Does the term 'evil' suggest a spiritual realm, but distorted, perverse, or somehow threatening of the well-being of spirit? One thing must be stated clearly from the beginning; by 'evil' we cannot mean 'nonspiritual', for the entire argument is this: evil is possible only if spirit is possible. If one's worth consists solely in one's morality, then there is neither spirit nor evil, for 'spirit' becomes a mere extension of 'good', and 'evil' becomes a mere extension of 'immoral'. (Deism seems, in fact, to support these reductions. It is extremely difficult to find any ground among deists for analyzing the notion of the holy: for them, the good and virtuous life is truly its own reward, and the wicked are the nonelect who deserve punishment but can never be forgiven. Cotton Mather, Benjamin Franklin, David Hume, and even Kant himself press the notion that 'religion' means the same as 'morality', and if there is anything to the notion of holy or sacred it is equated with the virtuous.)

The argument works both ways. If there is an autonomous notion of spirit which is not reducible to the virtuous life, then spiritual evil must be possible; on the other hand, if I accept a notion of evil which is not merely immoral, then I must accept the realm of spirit. For in the present context the term 'evil' is being used solely and exclusively as a spiritual term. If we assume this provisionally, then it should be beneficial for the inquiry to examine the meaning of evil as a way of illuminating just what spirit means, in the same way that the study of the wicked often reveals how we think of virtue.

But when we turn to a consideration of an autonomous notion of spiritual evil we find ourselves confronted with a powerful and impressive argument that seems to deflate the entire program. Nietzsche insists that there *is* a difference between what is merely 'bad' and what is 'evil', but his famous and persuasive argument in *The Genealogy of Morals* makes belief in the meaningful notion of evil *ignoble*. That is, those who accept the reality of evil are by definition ignoble; whereas those who accept the notion of 'bad' are noble. According to Nietzsche's analysis the difference between bad and evil is this: when a base or ignoble person does something wrong, he thinks of it as grounded in the power of the Evil Ones, those greater than we who seek our spiritual destruction (like Satan, for example). But when a noble person does something wrong, he thinks of it as an action not in keeping with his true character or calling, and thus is *bad*. To be bad is thus to be unworthy of one's nobility; so, if the noble person errs, he rejects his act as unworthy of himself, makes whatever recompense is necessary and forgets it. But the ignoble whimpers and whines beneath the dark shadow of impending evil; his errors are brought about by the influence of the devil, who hence terrorizes the guilty by burdening them with the weight of guilt which they do not deserve. "The devil made me do it." This is how we think of evil, because evil, in the guise of Satan or any other candidate, being more powerful than us, is a force or power *beyond* ourselves, *other* than ourselves. Of course, under this assumption, I cannot truly be held responsible. My sins are due to the possession of my soul by some foul fiend. Thus, for the noble, the distinction is between good and bad, where bad is simply that which the noble do not do; for the ignoble, the distinction is between the good (the weak) and the evil (the powerful), which not only denies our responsibility, but makes us terrified before the manipulative cunning of one more powerful than ourselves.

This is a brilliant analysis, and surely it contains much truth. However, it seems to deflate completely the present inquiry, for the overriding point of Nietzsche's analysis simply is the grounding of morality on nobility, and this makes the notion of spiritual evil an ignoble belief. Now I have far too great a respect for Nietzsche to dismiss his profound analysis; but the threat to the autonomy of spirit and evil wrought by this interpretation is formidable. It is, however, not irresistible. Indeed, I should argue that Nietzsche is quite right in his profound observation that 'evil' means "other"; but it is not another being or entity which is other; rather, it is being other that threatens us in the spiritual phenomenon of evil. In other words, it is not an external, powerful entity or person like Lucifer that threatens, it is the distortion or even perversion of one's spirituality, which is indeed 'other', but not excusatory. For the distinction between 'evil' and 'bad' is precious to us; we do not want to lose this valuable difference. We seem to need the ability to indict and censure by means of responsibility (the bad), and at the same time, to hold in dread and revulsion that which threatens us as a powerful force alien to ourselves (evil). This, it seems, Nietzsche recognizes; but his insistence that 'evil' be another *entity*, indeed a source of power outside ourselves, is simplistic. There is no doubt that many superstitious people do believe in wicked spirits, like elves, gnomes, ghosts, and devils, who roam about the world seeking entrance into souls. Such beliefs, even if lightly and nonseriously entertained, make for wonderful horror stories and thrillers. Where would Hollywood be without vampires, werewolves, and Satanic possessions? But, though the more critical amongst us may hold such beliefs in contempt, even these fairly harmless, imaginative entertainments help us understand something about evil: it is different from bad precisely in that it threatens by alienation. In this, Nietzsche is right. But that it is thereby an external reality is an unwarranted inference. Surely what we mean by evil is that threat of becoming alien to ourselves; becoming twisted, perverse, or unnatural. But we are still *responsible* for this transmogrification; hence Nietzsche's supreme complaint against it is reserved only for those who objectify it as other, not to those who recognize it as a possibility of one's own being.

It is a wicked and cruel thing to see a grown man break the legs of a child, and our sentiments in such a situation are outrage, disgust, and an impulse to punish. But when an African slaveholder clamps the youth's legs into distorted boxes so that the growing limbs will be thwarted in their natural development, making the child a cripple to evoke the pity of the almsgiver, we feel not only a moral outrage but a sickness of heart, a deep feeling of defilement and pity. If a young girl loses her voice by a car accident we consider it a terrible misfortune and deeply regrettable; but if she herself rips out her own vocal chords in some perverse spiritual ritual, we are horrified. There is something evil about the distortion and twisting of what is naturally radiant and wonderful into something grotesque and obscene. These are not mere aesthetic differences; they account for a genuine distinction which demands the presupposition of spirit. A moral offense is bad, a spiritual offense is evil. Nietzsche's definition of evil as an outside power actually reduces it to whatever causes superstition and fear. It is the otherness of both superstition and true evil that makes Nietzsche characterize this otherness as ignoble. To be sure, to tremble and quake before an external power greater than ourselves, thus forfeiting our responsibility, is ignoble; but to dread the possibility that one becomes alien to oneself and hence unworthy of being who one is cannot be seen as ignoble. Such dread merely manifests the high and lofty concern one has for who one is.

When the bad presents itself, one may be *tempted;* when evil portends, one may be fearful. I dread the possibility of *becoming* evil, but I am attracted or seduced by what is bad. To do what is bad benefits me at least on the baser level of my appetites; to become evil, however, is to lose or forfeit my own reality. Temptation (which is always of the bad, not of evil) is an appeal to my possible weakness and thus, by definition, is what attracts. Evil, though it too may be alluring, repels. Spiritual evil repels us because it threatens to make us other than we are, even though we freely, and hence responsibly, may submit to it. The Nietzschean insight is thus retained, though altered. There is a meaningful and nonignoble sense of evil, which is different from mere badness, in that it brings about an alteration of our very meaning and existence, but it is not, as Nietzsche seems to suggest, *simply* an external force which frightens us because of its superior power. Spiritual evil therefore, is not the timid and cowardly fear that 'Satan' will force us to ruin; rather it is the awesome dread that we ourselves will *become* satanic.

Nietzsche is correct that evil is thought of as a power and indeed an alien power. But it is not an external power. It is rather the power which we ourselves may become and which permanently alters us in such a way as to forfeit our ownness. It is for this reason that medieval thinkers often speak of evil as the loss of one's soul, not the mere doing of what is immoral. What does it mean to speak like this? What is meant by saying one can actually *lose* one's soul? Ordinarily it may be supposed that 'to lose one's soul' is the same as 'damnation'; but being 'damned' or being 'saved' implies that one still *has* one's soul, depending on which place one is in. To lose a soul is to be without a soul, not to have it in the wrong place. To be soulless must mean something else. To be soulless is to be without care, concern, or meaning for who one is. This is not submission, as in the case of worship or rapture, for in those modalities the soul is glorified by the presence of the beloved. Rather, in 'losing one's soul'—i.e., being evil—one is without the possibility of rapture and worship, for in the soullessness that is evil one has nothing to submit and nothing to offer. One cannot be 'rapt', for there is nothing that can be taken over by the magnificence of the other. And this, of course, reveals the true meaning of spiritual evil: it is to be without any existential worth at all. The horror of it lies in the even more dreadful realization that this loss of worth is one's own responsibility.

It is the terrifying realization that I and I alone am responsible for no longer having any worth; and so I become a mere shell of a man, a thing without purpose or meaning, but still real, and hence still capable of bringing about events for ill or good. But, having achieved a total submission of worth, nothing can matter. Evil, as Hannah Arendt so wisely points out, becomes banal. It is the very banality or meaninglessness of evil which is so terrifying, and which ultimately sets it off from the bad. Morally speaking, there is nothing as bad as being bad; but spiritually speaking, the attribute of evil is far worse, since the very possibility of caring or mattering is forfeit.

One can draw a cautious parallel between spiritual evil and madness. There are many terrifying and dreadful mental torments one can endure in the struggle for sanity and self-mastery. But none so dreadful as the total loss which is entailed by the notion of complete madness. It is what the tormented mental patient fears most. The moral wrongs we may commit are, as moral, bad; indeed they may be absolutely bad—as bad as you can get. But, as long as I have done these things, I am capable of responsibility, of being censured, and even of being forgiven. But spiritual evil is not a matter of doing bad things, it is a matter of being without any meaning whatsoever. The evil person is still responsible for his actions, since he is not mad; but being evil makes his responsibility empty. He does not care one way or the other. It is the very indifference to his own wrongness that so terrifies us about the evil person; and that terror is not directed toward what he may do to us, but rather what we may ourselves become. If spirit means, as is suggested in the previous chapters, the autonomy of meaningfulness, then evil is the vacancy or emptiness that threatens such autonomy. "As flies to wanton boys are we to the gods; they use us for their sport," Albany says in *King Lear*, suggesting that the youthful cruelty is all the more terrifying for its indifference, and that despair consists of raising that cruel indifference to the level of the divine.

Suppose all our internal struggles—the agony of courage, the battle with weakness, the trust that is so monumental in the threat of doubt—suppose all of these things are simply meaningless, they just do not matter. What would this mean? It would mean that doing ill or good is a matter of supreme indifference.

Like wanton boys we pull off the wings of flies, indifferent to this violation, to this pain, to this wantonness. But boys, we hope, will mature, and learn that things do matter. The meaninglessness of evil, however, cannot be redeemed through maturity. Since it is self-induced, evil cannot simply run its course. To torture someone to force him or her to reveal an important secret may be immoral, but it is at least relieved by the importance of what is achieved. To torture for the delight it brings a sadist is more horrific, but at least there is the pleasure the torturer receives in doing it. But to torture merely because this act debases both the torturer and the tortured is not bad but evil, for the act as such has no meaning; it is countermeaningful; it is, indeed, an *assault* upon meaning itself. I do it, the evil one would say, because it has no purpose, not even the hedonistic one of bringing me pleasure. I do it because I no longer have a soul—that is, the realm of spirit has canceled itself, forfeit itself, like some hideous Hegelian dialectic without the hope of the continuing reach toward an Absolute. Surely this notion, the true notion of evil, *is* to be feared: not as an external power, but as a possibility of becoming.

These reflections in no way suggest that there are any truly evil people in the world. I know there are bad people—for as human I have been bad myself and know it—and there may be truly wicked people, whose character is so distorted that they do bad things because of their natures. But evil threatens, not because there are evil people, but simply because it is a possibility. It is not a possibility which tempts, as does the bad, but rather a possibility that *lurks*, and indeed, it lurks solely within the realm of spirit, not the realm of morality. Because it does lurk as a deceitful but genuine possible *way to be*, I am fearful of it. It is, indeed, *rational* to fear evil. The metaphoric and unrealistic imagery of ghosts, monsters, devils, and the like are helpful in this sense: they show us that to be enthralled by such is to become debased. The vampire not only sucks the blood from its victim, it sucks the very meaning from the victim, making the victim himself one of them. The fear of vampires is the fear of *becoming* a vampire. No educated person believes in vampires, of course, but one can see in these depictions of fantasy a dreary truth: spiritual slavery, in which one's autonomy is surrendered to the meaningless, is evil and should be feared.

The difference between evil and bad is not a mere childish distinction, as may be suggested by these references to vampires and ghosts. Indeed, some of the greatest literary reflections in human history focus precisely on this point, with remarkable effect. It is curious that few critics have seen that the great enigma of *Hamlet* is precisely that of distinguishing bad from evil. How many countless articles and monographs, trying to come to grips with the great literary puzzle, *why does not Hamlet act?* lead us to labyrinthian distortions of speculative psychology and to no avail? We read that Hamlet is incapable of action because he is melancholy, or because he has an Oedipus complex for his mother, or because he is homosexual, or even because he is overweight. Perhaps Hamlet is simply too scholarly, or too young or too old, or illegitimate or impotent . . . the list grows longer and sillier. Of course, almost any resolution which relies on a psychological factor such as melancholy or academic intellectualism suffers precisely because, in most cases, Hamlet can and indeed does act very resourcefully and promptly. His thrust into the arras in his mother's room with his sword is swift and unhesitating, and he even then asks if perhaps his victim is the king. He leaps openly into Ophelia's grave without hesitation and certainly without due consideration of the bad political ramifications. Hamlet seems indecisive only with regard to one issue, the revenge against his uncle the king. If this hesitancy were due to a character fault or psychological perversion, it would manifest itself in other instances, not only the one's dealing with the revenge.

But the suggestion that evil must be distinguished from the bad is wonderfully illuminating of this great play without rendering the characters or the plot ridiculous. Hamlet obviously sees the murder of his father and the marriage of his mother to his uncle not merely as bad but as evil, and precisely because it is evil there is no human act which *can* avenge it. We see Hamlet tormenting himself, calling the marriage incestuous, which it is not (the kings of Europe did it all the time; even the great Elizabeth's own father did it). So dearly does he love his mother that the notion of being defiled by his uncle seems to him not a moral wrong but a sacrilege. He tells us that what upsets him is the brevity of the time between the death and the marriage, but we know that had Claudius waited five years it would still gall the young Hamlet. The point is very simple: as long as Hamlet sees the murder and marriage as violations of the *sacred*, he cannot obey the ghostly apparition of his father for the simple reason that *no one* can rectify a sacrilege by simple revenge. How then does Hamlet finally overcome this benumbing inability to act? With his discovery, on the field when he sees Fortinbras' army, that "rightly to be great,/ Is not to stir without great argument,/ But greatly to find quarrel is a straw,/ When honor's at the stake." That is, he recognizes it is not the *act* per se which is either bad or evil but the spirit in which the act is done. Hamlet, prior to his conversion of mind during his would-be journey to England sees the acts of Claudius and Gertrude as *evil*—and hence of the order of the sacred and thus incapable of being revenged by mere human action. Afterwards, however, he sees the acts merely as *bad,* and so he can act. Thus the greatest play in the English language becomes a resource for understanding the overwhelming significance of the distinction. At the same time, the Nietzschean distinction, altered somewhat by this analysis, becomes a resolve for one of the thornier questions in literature, why Hamlet hesitates. This, however, is not a literary monograph, and though a fully developed interpretation of *Hamlet* along these lines would be richly deserving of our attention, it is enough here merely to point at the suggestion. For in *Hamlet* we see the truth starkly and poetically revealed: there is a meaningful, indeed terrifying, distinction between what is evil and what is bad. (The very opening of the play, with talk of ghosts in the misty towers of Elsinore, should alert the sensitive viewer that here we are in the realm of spirit, not moral outrage or justification.)

With this refinement one can see more clearly that one *does* what is bad, but one *is* (or dreads becoming) evil. The rich psychological and phenomenological dimensions of this distinction are available for anyone who wants to read *Hamlet* seriously. Or, for that matter, to reflect seriously on any literary or musical work which reveals the spiritual in us as a kind of battlefield. Perhaps indeed the proper definition of spirit is as a place. What is spirit? It is that *place* where the greatest struggles, the most Herculean battles occur. It is thus just as ridiculous to deny there is spirit as to deny there are these struggles.

I should not like to leave the impression that any and all forms of wrongdoing within the realm of spirit are always and only evil, never bad. There are situations or occasions in which the reflection on spirit produce nothing evil but still produce something bad. For the very *notion* of spirit prompts a certain kind of delinquency, which though not evil, is bad enough.

The doctrine that we possess worth independently of what we do is a dangerous notion if misunderstood. For on an inauthentic reading it seems to suggest that one should become indifferent to moral restrictions; or worse, it could be taken to wallow in an orgulous fantasy that being loved is all that matters. As Auden so brilliantly reveals in his poem "In Praise of Limestone":

> What could be more like Mother or a fitter background
> For her son, for the nude young male who lounges
> Against a rock displaying his dildo, never doubting
> That for all his faults he is loved, whose works are but
> Extensions of his power to charm?*

The young son relies on his charm to evoke pardon and, certain of it, smiles at his power. But the poem tells us that these are the people of limestone, who are cheerful, happy, soft, wanton, and pleasant, but who have no heroes, no warriors, and no saints. To be sure, this kind of life attracts us, and we cannot escape the lure of its charm. But spirit is not charming. Somehow we sense that to bask in the warm sun of forgiveness and bestowal is as inauthentic as to deny forgiveness at all. So how are we to think about this?

A challenge may seem to exist in the thinking of Kant. According to his moral analysis, Kant argues that the sole worth of a human person lies in his adherence to the moral law. Note the emphasis: the *sole worth* lies in one's sense of duty. Is this not a counterargument to the presently offered suggestion that forgiveness proves that we have worth independent of what we ought to do? In one sense, of course, it is obvious that if I have some existential worth which is autonomous of the moral, then I cannot say that my sense of duty is the *sole* worth which I possess. But one must read Kant more carefully; and more importantly,

---

* W. H. Auden, *Selected Poems* (New York: Random House, 1979) and *Collected Poems* (London: Faber & Faber); quoted with permission of the publishers.

one must reflect on the autonomy of existential worth more profoundly, so that these two claims will not contradict.

Moral worth is fundamentally *mine*. Existential worth is *bestowed*. Insofar as I reflect on what I should do, how I should live,
what actions I should take, there can be no doubt that the moral
law is absolute, and in this sense adherence to its principles must
constitute the sole source of my worth. If someone *else*, however,
decides to *bestow*, the basis of that bestowal cannot be my adherence to the moral law. Thus, the worth of existence depends on
someone other than myself and is thus not absolute. I cannot
demand, as a right, that I be forgiven or that I be loved. Just
because I can be loved or forgiven, of course, does not invalidate
the more fundamental principle that I ought to adhere to the
moral law. Thus, precisely because I have not *earned* the worth of
my existence, but have merely *received* it as a bestowal, shows that
it cannot be absolute and as nonabsolute cannot be the *sole* determination of my worth. Kant argues that the moral law cannot
assure me happiness but insists only that being moral makes me
worthy of being happy. Now suppose I am happy even though I
am not good. This may be the result of fortune, fate, or perhaps
a bestowal by a mother forgiving her promiscuous son who knows
for all his faults he will be forgiven. Thus I have the benefit of
forgiveness bestowed upon me, but I do not deserve it. What
would it mean to delight, as the limestone boy does, in my very
sinfulness, knowing that it will be forgiven? It is to say, I receive
the boon but do not deserve it. Or, "I am not *worthy* of it." Hence,
the *sole* basis of worth remains the moral law, as Kant says; for
we have just admitted that the forgiven but still errant son is not
worthy of the maternal love that forgives perpetually. The term
'worth' in the moral sense simply means something different
than the term 'worth' in the existential sense. *Domine, non sum
dignus*. I am not worthy, yet I entreat all the same. If it is given,
the basis must be a kind of worth of which I am not worthy. This
is paradoxical to be sure, but not contradictory.

But it certainly *seems* a contradiction. What could it possibly
mean to say I have a kind of worth of which I am not worthy? In
the latter sense, 'worth' means: I have earned it. In the former
sense 'kind of worth' means a quality of meaning which explains
something, namely my being forgiven. The moral sense of worth

just means 'deserves', and the existential meaning of 'worth' just means a predicate of existential meaning. Thus, the two claims do not contradict. This reflection, however, is not carried out merely to salvage the Kantian ethical principle. Rather, it is meant to show the profundity of spirit.

The vile but cunning monk Rasputin helped bring down the corrupt government of the czars by his enormous influence on the Russian court, especially the czarina, Alexandria. It was Rasputin's theology that men should sin as often and as wantonly as possible, to proclaim their sinfulness and finitude and thus invite ever greater instances of divine forgiveness. Now, this despicable and noxious man lived according to these principles and in part established a tyranny over the czar's court precisely because of these teachings. But one cannot indict a theology by pointing to a single, disgusting manifestation of it. What is wrong with Rasputin's thinking? Why do those who rely, for their theological worth, upon being forgiven their many sins not represent the truest and deepest meaning to spirit? On the face of it, Rasputin sounds as if he has a point. Surely we *are* sinners, and surely being forgiven not only attests to our being loved, but the acknowledgment of it must be the greatest kind of glory given to the forgiving deity. So go out and sin with carefree abandon and wanton pleasure, beg forgiveness and thereby win heaven too. In this way one simply turns Pascal's wager upside down and gets the best of both worlds. Why ever not?

Such a view errs in three fundamental ways. First, it is antispirit; for it constitutes a kind of pragmatic calculating which reduces how we think about spirit to how we think about prudence. Secondly and more importantly, it focuses upon the wrong end of the worth in forgiveness. We admire, not those who are forgiven, but those who forgive. And finally, we do not say that the existence of a transmoral spirituality should be *immoral*. There are wholly independent and valid reasons for being moral which have nothing to do with spirit but which are still valid. If I argue that, in order to be forgiven, I must have a kind of worth which is "above" the moral, this does not mean I ought to be immoral. ("I ought to be immoral" is internally self-contradictory, obviously.) Nor does the term "above" mean "more important" or "of a higher rank." It merely means that, in canceling the exhaustive range of the moral, the realm of spirit is not rendered intelligible by the moral.

It might even be argued, of course, that a certain respect for morality is requisite for being spiritual, though not for being forgiven. The nude young man in Auden's poem is forgiven because of the power of his mother's love, not because of his wantonness. "Though your sins be red as scarlet, you shall be made white as snow" celebrates the power of a loving and godly father, not the making of the scarlet sins. The predicate of nobility suggests this: one must care about moral perfection in order to achieve spirit. And Nietzsche's analysis of bad and evil shows the close connection between spiritual nobility and the morally good. Nevertheless, the entire persuasion of this inquiry is to reveal the extent to which spirit is an autonomous and separate realm. It is enough to show this; we do not need to step to the ridiculous and assert that because spirit is autonomous from the good, the way to spirit is through the bad. No truly spiritual person could ever *want* to be bad, but that is what Rasputin and all the myriad sinners who take devilish delight in their own immorality suggest. This suggestion actually counters the very first insight: it reduces spirit to flesh.

12

Reflections

They rejoice as they suffer. They give of themselves often with no hope of reward or even recognition, but they writhe at the thought they may be fools in their bestowal. Their doubts are dark and massive, like threatening thunderheads portending torrential despair, but in this maelstrom of dubiety, they trust. In trust they are in danger, but they bestow these hazards as offerings, offerings to one who may not be there.

Their torment is often spectacular. In agonizing over soul and God and guilt, they are sneered at by their contemporaries as naive, foolish, childish, and even as bigots. These sneers bring hurt and doubt and ever greater demands on their trust. They wonder achingly if they are beguiled by nostalgia, for the zeitgeist is surely against them. The glitter of cheerful innocence in pleasure surrounds them, and they would gladly yield to it, but it beckons from the land of the void, and so they sadly turn away. They ache for solace, warmth, comfort, and nearness, but such things evade them, for they will not yield their tenacious and perhaps dubious hope that maybe their loneliness somehow matters, that sharing and closeness can deceive, that perhaps as abandoned and singularly alone they have more to offer and far, far more to lose.

Though seeming arrogant and haughty with their own suffering importance, they bend their knees and touch the ground, like unworthy dogs. They supplicate before what they cannot see and call it worship. The others, who know full well of sensuous rapture before the allure of wonderful flesh and real beauty, wonder at these kneelers who worship the unseen, the unsensed, the unfelt, and perhaps even the unbelieved. Their worship leaves them unsated, for they pray and worship all the more when denied. Even when their prayers reap only bitter doubts, they still worship, not even knowing who or why, not even rejoicing in their own worshiping; they simply fall down on the ground to acknowledge what is absolutely magnificent.

When, among the best of them, their entreaties are denied, which is often, they cannot find any hate or disgust, and not enough disappointment, to abandon their entreaties. And so they grimly continue to husband their inner meaning, unsure whether the soil may be unsustaining of nurture or growth. Despair haunts their past, their present, and their future, but perhaps against all reason, like one berserk with a lunatic notion, they forge impossible metals of courage to give iron to their flagging energies. They sacrifice nobly and expect nothing, and in the midst of unparalleled wretchedness they mock their own misery by thanking!

They are spirit. They are us.

Some, of course, protest they have achieved a peace that surpasseth all human understanding, and perhaps they have. Why not believe them? It is as easy to believe as to doubt. But we hear the same from newlyweds and drug users and yoga-sitters, and besides, they all seem passed by the racing clocks; they are yesterday. There was a time, perhaps, when spirit was something else, something less onerous. There was a time when it meant sublime tranquility and sweet submission to a loving and caring sire; or it meant simple, radiant goodness, like the sweet smile of a loving child, or a visitation to an undeserving earth by the celestial. These were then absolute beliefs, but what claim or authority do absolute beliefs have on us, the modern questioner? Beliefs, particularly past beliefs, cling like leeches to the skin of those who have labored through the swamps of theology or the bogs of despairing doubt, and if we pull off their blood-bloated bodies, the head remains under the skin to suck at our life and bloat again. To be spirit is to be nostalgic, to have the past lurking in our guts like a virus, causing cramps. Even those who now espouse a religious spirit, who build churches and temples, who sing hymns and light holy candles and put on long cassocks, all appear as players of a remote pageant. There is no modern spirit, there is only longing after an ancient spirit; and our rites and ceremonies take place inauthentically because the calendar is wrong.

But we are, in spite of our calendar and our derailed religions, spirit. Our errors and our time have, perhaps, left us both unaware and unweaponed in this arena of wonder and doubt. But modern and hedonistic as we are, dubious and cynical as our intellectualism demands, scoffing at religious beliefs as our academies insist, we still . . . thank and wonder, we still pray and doubt, we still worship and adore. But his famous sentence has now become inverted, for the modern truth is this: the flesh indeed is willing, but the spirit is weak. Jesus Christ has been replaced by Oscar Wilde. The modern permissive theology agrees with him: the best way to rid us of temptation is to yield to it. So we can fill our churches by making membership easy. Having satisfied our carnal wants and removed the terrible censures of moral inhibition, letting our youngsters mate uncensured with their friends of both genders, and middle-aged lust also given its due, we have no appetites that intrude. What itches must be scratched.

The question now is: Is it better to be spirit or to be not? We must acknowledge it is possible to be not and still be good. It is possible to be not and still be happy. Indeed it may be that we must be not to be happy. It is possible to be not and be moral. Thus it would seem that there is no compelling reason to be spirit, only reason to be not spirit.

But though we can be happy, and be good, and even be moral, without being spirit, it is not obvious that we can be worthy of our being without it; it is not obvious that we can be true to our own questioning without it; it is not obvious we can be our own selves without it. It is surely obvious that we cannot be free, or forgiven, or bestowed, or blest, without it. It loses so much of its force because we do not raise the right questions. And we do not raise these questions of spirit because such questions embarrass us. It seems it is shameful to be spirit. Thus, to continue to inquire we must be shameless; or at least we must confront our shame and dare to ask.

This is a philosophical inquiry. As philosophical it is solely concerned with truth and with nothing else. The extreme labors of this inquiry have not been carried out merely to give a description or definition; we define in order to ask: Is it true? Is there truth in spirit? Having struggled with the three paradoxes and the resistant essence, we can perhaps suggest what spirit means: *spirit is transcendent gratitude for drawing near.* This is not the perfect and only understanding, but it is close enough. It is a way of combining the three candidates for essence into a single notion. But we are no longer asking what it is; we have a provisional and workable definition that is achieved by the tough questioning of the inquiry: as spirit we are transcendent in our gratitude for being able to draw near or approach. But we now must ask: Is there truth in this? We do not ask if this definition is true, as if we were verifying a sentence; we are asking a more direct question: Is there truth in spirit so understood?

Is there truth in spirit? The response can be found only in the purity of absolute torment. It is far deeper than doubt, from which we can turn away in indifference; it is fiercer than the pangs of treachery or the mind-ravaging dubiety of the irresolute. This is the torment which comes when two unmitigated and opposing realizations congeal like a clot in our arteries and block the flow of our life's blood. The first of these is the acknowledgment that we long to know; the second of these is that we long to matter. These two realizations stem from opposing interests, yet we demand them both, and this conflict, or war, is the battlefield of spirit. As a phenomenon this struggle promises only madness or despair, but it is real. And the real is the ground of the true. So spirit is true because of the inevitability of this torment. Like a lover with two beloveds who cannot bigamize and hence must forfeit a love, which is unacceptable, so the enmity between reason as knowledge and reason as mattering tears apart the soundness of our heart, the authority of mind, and whatever peace or tranquility we can discover in being questioners. There is truth in spirit because it seems I care but cannot know, yet lest I know, how can I care? Spirit, then, is never a refuge, it is always an arena, and the struggle is timeless, endless, and absolutely real.

To be spirit is to reject solace or resolution. It is imperative to spot the many offerings of solace and the genuine attraction of therapy. And these therapies are good; they do indeed work. The therapy brings solace, contentment, happiness, and peace. The anguish of spirit can be cured, as Rosalind, disguised as

Ganymede offers Orlando the cure to his love-sickness. His reply, "But I would not be cured, youth," is the truth of love. It is also the truth of spirit. We would not be cured of it.

To say there is truth in spirit is not to say that the entities which would *justify belief* actually do exist. We would like to have this solution, but it is not available to philosophy. Kant has shown us that these metaphysical questions cannot be resolved by pure reason alone, and hence reason as knowledge is frustrated. But to insist on the question in the face of this repudiation of knowledge does not deny us *reason,* for we can still inquire, not into metaphysical entities, but into *meanings.* The rationality of such inquiry is no less authoritative, no less illuminating, than that of knowledge.

The professor asks the youth, "Do you pray?" and the boy says he does. The professor smiles wisely and says, "You pray but to yourself." The youth considers this, and says: "I cannot pray to myself; for I pray to a bestowing and forgiving magnificence, and I am not like that." The professor frowns and says, "But there is no such thing. You pray to what does not exist." The youth reflects, and then nods. "Perhaps that is true. Perhaps God does not exist. But then I am praying to nothing; I am still not praying to myself." The professor smiles again, "Ah, now you understand. You are praying to nothing at all." "Perhaps" the youth says. "But in that case I am simply gibbering. I must reflect on that. If my prayers are really just gibberish, I shall stop, for I do not wish to gibber." "But if you pray to what does not exist, that *is* gibberish." "How do you know I am gibbering? Because you claim God does not exist? But if I am not gibbering, then you cannot be so sure. So I must reflect if my prayers are gibberish; I cannot reflect on whether God exists. And I rather doubt I am gibbering, you know. But I must think about it."

People pray; they do not do so because they first believe in God; rather, they believe in God because they pray. It is possible that their praying is a form of self-deception or gibberish; but their praying cannot be forfeit by the mere fact that we lack an absolute implacable proof for God's existence. The existential meaning of being a worshiper comes before the metaphysical assertions or denials of a supreme entity. This does not make the existential any less authoritative, nor does it make it subjective. It merely makes the inquiry more difficult. It might possibly make the inquiry more true.

If there is no truth in spirit, then although an *abstract* notion of truth is still possible for the epistemologists, an authentic and existential realization of truth as our own would be impossible. If the struggles of our inner meaning are genuine, where do they take place? How do they take place? This place, or this 'how' is what is meant by spirit. So if the struggle is genuine, the arena must be true. The true arena for these struggles is spirit. As Plato first recognizes in the *Republic:* I am mind, and I am body. But I cannot be both unless I am spirit; and without spirit I am neither. Hence I am spirit.

It is less the truth of spirit than the falsity of nonspirit that evoked the beginning of this inquiry; now, however, it is necessary to go beyond the mere negative rejection of flesh and seek to isolate how truth is possible in being spirit. This truth in being has nothing whatsoever to do with 'beliefs'. If by 'belief' one means the subjective appraisal of what exists externally, it is of no interest to this greater quest. If I believe in a soul, or even in God, I am not necessarily spiritual; and if I do not believe—out of doubt, confusion, or persuasion—I am not necessarily nonspiritual. If being an atheist merely means not believing in something, how can that matter since we are not talking about the existence of anything? If, however, being an atheist means acting without concern for transcendent meaning, or worse, if by being an atheist one means existing in such a way as to be without worship, then it does become a serious impediment to understanding. Being spiritual is beyond the dispute between atheism and theism, not because such questions are not important—they are indeed—but they are not *this* question. This question is, to reiterate: Is there truth in spirit?

The analysis of the ontological pronominal tandems shows that there is a difference between I-It or All-It and I-Thou or He-Us. It is precisely because we can understand this difference and recognize the authority of I-Thou and He-Us as modes of existence that we recognize the truth of spirit. It is tempting to argue that one who cannot acknowledge worship, suffering, mystery, sacrifice, and rapture is simply *lacking* in so fundamental a way that such a one is in untruth. This realization may be so, but it suffers from a mere appraisal, and hence is subjective. It is required, rather, to show that worship, suffering, and sacrifice are essential for *meaning;* and this approach, if successful, reveals nonsubjective and hence nonpersonal or universal truth. We may evoke certain sensitivities by appealing to the emptiness of the spiritless existence, but unless this is grounded in an understanding of our modes of being it cannot ever go beyond our subjective sensitivities and appraisals. The inquiry is far too agonizing to become a mere stirring of emotional fervor. The analyses of the ten predicates reveal fundamental ways of being and shows that in their absence *a way of being reasonable* is lost. But the analyses also show that in acknowledgment of these modalities, a way of being reasonable is not only uncovered but affirmed. We do not merely show that the spiritless is empty, we also show why spirit fulfills. Spirit is true because it matters that and how we exist. In the absence of spirit there is no way to acknowledge that we matter. Not even knowledge would provide us with this kind of care. Suppose I were to *know* with absolute certainty that God either exists or does not exist; but suppose I also lack any capacity for caring about this question. The knowledge becomes not only useless but literally impossible. (How can a finite being *know* an infinite being, Descartes asks in the Third Meditation. He should have thought further and deeper about the question, and less eagerly on his dubious solution. It is impossible for a finite being to know the infinite. It is not impossible, however, for a finite being to wonder about what such ignorance means and to care deeply about the possibility of worship and the even greater possibility of rapture.)

Truth is not first and foremost a matter of knowledge; it is rather first and foremost a matter of existence. To know is to objectify, and if I objectify my own knowing I commit an epistemic error by reifying what is not an objective entity. Yet, even though I cannot strictly know my own knowing without objectifying the subject, there can be no doubt that I, as subject, am meaningful and, as meaningful, can be thought about. But once I begin to think about my meaning, I realize that being a knower is not and cannot be the fundamental way to be. Rather, I discover I am already involved with existence, and the ways of involvement are at least as many as the various tandem pronouns. To uncover what these tandem pronouns *mean* is the task of philosophy. To be sure, to understand the tandem I-It or We-It has received considerable attention from the epistemologist, but truth is not restricted to epistemology. Indeed it is not even primarily epistemology, or even what epistemology considers, namely science.

It is often suggested, in vernacular discussions, that by spirit we mean 'something beyond the physical'. There is nothing wrong with this, of course, but there is a danger. And that danger is that the presupposition behind this definition is that the 'physical' is understandable whereas what is 'beyond' the physical—spirit—is not. This is simply false in the most obvious and casual of reflections. In fact, we are probably more alert to the meanings of sacrifice, suffering, worship, nobility, and radiance than we are of molecules, atoms, electricity, and the theory of relativity. There is, in spirit, an immediacy and familiarity which any epistemologist would dearly long to have in the case of knowing efficient causes in nature. It is, perhaps, this very immediacy and familiarity with spirit that causes us to overlook it as an object of our thinking. It is possible, of course, to lose our familiarity with spirit, and when this happens a distorted notion of truth is inevitable. Ours is an age in which the physical is fascinating just because our advances in technology have made such studies *mysterious.* We consider ourselves enlightened when we humbly admit that our grasp of nature is yet but small. Yet the suggestion of mystery in spirit is seen as reason for foreclosure. The truth is, this mystery is familiar, and the the attempts to foreclose by some scientific epistemologists are unfounded and misguided. Spirit has always, and probably always will, belong to us as a legitimate field of inquiry and endeavor. But as spirit, the questions simply must always be reawakened and reasked.

This inquiry is into spirit and not into religion. Nevertheless, religious spirituality is a dominate mode of being spirit, and so it is not inopportune to use religious modes of spirit in our analyses. This we have done even as the distinction between spirit and religion has been clearly retained. And since ours is primordially a Christian civilization, it is not amiss to focus on that tradition. This is a philosophical inquiry, not an anthropological or sociological one, so there is no necessity in comparing religions or in trying to strike a difficult balance with examples from differing traditions.

Those whose spirituality is religious, however, ought to howl and shriek and revolt against many of their churches, precisely because they too often have ceased providing us with any understanding of spirit whatsoever. Where can one go now to hear a sermon (not a 'homily') on how to approach the divine? Where does one learn how to understand the mystery of sacrifice or thanksgiving? Who tells us of the ways of worship, the trust of mystery, or radiance, or the ways of prayer? They tell us rather how we ought to feed the poor, to stop wars, to vote correctly, to keep our children away from drugs and handguns. These things are perhaps necessary to hear. We need to be reminded of our civic duties. The poor do suffer, and we ought to feed them, though the instinct today is to achieve this, not by alms or genuine giving from our own pockets, but by tinkering with political powers. Wars do threaten, and we should do something about that. But such things are the task of kings, presidents, senates and newspapers, not our priests, our saints, our preachers. In making us better they have made us less. In making us morally upright, they have darkened our spirit. How could they have forgotten the great truths: one does not become different by doing good things, one does good things because one has become different.

With the despiritualization of the great established religions, some have turned to private, evangelical sects, in which the person himself can seek a private and personal intimacy with the divine. In the absence of spirit in the great churches, it is easy to see why these curious sects flourish so, especially among the young. For, deprived of spirit in churches that seek to make us good rather than holy, where else can they, the young, who always know their hungers at least, go to seek relief from the impoverishment sketched out in the opening paragraphs of this book? These Jonestown-type cults, however, are even more tragic, for they turn spirit into psychological fervor, which is what the atheist has maintained all along. The pious has become the pietistic, or worse, the fervent. And once again, although in a different context and meaning, the 'good' has become the enemy of the great.

This, however, is not a mere protest against an age sated with indulgence. It is always easy to do that, to look back to a 'golden age' and lament one's present times. No, this present indictment is done not for the sake of looking back, but to realize two things: (1) that spirit is something we can lose; and (2) elements of our present consciousness can help us to lose it. There is no reason to long for an earlier period: that in itself is inauthentic. We must seek to rediscover what makes spirit possible for ourselves, for this age is after all our own. As an inquirer I am also interested in my own personal search: have I lost spirit? If so, can I regain it? Is it worth the effort? How am I to understand it? Thus, these protests against the 'age' are not the cranky harpings of one displeased with the current of his contemporaries but an attempt to isolate the universal distractions from spirit. As a philosophical inquiry the truth, if there is any, which is discovered by thought is universal and transcends the petty disappointments of an epoch. Thus, to regain spirit is done for the sake of ourselves and our own time.

Botticelli is reported to have said of Fra Lippo Lippi that his paintings of the Madonna were accomplished with such sheer loveliness and grace that they made the mystery of the incarnation intelligible. This remark tells us almost as much about Botticelli as it does about the genius of Fra Lippo Lippi. But if Heidegger is right, and art speaks the *truth*, then there is truth both in Lippi's Madonnas and in Botticelli's remarks. It is curious when we read or hear such things, we sense their truth. Surely if anything makes the incarnation—which is presented *as* a mystery—*intelligible*, it must be beauty; indeed artistic beauty. That in itself is spirit; and it is something we desperately do not want to lose. Let us assume, just for a moment, that Botticelli is correct in his claim. To assume this does not mean we believe in the incarnation, rather it means the incarnation is intelligible. The Madonna, representing humanity, has in this face such tender loveliness, such transcendent radiance, that one could understand that a god would visit her and become one of us through her femininity. This is neither romantic dreaming nor sacrilege: it is a realization of our being spirit. Such things matter. And because they matter, we must think about ourselves differently, and like a circle, though not a vicious one, such thinking *makes* us different. There is, to be sure, that wonderful persistence of caution which almost approaches skepticism among the highly developed, that warns us of not accepting too much too easily. But there is the other side of our inquiring natures that is willing to accept a truth when it is blatantly set before us, as Lippi's Madonnas reveal the truth of what it would mean to acknowledge the incarnation. Such surety is not technologically verifiable; it is, perhaps, more believable than that. We must remember who we are. Emily Dickinson reminds us:

> I never saw a Moor—
> I never saw the Sea—
> Yet know I how the Heather looks
> And what a Billow be.

> I never spoke with God
> Nor visited in Heaven—
> Yet certain am I of the spot
> As if the Checks were given—